Rethinking Human Resources for Health: on the edge of the post-modern era

Rethinking Human Resources for Health:

ON THE EDGE OF THE POST-MODERN ERA

2020

COORDENADORES
Inês Fronteira, Gilles Dussault, James Buchan

ALMEDINA

RETHINKING HUMAN RESOURCES FOR HEALTH

COORDENADORES
Inês Fronteira, Gilles Dussault, James Buchan

EDITOR
EDIÇÕES ALMEDINA, S.A.
Rua Fernandes Tomás, 76-80
3000-167 Coimbra
Tel.: 239 851 904 · Fax: 239 851 901
www.almedina.net · editora@almedina.net

DESIGN DE CAPA
FBA

PAGINAÇÃO
Aresta Criativa – Artes Gráficas

IMPRESSÃO E ACABAMENTO
?????

1.ª edição: janeiro, 2021

DEPÓSITO LEGAL
?????

ALMEDINA | GRUPOALMEDINA

BIBLIOTECA NACIONAL DE PORTUGAL – CATALOGAÇÃO NA PUBLICAÇÃO

RETHINKING HUMAN RESOURCES FOR HEALTH

Rethinking human resources for health : on the
edge of the post-modern era / coord. Inês Fronteira,
Gilles Dussault, James Buchan
ISBN 978-972-40-8941-6

I - FRONTEIRA, Inês
II – DUSSAULT, Gilles
III - BUCHAN, James

CDU 614

CONTENT

PART II

INVESTMENT IN HRH AND FUTURE NEEDS OF POPULATION AND HEALTH SYSTEMS

PART III

EFFECTIVE PUBLIC POLICY STEWARDSHIP, LEADERSHIP AND GOVERNANCE

PART IV

STRENGTHENING INFORMATION SYSTEMS ON HRH

FOREWORD

The project of this book originated from the observation that for decades health workforce (HW) problems existed without raising much alarm at the level of policy-making. Almost all countries of the world have difficulty in providing access to all to a competent, effective and motivated health workforce. Problems such as shortages of health workers, their inequitable geographical distribution, or an inefficient division of labour and organization of work, are obstacles on the road to achieving universal health coverage (UHC) by 2030, as per the United Nations commitment of 2015. To overcome these obstacles, countries will need to design and implement policies and strategies, informed by valid data and information on the state and dynamics of the health labour market. First, the issue of the development of a health workforce that meets the needs of the population should be much higher on the political agenda. This is not easy because reforming the health labour market takes time, well beyond the typical political cycle, and requires the support of the many stakeholder groups whose interests do not always coincide.

The awareness of the critical role of health workers in ensuring that health services produce high quality results in an efficient way, i.e. in using available resources in as an optimal manner as feasible, has been raised since the adoption of the Millennium Development Goals (MDGs) in 2000. At first, the accepted thinking was that if sufficient financial resources were available, these ambitious goals would be attained as planned by 2015. Seminal reports, such as those of the Joint learning Innitiative in 2004 and others by the World Health Organization) alerted to the existence of a "health workforce crisis" and raised the awareness of the need to react at policy level, making the point that human resources were just as important as finances when trying to improve services and population health. In the last 10-15 years, flows of research have helped document the extent of problems, and throw light on how countries tried to cope with them. Debates about what needs to be done and how to do it have tended to be limited to circles of researchers, hence the need we felt to reach out to a broader range of actors with an interest in health labour market reform.

This book targets non-specialists in health workforce studies, who want to have a good overview of the main issues to address in order to make UHC a reality. Potentially interested readers included those from education institutions, of professional organizations, such as councils, trade unions or associations of scientific interest, of regulation and accreditation bodies and other quality assurance agencies, of student organizations, and of provider organizations. Individual educators, health professionals, and health services managers should also find useful to have access to the type of information this book provides.

The selected topics include the performance, quality and impact of the health workforce, related issues of education, training and professional development, barriers to defining the desirable mix of the health workers, the deployment, retention and mobility of health workers, and the economic impact and relevance of investing in the health workforce. The specificities of the health market are identified, including a focus on the issue of work flexibility, its drivers and enablers. At a more macro level, the topics of stewardship, leadership and governance of health workforce public policies, and of the importance of human resources for health (HRH) information systems are discussed as critical to the development of policies based on sound data and information. Authors of the chapters present complex issues in a way that makes these accessible to a general public. We are grateful for their contribution and we hope that readers will learn enjoy reading and learning from their work.

Inês Fronteira
Gilles Dussault
James Buchan

INTRODUCTION

Inês Fronteira, Gilles Dussault, James Buchan

Background

A 2016 report by the International Labour Office, the Organisation for Economic Co-operation and Development and by the World Health Organization argued — and demonstrated — that investing in health services, in particular in the workforce that delivers them, generates wealth, promotes social protection, cohesion, and innovation, beyond improving the health status of the population (UN 2016). This conclusion goes against the traditional dominant view that health was essentially an economic drain, not a source of growth, and that the health workforce was a cost, rather than an investment.

To make sure that expenditure on health services, from promotion and prevention to curative, rehabilitation, and palliative services, is a real investment, it is critical that its main component, human resources, is managed in the most effective manner. Human resources for health (HRH), i.e. all people who contribute directly to the delivery of health care, in a clinical or in a support role, are a fundamental pillar of any health system. No matter the social or economic context, the type of health system or the overall organization of the provision of care, the success of health policies and the achievement of Universal Health Coverage are largely dependent on their performance. The provision of socially just, timely, integrated, people-centred and ethically delivered services, requires a health workforce that is available in sufficient numbers, accessible and acceptable to all and performs at the highest quality standards possible (WHO 2016a).

If everyone agrees with that objective in principle, designing policies that will develop such a health workforce, let alone implementing them, remains a daunting challenge. Most countries struggle with HRH problems: some face shortages, as in the case of the English National Health Service that in 2019 had more than 40 000 unfilled nursing positions. Others have two few health workers, because their capacity to produce them is insufficient or because they cannot mobilize the resources needed to do so or because those they produce move to other countries. With the exception of some very small countries, everywhere there are imbalances in the geographical distribution of health workers, with rural, remote and isolated areas, also poor urban ones, with limited, sometimes no access to qualified providers. Other problems typically include an inefficient combination of skills, such as when there are too few primary care practitioners, or when there are two few nurses and other paramedical staff to support the work of physicians, which limits the overall productivity of the health workforce. In many countries, poor productivity also results from a division of tasks that does not make an optimal use of the potential of each category of workers, such as when the potential contribution of nurses is constrained by legal definitions of their scope of practice that limit their autonomy.

What the book intends to do

In this book, we do not seek to overdramatize these problems, as it is often done by characterizing them as too complex or too political. Too complex because they can be addressed only by a well-articulated mix of interventions that take time to produce results. Too political, because they involve too many actors with conflicting interests and with a strong capacity of resistance to change. While there is truth in those arguments, we submit that a better understanding of HRH issues and evidence-informed strategies, with a tested degree of feasibility, can contribute much to mitigating the effects of current HRH problems, and preventing future problems. With that in mind, we set the objectives of the book as:

- To inform actors linked to and affected by health workforce problems of current knowledge of their nature and of their causes. This can help promote a common understanding of what needs to be done and of what can be done, based on valid data and information. This in turn helps frame the policy debate in a more rational and less ideological manner.

- To raise awareness of the need for more proactive policies to address the causes of these problems and of examples of good practices that have shown positive effects. For example, the demonstration is clear that nurses can contribute a good deal more, for instance if authorized to prescribe medicines or exams under certain conditions (Maier et al. 2017).
- To stimulate engagement in policy development and implementation of actors who have a stake in improving how health workers are educated, and how conditions of employment and the work environment can foster their performance. In addition to educators and health workers themselves, stakeholders such as students and users of services can bring policy-makers to pay greater attention to health workforce issues.

What you will find in the following chapters

The book presents an analysis and discussion of the main structural issues and challenges that policy-makers face in relation to the health workforce, in the context of global economic, social, demographic and epidemiological changes. The contents isaligned with the four objectives proposed by the WHO *Global Strategy on Human Resources for Health: Workforce 2030* (WHO 2016) which are:

- To optimize performance, quality and impact of the health workforce through evidence-informed policies on human resources for health, contributing to healthy lives and well-being, effective universal health coverage, resilience and strengthened health systems at all levels;
- To align investment in human resources for health with the current and future needs of the population and health systems, taking account of labour market dynamics and education policies, to address shortages and improve distribution of health workers, so as to enable maximum improvements in health outcomes, social welfare, employment creation and economic growth;

- To build the capacity of institutions at subnational, national, regional and global levels for effective public policy stewardship, leadership and governance of actions on human resources for health;
- To strengthen data on human resources for health for monitoring and accountability of national and regional strategies, and the Global Strategy.

Part 1 of this book is dedicated to the performance, quality and impact of the health workforce. Maeda, Berland, and Socha-Dietrich show how education, training and professional development of HRH can better align with changing population needs and expectations if they are to prepare health workers to deliver people-centred care. They identify transversal skills that all future health professionals, as well as those currently practising, should acquire or strengthen in areas such as teamwork, communication, artificial intelligence and big data and new technology, and socio-cultural sensitivity. These skills add to those required by the performance of the tasks specific to each occupational category. The authors discuss how actors involved in health workers' education, training and life-long learning can adapt to these new requirements, including by reforming programs and learning strategies, and even retraining the educators and trainers themselves.

Temido and Gonçalves discuss how at a time of growing pressures on healthcare systems, achieving an optimal skill-mix offers promising paths to improve the performance of the health workforce and services. Their chapter reviews the rationale for changing the skills-mix, experiences, implementation approaches, and future challenges. First, they define those concepts that often have different meanings, which they illustrate with examples. They briefly discuss how skills-mix can be assessed in terms of its impact. They then identify factors that typically motivate policy-makers to change the skills-mix, and barriers and facilitators that make it difficult or possible. Studies of such changes have mainly focused on doctors and nurses, though some have also looked at other professions; the authors present examples of both categories and show that there is a typical "implementation cycle" in the process of changing the distribution of tasks among diverse occupational groups.

Kroezen shows that deployment, retention and mobility of health workers are fundamental aspects to take into account for the development of a sustainable health workforce. Her chapter introduces these dimensions and discusses what they encompass, how they are measured and what evidence is available on each. Most importantly, it reviews interventions implemented to correct deficiencies in relation to each dimension. Few interventions have been properly evaluated, but enough is known to give information on what seems to work and on what does not work. Research tends to conclude that single interventions have only limited effects and that corrective policies should be defined in accordance with the specific context of the country.

Pita Barros and Costa argue that policymakers need to consider the economic impact of HRH to ensure that health care is delivered efficiently, i.e. at the minimum possible cost. They provide an assessment of the efficiency of health systems, and estimate the excess cost faced by the health system associated with non-optimal nurses to doctor ratios. It is difficult to obtain a precise measure of HRH spending across countries given the lack of comparable data on the number of doctors and nurses, and of their respective wages. Based on available OECD data, they estimate that core HRH expenditure, including only physicians and nurse's wages, amounts to at least one fourth of total healthcare expenditure. If all other staff are included, estimates are that high-income countries' HRH expenditure amounts to 38% of total spending. Looking at OECD countries, they observe striking differences among the nurses to doctor ratio. This raises immediate questions: what is the optimal combination between nurses and doctors? Is such optimal combination common to all countries? This brings the authors to expand on the discussion of skills-mix initiated by Temido and Gonçalves in a previous chapter. They estimate that countries face, on average, a 7% excess cost due to non-optimal nurses to doctor ratio and conclude that ignoring substitution effects between nurses and doctor increases the inefficiency of the health system and leads to higher costs.

Part II looks at the health workforce as an investment and at how to plan to make this investment productive. Campbell, Zurn, and McIsaac argue that the health sector contributes to direct and indirect employment, productivity gains, economic growth and has important impacts on other economic sectors and on sustainable and equitable development. They note that the health and social workforce represents one in every ten jobs in OECD countries (OECD, 2016), a proportion that is expected to increase in the coming 15 years. They build on the work of the UN High Level Commission for Health Employment and Economic Growth and of the *Global Strategy on Human Resources for Health: Workforce 2030* (UN, 2016; 2016) to show the contributions employment in the health sector makes to economic growth and to wider social goals, such as achieving universal health coverage and meeting the Sustainable Development Goals (SDGs). The authors conclude that evidence suggests that, rather than being only a cost, strengthening the health workforce, if well done, can be a wise investment.

In their chapter on "Planning the future health workforce", Lopes, Castro and Simões show that rational planning is needed to bridge the gap between need, demand and supply of HRH, and mitigate its consequences, such as when shortages lead to underservicing and unmet healthcare needs, overworked practitioners, unfilled public positions and higher costs; or as when oversupply or surplus of certain categories of health workers generates a waste of human resources (unemployment or underemployment) and declining average incomes. They argue that health workforce planning is even more critical in the context of limited resources and the hard-to-predict changes, such as in the roles and responsibilities of different health providers, in the structure and organization of the health service delivery, and in the demand for health services.

They briefly review the recent literature on approaches to health workforce planning, before using the example of the methodology they developed and applied in Portugal to the medical and nursing professions. They present their HEALTH2040 model that aimed: (i) to estimate the future needs of physicians and nurses to 2040; (ii) to calculate the training needs to meet them; and (iii) to determine the number of students that should enter medical and nursing schools. The authors added a technical annex detailing the process of using the model. As they present the results of the application of the model, they recognize its limitations, in part related to the lack of comprehensive data, and to the necessarily speculative character of the assumptions about future epidemiological and organizational changes. Nevertheless, these results provide a basis for further analysis, and for more informed policy decisions on health workforce development.

Part III is about the management of the health workforce at the macro level and at the organizational level. Kuhlmann discusses governance issues ("Transparency, Accountability, Participation, Integrity and Capacity building") in the development of the health workforce. She notes that policy support for the building of a people-centred health workforce is still weak, and appropriate funding and research programmes are lacking. She focuses on Europe and draws on published research and on secondary sources to provide a synthesis of approaches to governance from the sociology of professions and governance studies with a focus on the healthcare sector. Then she introduces a comprehensive framework for researching governance and health workforce development, in order to improve empirical research that informs decision-making and policy. She illustrates the usefulness of a comparative governance approach by using an empirical case study of selected EU healthcare systems (England, Germany, the Netherlands and Sweden). She finally shows how innovation in governance may contribute to the rethinking of human resources for health to serve better the changing population needs. The main governance challenge is to break the "silo approach" whereby policy-making and management are conducted occupation by occupation rather than in a systemic way.

The author argues that health workforce development must become a high-level policy issue and needs health system changes, namely at governance level. Efforts to improve more integrated professionalism and collaboration between and within health professions must take into account that institutional settings matter and create different forms of governing health workforce innovation; this, in turn, creates different modes of collaboration, management and leadership in the health workforce. It is therefore important to strengthen sensitivity to local contexts instead of searching for a uniform big bang solution.

Nancarrow and Buchan address the need for innovative solutions to use existing workforce resources more efficiently. They suggest that health workforce flexibilities are a management response to increase organisational efficiency, address workforce shortages, and better meet population needs. However, the introduction of flexibility in the utilization of the health workforce is a major challenge. The chapter explores the drivers, enablers and models of flexibility within the health workforce, recognising the tensions between professionalization and management objectives.

Professional groups use strategies to prevent other groups from encroaching into their task and knowledge domains, a process called "social closure". Consequently, scopes of practice have evolved, historically, through market opportunism and strategic negotiation, rather than through logic, evidence, assessment of needs, or health policy objectives, as good management would require in the pursuit of the goals of increasing health services safety and efficiency and responding to workforce imbalances.

The key drivers of health workforce flexibility are changes in need and demand, supply, and distribution of health workers. As to enablers, they include: (1) increasing training and international recruitment; (2) structural adjustments that allow workforce capacity to adjust to service needs; (3) the renegotiation of roles within a team or organisation to ensure the appropriate deployment of skills; (4) technology like eHealth providing opportunities for the delivery of health services closer to the home and for new ways of accessing care; and (4) pay levels based on demand and on individual costs of employment, rather than on a collective basis. While the notion of workforce flexibility supports the managerial objectives of increased efficiency, patient focussed care and addressing workforce shortages, it is at odds with the current division and organisation of professional work.

In the last Part of the book, Boniol, Diallo, and Saares present a strategy to strengthen HRH information systems. It consists in producing National Health Workforce Accounts (NHWA) on the model proposed by WHO (WHO 2018) in response to one of the recommendations of the *Global Strategy on Human Resources for Health: Workforce 2030* (WHO 2016). The authors present NHWA as a system strengthening approach for countries to address the challenges they face in producing and using quality HRH information and evidence. The NHWA model introduces 78 indicators for improved collection, reporting, analysis, monitoring and use of harmonized and comparable statistics on HRH. NHWA indicators are aligned with the various domains of a health labour market framework covering topics such as HRH education, distribution, migration, and gender. NHWA can help answer key policy questions, such as: How to improve planning through better alignment of HRH production and needs? How to address geographical imbalances and improve access in underserved areas? How to monitor and address HWF migration? and others.

The chapter introduces the 10 modules that compose NHWA and gives directions on how to collect the data and information to build the various indicators. Traditional HRH data sources include Ministry of Health databases, and data collected by regulatory bodies, councils and professional associations. This information is usually partial (e.g. only includes public-sector employees) or unfit for the purpose (e.g. includes licensed health workers without specifying who is actively practicing). HRH employed by private and non-profit sectors should also be captured as well as those employed by training institutes and academia, military services, or ministries and other government entities in non-clinical assignments. Additional potential sources of HRH data include administrative records such as payrolls, tax and pension funds databases, among others. The authors also present the various tools available to guide the implementation of NHWA, to analyse the information they produce, and to communicate the findings to inform planning and decision-making processes and to raise awareness on HRH issues among stakeholders and the general public. They submit that the effective implementation of NHWA will contribute to building a stronger health system through identifying HRH challenges, bottlenecks, requirements and opportunities for significant improvements in health service coverage and health outcomes.

A final chapter, by the editors, summarizes the key messages and lessons learned to retain in the process of building a health workforce with the capacity and the motivation to produce effective and efficient health services that meet the needs and expectations of a country's population.

PART I

PERFORMANCE, QUALITY AND IMPACT OF THE HEALTH WORKFORCE

Education, training and professional development to deliver people-centred care

Akiko Maeda, Alex Berland, Karolina Socha-Dietrich

1. Introduction: the *status quo* cannot meet current systemic challenges or new expectations

"People-centred care" may well be the disruptive force that transforms our thinking about the education of newly graduated health professionals and the training or Continuing Professional Development [CPD] of those already working. The disruptive effect arises because people-centred care, supported by enabling technology, increases the complexity of delivering services - yet another challenge for health systems already struggling with low productivity growth and high levels of inefficiency (OECD, 2017). We propose that educators will play a critical role in shaping delivery systems that can balance the "iron triangle" of access, cost and quality, the key metrics for evaluating our progress toward people-centred care.

Over the past two decades, policy-makers in OECD countries have tried to push their health systems towards more efficient and responsive models of care. But their reforms have not resulted in improved productivity - even as expenditures increased (Scheiner & Malinovskaya, 2016). In addition to low productivity gains, the sector is prone to significant waste, which has not improved significantly despite the emphasis on the "positive" dimensions of quality and safety (Blumenthal, Stremikis, &

Cutler, 2013). Disappointingly then, many economists predict that productivity growth in healthcare will lag other sectors for the foreseeable future (Shatto & Clemens, 2015). In addition, new demands will add even greater complexity and likely raise costs.

One of the factors contributing to this stagnation could be the inability of current education and training processes to adopt advances in pedagogy and social sciences in order to effectively prepare the workforce for people-centred care, automation, as well as advances in precision medicine and biomedical technology. The pace of reforms in education and training systems appears to be lagging behind the reforms in service delivery. Exacerbating gaps in the preparation of health care workers (HCW) is the inability of employers to maximize the benefit of new graduates' skills as seen, for example, in a recent study of skills mismatch (Schoenstein M, 2015). Compared to other professions, physicians across OECD countries reported significantly higher rates of feeling insufficiently prepared or "under-skilling". Advanced practice nurses, on the other hand, reported significant "over-skilling" in their jobs, suggesting that their skills are not well utilized. In addition to inefficiency, misalignment of skills and jobs contributes to the widespread reports of job-related stress and attrition among all categories of health professions (Dyrbye, et al., 2017).

Summing up the problem, training and education must be viewed as components of a complex adaptive system. Without such a perspective, broad goals such as, "Become a high-performing organization" or "Empower people to have a more active role in their own health" may be immune to isolated cause and effect solutions such as payment reforms. Health care workers are everywhere in great demand; many countries have standardized payment schemes. Therefore, any organization "squeezing" its staff for greater efficiency could experience higher turn-over rates; nationally, policy-makers might exacerbate emigration of skilled HCWs.

How can we move beyond this impasse to find a workable solution? A first step will be to recognize that a significant change such as people-centred care cannot be accomplished by the status quo in education systems. In this chapter, we explore some of the changes in the skills required for healthcare jobs in the near future. We link these and highlight key features of education and training systems that warrant deeper reforms. We conclude with broader observations about reform as a collective effort: educators, funders, regulators and employers need to work collaboratively, developing resilient and resourceful HCWs capable of harnessing the potential of new technology and new ideas to unleash large-scale productivity gains that will, in turn, support people-centred improvements.

2. People-centred care requires additional skills

2.1. Building resilience and adaptability through transversal skills

Today's health professionals are trained and equipped with specialized knowledge and skills for handling well-specified clinical functions, and these remain the primary focus of professional education. But the demand for people-centred care will require HCWs to function in multi-disciplinary teams. There is a growing recognition of a core set of professional practice skills, such as teamwork, communication, and socio-cultural sensitivity, that are shared across all categories of health professionals

Figure 1. Transversal skills required for people-centred care

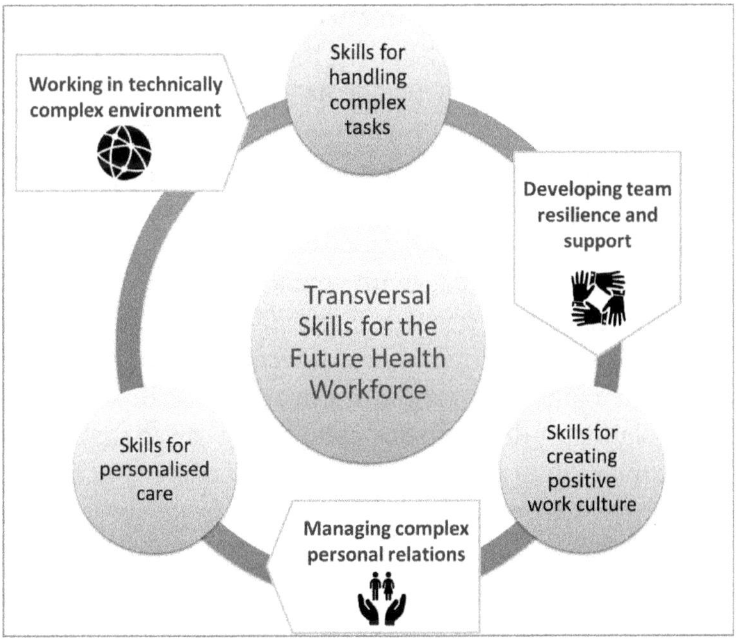

Source: Adapted from OECD, 2018a

(Braithwaite, et al., 2012; Braithwaite & Lamprell, 2013). These would build upon common "foundational" clinical skills such as holistic patient assessment, care coordination, system navigation and counselling for adaptation to chronic illness. Figure 1 shows that care providers will need to develop these crosscutting or "transversal" skills, so they can function across professional boundaries, adapt to different work settings and interact appropriately with diverse types of patients and non-team members (OECD, 2018a). At a minimum, educators will need to teach these transversal skills in discipline-specific programs; ideally, students will learn transversal skills in multi-disciplinary classes where they can begin experiencing the reality of the people-centred workplace.

Figure 1 illustrates the constellation of transversal skills that are shared capabilities across all health disciplines. It should be emphasized however that these transversal skills do not replace the specialized intra-disciplinary skills of competent professionals in their own field of expertise. Rather, these transversal skills enable inter-disciplinary team work such as sharing knowledge more effectively, creating a positive environment, and using all team members' contributions effectively. The diagram shows, in each circle, the skills required in response to expectations or conditions in the work environment. We explore each of the skills areas in more detail in the context of those environmental demands.

2.2. Working in technically complex environments requires skills for handling complex tasks

People-centred care is one of many trends affecting delivery of health care. Emerging technologies interact with people-centred care with complex effects, both negative and positive. Figure 2 illustrates various types of technological applications that we can expect in the care setting. All will have significant implications for the health workforce; to some extent this will be an evolutionary development, although we can already see all types in use simultaneously. In all sectors, technology is taking over many human tasks while fundamentally changing the nature of all jobs. Many routine and repetitive tasks are already completed by machines, while advances in artificial intelligence (AI) and robotics tackle even more complex tasks requiring dexterity and cognitive capacity. This trend has contributed to anxiety about negative impact on employment through the displacement

Figure 2. Different categories of automation of tasks in healthcare

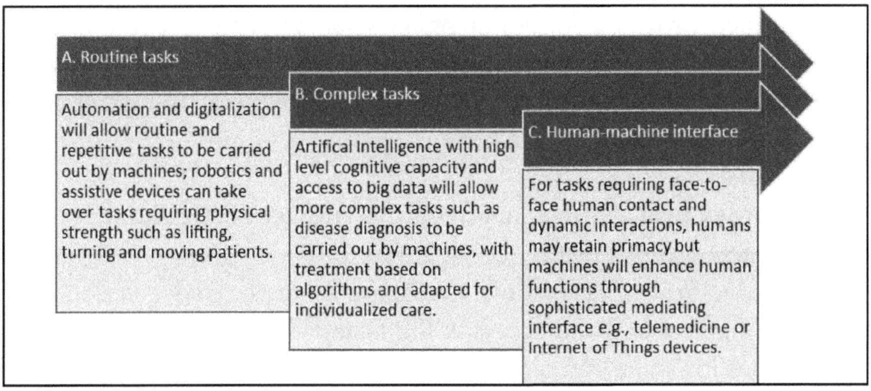

of human labour. In many OECD countries, employment growth in health care is increasing for low and high-skilled workers, but declining for middle-skilled workers (Cedefop, 2012). The emergence of new technologies will not only affect existing jobs as discussed above, they will also create new jobs which could not be imagined a decade ago.

2.3. Routine tasks – improving productivity directly

Historically, periods of intensive automation have coincided with the emergence of new jobs to carry out new types of labour-intensive tasks. For example, in the banking sector expansion of ATM machines did not result in overall reduction of bank staff: rather, productivity gains enabled banks to retrain employees for more complex labour-intensive tasks (Acemoglu & Autor, 2011). Similar displacement of routine and repetitive activities is occurring in healthcare, where some of the tasks most affected by automation and digitalization have been drug dispensing, laboratory specimen acquisition and voice recognition for medical reporting. As a result, for example, pharmacist associations are seeking to expand their professional role into counselling and consulting in community settings, reducing physician shortages (International Pharmaceutical Federation, 2012). Such role transition involves retraining and "skilling up" the HCWs to manage novel and usually more complex tasks. As technological innovation advances, processing activity with greater speed and precision by machines will further reduce low-skilled human effort, but will expand employment for more complex tasks such as quality assurance, program development and user training. The implications for the education system will include greater emphasis on assessment and retraining of displaced HCWs, especially for analytical and supervisory skills as well as training of trainers.

2.4. Complex tasks – the transformative impact of Artificial Intelligence and Big Data

In the second type of tasks shown in Figure 2, we place advances in Artificial Intelligence [AI] and access to Big Data, which are already creating possibilities for some complex tasks to behandled by machines. Already, firms using AI in their work process are adding new tasks related to design, management and maintenance of AI. These new roles include: "trainers" for AI systems; "explainers" to communicate and explain the outputs of AI systems to users; and "sustainers" to monitor the performance of AI systems including adherence to ethical and regulatory standards.

A health care example would be a decision support system for infectious disease management, that links clinical data of an observed patient with their specimen results from the microbiology lab, matched to antibiotic prescribing protocols developed by infectious disease specialists and patient-handling guidelines developed by infection control practitioners, all coordinated by a clinician who adapts the AI advice to the patient's unique situation, such as a history of poor medication adherence due to poverty. This scenario, while simplistic, illustrates the challenge of legacy terminology like "compliance", "doctor's orders", "prescription" and "most responsible physician". In the people-centred future, there will be many "advisors" and "coordinators" - as well as the "trainers", "explainers", and "sustainers".

Learners will need to understand the limits of the knowledge they can "carry in their head", and how to work with AI advisors, navigate Big Data and analyse their own role in care processes mediated by machines. Pedagogical applications of AI will enable the educational system to become more customized. For example, using large-scale assessments of learning needs and curriculum tracking software, faculty will be able to identify every point in the syllabus where a specific topic is discussed, enabling them to reinforce prior learning. This combination of high-tech and high-touch educational approaches will add value to the learner's experience, thus improving academic productivity. For care delivery organizations, the potential impact of individualized learning and progress monitoring programs will be an incentive to create more educator jobs, and to invest in educational technology. For instance, patient simulators mitigate the risk of student practice on the acutely ill patients typically found in modern hospitals; asynchronous lesson delivery can improve productivity by making use of periods when staffing exceeds workload.

2.4. The human-machine interface combines High Tech with High Touch

Prosthetics have been used in healthcare for a very long time, and some of the more sophisticated tools, such as systems for speech recognition based on eye movements demonstrate the close interaction between bio-medical engineers and clinicians. We are now seeing a deepening of human-machine interaction through the application of more sophisticated interfaces, such as the Internet-of-Things (IoT). As an example, in health care, improvements in the power and portability of computing systems have stimulated development of "cognitive prostheses", particularly for treating effects of injury and disease affecting neurological systems, which have an enormous impact globally. More recently, human-machine interface systems have been developed for people with spinal cord injury, using robotic assistant devices that assist social reintegration and reduce cost of caregiving (Hazlett-Knudsen, Smith, & Behal, 2011). In dementia care, a number of research prototypes have been developed to support people with dementia in specific areas of functioning, such as carrying out everyday activities, holding a conversation, being entertained, and being creative (Alm, et al., 2011). This intersection of rehabilitation therapies, engineering, physiology and computer sciences is already creating new jobs for services that significantly improve individual quality of life and help reduce costs.

Health care is unique in that it requires skilled and experienced HCWs who are able simultaneously to handle highly technical tasks while managing emotionally charged and often ethically challenging human interactions. This requires educators to prepare graduates for a complex environment where they must collaborate with colleagues trained in other disciplines, manage unrealistic expectations from patients, and handle conflict. One response to this complexity is "Human-Centred Design" (HCD) in which psychological responses are considered in technical design to make interactive systems more usable, based on direct input from users. Over the past decade, this participatory process has been applied in some areas of healthcare. For example, HCD principles guide innovations in user interfaces for clinical decision support systems and Electronic Health Records, and collaborative tools for shared decision-making, such as Patient Reported Outcome Measures for cancer (Hartzler, Chaudhuri, Fey, & Flum, 2015). In the USA, Kaiser Permanente has developed a training program in quality improvement that embeds predicted emotional responses of both patients and HCWs into critical points of clinical pathways. A "High Touch" aspect of this approach is exemplified in an education program that trains staff to deliver "equity-oriented care" for marginalized populations based on three components: cultural safety, trauma and violence-informed care, and deep understanding of the community that is being served (Browne et al. 2018).

It is beyond the scope of this chapter to speculate in depth on how technological solutions might affect health care, but we can note that as the domain of machine-managed ("High Tech") care expands, healthcare will still require human-to-human ("High Touch") interaction. For instance, IoT can play an important role in supporting personalization of care by connecting individuals and systems data, by facilitating connection between the patient and the healthcare provider, and by enabling remote monitoring and provision of care outside formal settings (Dey, Ashour, & Bhatt, 2017). At least for now, humans still retain primacy over machines in providing essential dimensions of care, such as empathy, adaptation to personal transition and loss, and situational problem-solving and system navigation. In the future, the quality and reach of High-Touch care could be significantly enhanced by the machine interface, raising the productivity of this labour-intensive dimension of care. An imperfect example would be the use of telemedicine to deliver psychiatric services for patients in remote communities where mental health staff are scarce. While not a particularly sophisticated application, already we have learned much about the benefits, acceptability and limitations of the technology, and especially about how traditional clinical skills must be adapted for this form of machine mediation. In addition to the learning tasks for complex problems, HCWs will need to learn how to analyse their own role in care processes where the other team members include machines.

Summing up, emerging technologies will facilitate the creation of new categories of jobs and also require those in current jobs to learn new skills. These developments will not advance everywhere at the same pace. Nonetheless, the potential benefit of new technologies coupled with the global mobility of the health workforce suggest that we will need significant investments in re-skilling HCWs. If education and training systems are not adequately preparing HCWs, the adjustment will be impeded, and potential productivity gains will not be realized.

2.5. Developing team resilience and support requires skills for creating a positive work culture

At the system level, ongoing changes are placing enormous strains on the health workforce and creating a more supportive and positive work culture is essential. Looking ahead, we see greater demand for skills in stress management, maintaining professional standards and ethics, continuous learning and practice quality improvement. Mentoring and teaching skills are important for shaping positive work culture, since they influence how well young health professionals are prepared for their practice.

At the program level, where most HCWs spend their days, tackling social determinants of health, and providing holistic, community-based forms of care for people with chronic illness requires multi-disciplinary teams. These teams may be composed of different disciplines and professional categories, such as pharmacists, dieticians, community health workers, social workers, and rehabilitation therapists, as well as the traditional physicians and nurses. Multi-disciplinary teams have been promoted for decades, but strong examples of truly inter-disciplinary care are much less common. Recent evidence supports the concept. Page (2017) highlights the benefit of cognitive diversity—differences in how humans perceive, interpret, reason and solve—in human groups. Teams with more diverse participants discover novel insights and approaches, perform better in problem solving and predicting results and generally outperform homogenous groups on complex tasks (Page, 2017).

But collaboration also poses different challenges, especially in diverse, heterogeneous teams. Conflict may arise among team members holding different views, or tasks may not be divided equitably or efficiently. Effective collaboration demands each member to gain skills, knowledge and experience in handling and overcoming these difficult issues. Obviously, communication is an essential task for the individual practitioner, but it is also a team activity. Communication is now an essential subject in the basic training of most disciplines in OECD countries' pre-service education programs, but may be less common elsewhere. This is unfortunate because the gaps in High-Touch activities that are yet to be addressed by most educators have profound effects on the patient experience. These gaps include standardization of best practices across the disciplines, ideally people-centred, or at least tailored to a specific condition ("What should we communicate?"); roles of each discipline in communicating with the patient ("Who should say what?") and planning, coordination, documentation and evaluation of communication with patients ("How well did we communicate to this patient?"). Naturally, team members have other duties beside communication. At different times in the patient's or community's pathway to wellness, different team members will contribute their unique perspectives to the team's common tasks of assessment, diagnosis, treatment, coordination of care, system navigation, and counselling or teaching. Understanding others' roles and contributions is essential. We discuss below how inter-professional education will assume greater importance as an essential aspect of building workforce capacities to function effectively in complex settings.

2.6. Managing complex personal relations requires skills for providing personalized care.

Successful transition towards value-based and people-centred care will require a collaborative process between the patient and health professionals in treatment decisions, taking into account the best scientific evidence available, as well as an understanding of what matters to patients in terms of health outcomes, social values, personal goals and preferences (Kon, Davidson, Morrison, Danis, & White, 2016). In this context, social and communication skills take on a paramount importance: these will include the ability to engage patients in shared decision making; the ability to collaborate across professions in a multi-disciplinary team setting; and, in an increasingly diverse and multi-cultural context, the ability to function with socio-cultural sensitivities with people belonging to different social, cultural, and age groups. The increase in jobs requiring a high level of social skills has been accompanied by an increase in the wages for such jobs, suggesting that there is higher demand from employers for such skills, instead of simply a surplus of workers who hold such skills (OECD, 2018b).

3. Educational implications of future jobs for today's health workforce

In a labour-intensive sector like healthcare, education of the workforce will be critical. Generally, though, the adoption of automation has been relatively slow due to difficulties in meeting technology compliance standards and human resource capacities. Moreover, with task-shifting to machines, human workers will need retraining to focus on "reflective practice" - empathetic and creative approaches – and on harnessing the benefits of automation while mitigating its negative effects. Thus, transformation of the education and training systems will be a complex, continuous process, which we frame within four themes: (1) harnessing digital technology and automation in education and training; (2) integrating Human Centred Design into approaches into education and training; (3) facilitating inter-professional collaboration and multi-disciplinary education; and (4) sustaining lifelong learning and flexible career progression. In discussing these themes, we assume there will be a complex interplay of responsibilities amongst regulators, accreditation bodies, ministries of government and professional organizations, requiring explicit focus on harmonization of goals, coordination of plans, special consideration for innovative practices and agreed accountability functions. It is also important to recognize basic elements of the teaching environment. In their current enthusiasm for technological "silver bullets", funders appear to overlook important opportunities to enhance basic tools, especially for novice educators struggling with complex challenges.

3.1. Harnessing digital technology and automation in education and training

Across healthcare professions, there is a shortage of qualified faculty in many academic institutions – often a severe shortage. As with the supply of practitioners, the availability of educators cannot match demand.

The situation may be even more constrained for Continuing Professional Development because many expert practitioners face a heavy workload with little time to share their knowledge. Likewise, junior practitioners have their own busy schedules.

Innovations in education delivery, such as massive open online courses (MOOCs) can help tackle the shortage of specialty educators. In addition to recorded lectures, some MOOCs now include student readings, critical thinking exercises, and even interactive features such as user forums. Making best use of these, however, will require user-site resources so that faculty members can facilitate integration with local contextual factors and the host institution's requirements. Digital applications, social networking platforms and simulation tools can all help distribute the deep, experience-based knowledge of expert practitioners to larger numbers of students with less burden on limited educator resources. Digital technology can also increase the effectiveness of education, particularly its relevance, consistency and currency with for example, customized self-learning for individuals. A particularly powerful innovation is Open Education Resources. These open access, topic-based repositories are usually aimed at learners, for example in cancer or maternal care, preparation for certification exams, or occupational health and safety. One early stage project is producing open access materials to assist junior faculty withresources for pre-registration nurse education (Nurses International, 2018).

Unfortunately, we know that many workplace barriers affect CPD accessibility and utility, such as the lack of relief cover, insufficient funding for paid study leave, the burden of low-value mandatory training, and organizational issues that hinder knowledge transfer to benefit patients (Coventry, Maslin-Prothero, & Smith, 2015). To the extent that new technologies can help reduce the current workload, any gain should be used to support HCWs, both in formal programs as well as through experience on the job. For example, ultra-short, case-specific learning experiences incorporated in the design of multi-disciplinary work processes could connect novices with experts to provide timely feedback with minimal interference for both parties. Such approaches require two things concurrently: re-organization of the workplace based on automation reducing low-value activities, combined with tightly-focused "up-skilling" so that HCWs can assume new tasks based on people-centred care. Innovative approaches will require different organizational supports if they are to navigate the existing constraints. A recent initiative, "Innovations in Healthcare" at Duke University in the USA hosts a global network of innovators in an interesting model for driving change.

3.2. Integrating Human-Centred Design approaches into education and training

According to a recent OECD report, learners need to develop agency in order to achieve goals. The authors state, "two factors... help learners enable agency. The first is a personalised learning environment .... The second is building a solid foundation: digital literacy and data literacy are becoming increasingly essential, as are physical health and mental well-being" (OECD 2018c). Digital learning and data literacy should be fundamental components of all pre-registration education, with CPD opportunities for older HCWs. Personalized learning can be enhanced through HCD which applies participatory methods to design tools and products based on feedback from users, both patients and HCWs. HCD principles are also being applied in education and training to inculcate skills such as empathy, collaboration and innovation as foundations of job-readiness. Importantly, the approach also incorporates qualitative and divergent thinking into curricular development (Gottlieb, Wagner, Wagner, & Chan, 2017). For example, in the USA, Australia, New Zealand and Canada, complaints about discrimination towards Indigenous patients have led to staff training in cultural sensitivity (Churchill, et al., 2017) Browne et al. 2018). Such methods help prepare HCWs better anticipate how patients and their families or co-workers may react psychologically in the care environment. Similarly, HCD methods have been used to explore preferences of indigenous Mayan women, and the findings were integrated in creating a cervical cancer focused educational curriculum that included culturally-respectful in-class learning activities (Schutzenhofer, Williams, Archila, Gonzalez, & Burt, 2017). Ultimately, human behaviour modelling, using HCD principles, can be used to incorporate research from behavioural sciences in the design of self-directed learning elements to stimulate learner interest for lifelong professional knowledge development (Ahram & Karwowski, 2011). An important consideration in HCD, which will be challenging in authoritarian-style educational settings, will be to ensure the full range of human diversity is considered as well as the importance of learner agency.

3.3. Facilitating inter-professional collaboration and multi-disciplinary education

Most tertiary-level education systems still divide trainees by traditional subjects and professional specialties, with few opportunities for collaborative learning and problem solving. There exist several constraints for multi-disciplinary education: first, during the 20th century advances in biomedical sciences meant that healthcare students had to absorb an unprecedented volume of information in a short time. The resulting specialization promoted deep acquisition of knowledge within a narrow topical subject, with the unintended consequence of segmentation and entrenchment of disconnected domains of expertise. There is now increasing recognition of the need for inter-professional education to help HCW understand professional roles and use their varied expertise to improve care quality (WHO 2010; Barr and Low 2013). The phenomenon is not unique to healthcare (McLaughlin, Kennedy, & Reid, 2015). Post-graduate training and CPD are also segmented by professional groupings. The positive aspect is that professional groups provide valuable support and sense of identity while maintaining standards; but this structure also creates barriers to inter-professional learning, despite decades of recommendations to use integrated curricula (Barr and Low, 2013). A major transformation in the general education sector could herald a future shift in health professional education. The latest survey by the Programme for International Student Assessment (PISA) included a module specifically designed to evaluate collaborative problem solving capacities (OECD, 2018b). Currently, countries such as Finland and Japan are reforming their secondary education systems to develop cross-curricular or transversal competencies, requiring collaborative problem solving across the boundaries of individual subjects (OECD, 2018b).

The demand for people-centred care, as well as other factors, will likely accelerate the pace as well as stimulate development of novel training methods. Team-based training and simulation can improve patient safety, by improving communication, decision making, and performance of team members. (Grogan, et al., 2004) (Guise & Segel, 2008) (Crozier, et al., 2015). Much more work is needed however, to establish the validity of teamwork tools for evaluating team effectiveness in health care contexts (Onwochei, Halpern, & Balki, 2017). Further research is also needed to assess how outcomes, such as service quality and patient safety, are impacted through team building activities. For example, in some societies the over-emphasis on authoritarian workplace culture, creates a significant barrier for improving patient safety. Paradoxically, this is an area where top-down influence by government officials and regulators may be needed to buttress the bottom-up voices of patients and junior staff. Alternatively, changing deep-rooted cultural practices may not be possible on a large-scale and could best be tackled at the institutional level, where "better practice" innovations such as "model wards" or even "magnet hospitals" could serve as examples for wider change.

A special instance of collaborative practice involves leadership and supervision. In the future, this is likely to affect all job classifications: senior staff and those with formal responsibility will continue to oversee others' activities; students and novices will be coached by more experienced staff; the global increase in use of Community Health Workers and non-certified workers can only succeed with "supportive supervision"; in the multi-disciplinary context, different professional groups will lead in various stages of each patient's care journey and will share quality improvement responsibilities equally. Management and leadership skills must therefore feature more prominently in education and CPD training to ensure that other education investments can be realized.

3.4. Sustaining lifelong learning and flexible career progression

For decades, health professionals have expressed commitment to "lifelong learning" (Figure 3), yet this principle has never been implemented in the full sense of the meaning, and at best it has only been marginally applied. Most health professionals are expected to acquire the major bulk of knowledge during the pre-service education period, followed by marginal updates on this foundation over the course of their professional career. But the rapidly changing technology and knowledge base and the longevity of workers have combined to make this approach obsolete. Health workers may wish to (and may be required to) change their career more than once in their lifetime. They will need time, resources and organizational support to make these choices.

The challenge for today's employers is to address the needs of two different groups: firstly, induction for new entrants, typically younger and more technologically capable; secondly, upgrading for older employees, experienced in leadership and the realities of care-giving, but needing to adapt to fresh tasks, emerging technologies and a rapidly evolving workplace. Health care settings need both skill sets, as well as the capability to think about workplace roles and relationships in ways that may be unfamiliar to both groups.

Generally, the education and training programs of HCWs are not determined solely by an employer, but are prescribed by relevant professional bodies. Given the scope and scale of educational needs, it is now more important than ever for educators, regulators and employers to collaborate. Some of the more progressive international organizations may be able to play a role in establishing planning events and other opportunities to discuss standards and competencies. For example, critical shortages of HCWs in many countries has led to development of bridging courses and associate degrees; clarification of these roles, articulation of competencies and support for curriculum development and standardization will likely provide on-going benefit. Such efforts will require coordination among decision-makers.

Experiential learning does not happen haphazardly under any condition or with any person or on every occasion. It happens most effectively in environments where feedback on performance is rich with deliberately planned opportunities for integrating prior study or classroom learning through expression and reflection (Benner, Tanner, & Chesla, 2009). In other words, educators must actively encourage experiential learning using timely clinical situations and other "teachable moments" to achieve carefully planned educational objectives. In turn, curriculum planners need to ensure that objectives at course level articulate with prior in-course learning, include opportunities for meta-cognition and problem solving, promote inter-professional learning and introduce students to related aspects of other disciplines. These are significant tasks helped by emerging new technologies such as topic mapping software, including open access tools.

Unfortunately, there are many institutional barriers to practicum learning, especially to provide options for major career changes and, to a lesser extent, for access to precise just-in-time skill development for emerging models of care. Extracting maximum benefit from the resources invested in CPD will require both bottom-up and top-down approaches. Using HCD principles, the design and delivery of both pre-service education and CPD should be based on increased involvement of current HCWs and their employers. To manage the new realignment of skills, performance measures must be designed to assess and incentivize individual and team contributions to these new healthcare goals. Professional bodies and regulators responsible for accrediting, evaluating competency and licensing will need to accommodate these changes in their governance roles.

In a formal professional education setting, the curriculum typically emphasizes the progressive accumulation of a body of knowledge and skills prescribed and regulated by the professional body (Dall'Alba & Barnacle, 2005; Dall'Alba & Sandberg, 1996). Aspiring professionals are initially expected to acquire basic knowledge and skills relevant to the profession and, later, more advanced knowledge and skills. Subsequently in practice, formal and informal CPD programs are designed to promote continuing accumulation of knowledge and skills, but always within the boundaries defined by the professional body. Under this structure, health professionals

Figure 3. Rethinking the education and training of health workers

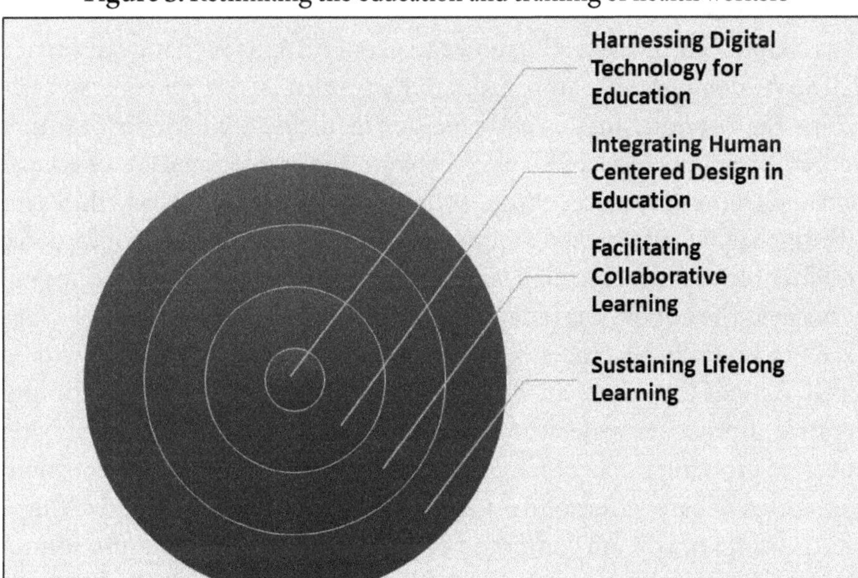

face great difficulty in moving across occupations or in combining expertise in other fields, such as bioengineering, software development or social and behavioural sciences. People-centred care and other new tasks arising from the expansion of technological solutions are not always supported by the existing formal educational structures.

Some organizations in sectors experiencing rapid technological changes are moving towards a "career lattice" structure to support the training and career development of employees (Tata Communications, 2018). The training strategies create new opportunities for HCWs to make task and career changes or develop new hybrid professions that combine areas of professional expertise. The lattice structure promotes the development of workplaces that encourage inter-professional education, collaborative practice, self-evaluation, and continuous learning (Frogner & Skillman, 2016). Transitioning to a career lattice structure would require deep collaboration among all the major health professional groups and education institutions, and a willingness to transform and reorganize the existing well-established structure. The challenge is enormous, but the relentless pace of technological changes and the strong demand for personalized care may provide the necessary impetus.

4. Conclusion

This chapter started by asking how the major drivers for change in service delivery – demographic and productivity pressures, people-centred care, AI and Big Data, automation and precision medicine – will influence future job requirements of HCWs and accelerate the transformation of education and training systems. Progress in technology creates possibilities for offering highly customized and personalized healthcare in an affordable and feasible manner, but this is only possible if HCWs can be skilled-up to harness the benefits of technology while mitigating the risks.

As more tasks become assigned to machines, human workers will be freed to focus their time and effort on tasks that require empathetic and creative approaches which the machines are not (yet) capable of carrying out. The growing importance placed on providing holistic and personalized forms of care will require a new approach to healthcare, involving a multi-disciplinary team composed of members from different disciplines and professional categories.

In practice settings, appropriate application of new technologies will allow clinicians to focus on tasks that require judgment, emotional engagement and creativity, releasing resources to engage in quality improvement and reflection as well as sharing knowledge and experience with others. Digital technologies in education offer a potential solution to the critical bottle-neck in the availability of pre-service educators and enable the delivery of customized CPD for individuals. These innovations could raise morale and motivation of clinicians as well as educators.

Balanced against this positive aspect of the future, today's graduates, working thirty, forty and even fifty years, will face significant demographic, technological, environmental and social change in their careers. Already we see high levels of job-related stress: how will these new workers navigate the turbulence ahead to create for themselves a fulfilling career over a long life? Can the health sector recruit in a highly competitive market those resilient and resourceful HCWs it needs? Can employers and HCWs apply lifelong learning and adapt rapidly evolving technologies to deliver empathetic and people-centred care as members of multidisciplinary teams?

Realizing the potential benefits of new ways of working will require a concurrent re-organization of the workplace, not simply introducing new technologies but reengineering work processes, infrastructure supports and human resource development tools. This also requires significant new thinking about the structure and content of education and training systems, for instance, to "retrain the trainers" about using new tools and applying different skills. Educators will need to engage in and contribute to the development of learning organizations across the entire health sector to respond to the needs of people-centred care.

References

3. Acemoglu, D., & Autor, D. H. (2011). Skills, Tasks and Technologies: Implications for Employment and Earnings. In O. Ashenfelter, & D. E. Card, Handbook of Labour Economics. Amsterdam: Elsevier.
4. Acemoglu, D., & Restrepo, P. (2018, January). Artificial Intelligence, Automation and Work. NBER Working Paper Series.
5. Ahram, T., & Karwowski, W. (2011). Social Networking Applications: Smarter Product Design for Complex Human Behaviour Modeling. In M. K. (Editor), Human Centered Design: HCII 2011 (pp. 470-481). Berlin Heidelberg: Springer-Verlag.

6. Alm, N., Astell, A., Gowans, G., Ellis, M., Dye, R., Vaughan, P., & Riley, P. (2011). Cognitive Prostheses: Findings from Attempts to Model Some Aspects of Cognition. In e. M Kurosu, Human Centered Design: HCII 2011 (pp. 275--284). Berlin Heidelberg: Springer-Verlag.
7. Ashley, E. A. (2015, June 2). The Precision Medicine Initiative: A New National Effort. JAMA, 313(21), pp. 2119-2120.
8. Autor, D. H. (2015). Why are there still so many jobs? The history and future of workplace automoation. The Journal of Economic Perspectives, 29(3), 3-30.
9. Benner, P., Tanner, C., & Chesla, C. (2009). Expertise in Nursing Practice, Second Edition. New York: Springer Publishing Company.
10. Blumenthal, D., Stremikis, K., & Cutler, D. (2013). Health Care Spending - A Giant Slain or Sleeping? The New England Journal of Medicine. doi:10.1056/NEJMhpr1310415
11. Cedefop. (2012). Future skills supply and demand in Europe, Forecast 2012. Retrieved from Future skills supply http://www.cedefop.europa.eu/en/publications-andresources/publications/5526
12. Churchill, M., Parent-Bergeron, M., Smylie, J., Ward, C., Fridkin, A., Smylie, D., & Firestone, M. (2017). Evidence Brief: Wise Practices for Indigenous-specific Cultural Safety Training. London, Ontario: Southwest Ontario Aboriginal Health Centre. Retrieved October 2, 2018, from http://soahac.on.ca/wp-content/uploads/2015/01/CS WisePractices FINAL 11.02/17.pdf
13. Clark, K. A. (2011). Human Interaction and Collaborative Innovation. In M. K. (Editor), Human Centered Design: HCII 2011 (pp. 13-21). Berlin Heidelberg: Springer-Verlag.
14. Collins, F. S., & Varmus, H. (2015, February 26). A New Initiative on Precision Medicine. NEJM, pp. 793-795.
15. Coventry, T. H., Maslin-Prothero, S. E., & Smith, G. (2015, December). Organizational impact of nurse supply and workload on nurses continuing professional development opportunities: an integrative review. Journal of Advanced Nursing, 71(12), 2715-2727.
16. Crozier, M. S., Ting, H. Y., Boone, D. C., O'Regan, N. B., Bandrauk, N., Furey, A., . . . Hogan, M. P. (2015, January/February). Use of Human Patient Simulation and Validation of the Team Situation Awareness Global Assessment Technique (TSAGAT): A Multidisciplinary Team Assessment Tool in Trauma Education. Jornal of Surgical Education, 72(1), pp. 156-163.
17. Dall'Alba, G., & Sandberg, J. (2006). Unveiling professional development: A critical review of stage models. Review of Educational Research, 76(3), 383-412.
18. Deloitte and The Manufacturing Institute. (2011). Boiling Point? The skills Gap in U.S. Manufacturing. Retrieved from www.themanufacturinginstitute.

org: http://www.themanufacturinginstitute.org/News-Articles/2011/10/17-2011-Skills-Gap.aspx

19. Dey, N., Ashour, A. S., & Bhatt, C. (2017). Internet of Things Driven Connected Healthcare. In C. Bhatt, N. Dey, & A. S. (Editors), Internet of Things and Big Data Technologies for Next Generation Healthcare (pp. 3-12). Springer International Publishing. doi:10.1007/978-3-319-49736-5_1
20. Dyrbye, L., Shanafelt, T., Sinsky, C., Cipriano, P., Bhatt, J., Ommaya, A.,... Meyers, a. D. (2017). Burnout among healthcare professionals: A call to explore and address this underrecognized threat to safe, high-quality care. Washington, DC: National Academy of Medicine.
21. Franklin, A. E., Gubrud-Howe, P., Sideras, S., & Lee, C. S. (2015, September). Effectiveness of Simulation Preparation on Novice. Nursing Education Perspectives. doi:10.5480/14-1546
22. Frogner, B. K., & Skillman, S. M. (2016). Pathways to Middle-Skilled Allied Health Care Occupations. Issues in Science and Technology, 33(1), pp. 52-57.
23. Gottlieb, M., Wagner, E., Wagner, A., & Chan, T. (2017). Applying Design Thinking Principles to Curricular Development in Medical Education. AEM Education and Training, 1(1), 21-25.
24. Grogan, E. L., Stiles, R. A., France, D. J., Spreoff, T., John A Morris, J., Nixon, B., . . . Pinson, C. W. (2004). The Impact of Aviation-Based Teamwork Training on the Attitudes of Health-care Professionals. J Am Coll Surg, 199(6), pp. 843-848.
25. Guise, J., & Segel, S. (2008). Teamwork in obstetric critical care. Best Pract Res Clin Obstet Gynaecol, 22, pp. 937-951.
26. Hartzler, A. L., Chaudhuri, S., Fey, B. C., & Flum, D. R. (2015). Integrating Patient-Reported Outcomes into Spine Surgical Care through Visual Dashboards: Lessons Learned from Human-Centered Design. eGEMs (Generating Evidence & Methods to improve patient outcomes), 3(2). Retrieved from http://repository.academyhealth.org/egems/vol3/iss2/2
27. Hazlett-Knudsen, R., Smith, M. A., & Behal, A. (2011). Knowledge Based Design of User Interface for Operating an Assistive Robot. In M. K. (Ed), Human Centered Design: HCII 2011 (pp. 304-312). Berlin Heidelberg: Springer-Verlag.
28. International Pharmaceutical Federation. (2012). Pharmacy Education Taskforce: A Global Comptency Framework . Geneva: International Pharmaceutical Federation.
29. Jain, S. S., & Schulman, K. A. (2018, September 21). Committing to Transformation: Chief Innovation Officers and the Role of Organizational Redesign. doi:10.1377//hblog20180920.793517

30. Jiang, F., Jiang, Y., Zhi, H., Dong, Y., Li, H., Ma, S., . . . Wang, Y. (2017). Aritificial intelligence in healthcare: past, present and future. Stroke and Vascular Neurology, 0: e000101. doi:10.1136/svn-2017-000101
31. Kaddurah-Daouk, R., & Weinshilboum, R. (2015). Metabolomic Signatures for Drug Response Phenotypes: Pharmacometabolomics Enables Precision Medicine. Pharmacometabolomis Research Network. American Society for Clinical Pharmacology & Therapeutics. doi:10.1002/cpt.134
32. Kon, A., Davidson, J., Morrison, W., Danis, M., & White, D. (2016). Shared decision making in intensive care units: An American College of Critical Care Medicine and American Thoracic Society policy statement. Critical Care Medicine, 44(1), 188-201.
33. Kuntz, T. M., & Gilbert, J. A. (2017, January). Introducing the Microbiome into Precision Medicine. Trends in Pharmacological Sciencs, 38(1), pp. 81-91.
34. Kuznets, S. (1966). Modern Economic Growth. New Haven: Yale University Press.
35. Laubli, T., Gassert, R., & Nakaseko, M. (2011). Human-Centered Design in the Care of Immobile Patients. In M. Kurosu, Human Centered Design: HCII 2011 (pp. 321-326). Berlin Heidelberg: Springer-Verlag.
36. Lent, R. W. (2013). Promoting Meaning and Purpose at Work: A Social-Cognitive Perspective. In B. J. Dik, Z. S. Byrne, & M. F. (Editors), Purpose and Meaning in the Workplace (pp. 151-170). Washington, DC: American Psychological Association .
37. McLaughlin, P., Kennedy, B., & Reid, J. (2015). Navigating the lifelong learning boat through uncharted waters. In T. Thomas, E. Levin, P. Dawson, K. Fraser, & R. Hadgraf, Research and Development in Higher Education: Learning for Life and Work in a Complex World, Vol 38 (pp. 344-355). Melbourne, Australia.
38. OECD. (2017). Tackling Wasteful Spending on Health. Paris: OECD. doi:10.1787/9789264266414-en.
39. OECD. (2018a). Feasibility Study of Health Workforce Skills Assessment: Supporting Health Workers Achieve Personalised Care. Paris: OECD. Retrieved from http://www.oecd.org/health/health-systems/Feasibility-Study-On-Health-Workforce-Skills-Assessment-Feb2018.pdf
40. OECD. (2018b). PISA 2015 Collaborative Learning Vol 5. Paris: OECD.
41. Onwochei, D. N., Halpern, S., & Balki, M. (2017, June). Teamwork Assessment Tools in Obstetric Emergencies: a Systematic Review. Simulation in Healthcare, 12(3), pp. 165-176.
42. Page, S. E. (2017). The Diversity Bonus: How Great Teams Pay Off in the Knowledge Economy. Princeton and Oxford: Princeton University Press.

43. Pronovost, P., Ravitz, A., & Grant, C. (2017, February 9). How Systems Engineering Can Help Fix Health Care. Harvard Business Review.
44. Scheiner, L., & Malinovskaya, A. (2016). Productivity in the Health Care Sector. Hutchins Center on Fiscal & Monetary Policy at Brookings. Washington, DC: Brookings Institution Press. Retrieved August 2, 2018, from https://www.brookings.edu/wp-content/uploads/2016/08/hp-issue-brief_final.pdf
45. Schoenstein M, O. T. (2015). Skills use and skills mismatch in the health sector: What do we know and what can be done? In M. L. LaFortune G, Health Workforce Policies in OECD Countries: Right Jobs, Right Skills, Right Places (pp. 163-183). Paris: OECD.
46. Schutzenhofer, E., Williams, B., Archila, F., Gonzalez, J., & Burt, D. (2017). Human-Centered Design of Women's Reproductive Health in Guatemala: Promoting Education and Understanding about Cervical Cancer. Annals of Global Health, 83(1).
47. Shatto, J. D., & Clemens, M. K. (2015). Projected Medicare Expenditures under an Illustrative Scenario with Alternative Payment Updates to Medicare Providers. Centers for Medicare & Medicaide Services, Office of the Actuary . Washington DC: US Department of Health and Human Services. Retrieved August 4, 2018, from https://www.cms.gov/Research-Statistics-Data-and-Systems/Statistics-Trends-and-Reports/ReportsTrustFunds/Downloads/2015TRAlternativeScenario.pdf
48. Tata Communications. (2018). Cognitive Diversity: AI & the Future of Work. Retrieved September 3, 2018, from www.tatacommunications.com:https://www.tatacommunications.com/wp-content/uploads/2018/09/Report_Cognitive-Diversity_AI-and-The-Future-of-Work.pdf

Skill-mix changes and advanced practices in health

Marta Temido, Andreia Gonçalves

1. Introduction: skill-mix changes for improving health systems performance

The statement that achieving the right mix of human resources is one of the most important challenges faced by health systems is not a novelty (WHO, 2000; Buchan et al., 2001; Buchan et al., 2002; WHO, 2006; Dubois et al., 2006; WHO, 2016). At least since the introduction of the role of nurse practitioner, in the late 1950s in the United States (Ford, 1986) and in the 1970s in some provinces in Canada (Kaasaleinen et al., 2010), healthcare systems developed initiatives to improve their performance, through maximisation of the competencies of their workforce.

It is also not a novelty to state that achieving an optimal skill-mix (Bourgeault et al., 2008) is not only an option for low income countries (WHO, 2008; Dubois et al., 2009; Lehmann et al., 2009; APPG, 2012), but also for most high and middle income countries. In virtually all countries, skill-mix changes are ongoing either formally, through the development of pilot initiatives, or informally (Maier, 2016).

Available evidence consistently shows that reviewing skill-mix can lead to improvements in access and quality of care (Buchan et al., 2004; Delamaire et al., 2010, Laurant et al., 2018). It is a response to social expectations that policy-makers and managers provide the best value-for-money healthcare (WHO, 2018). Therefore, deepening the knowledge on skill-mix, and learning from relevant experiences in skill-mix changes is an ethical imperative in the context of changing demographic and epidemiological trends that deeply affect achieving universal health coverage for all.

This chapter aims to synthesise issues related to the skill-mix of the health workforce. It discusses its theoretical foundations, experiences and evidence of changes, implementation approaches, and future challenges.

2. Theoretical foundations

2.1. Basic concepts

Skill-mix is a broad concept that is defined in different ways. Skill-mix or personnel mix may refers to *"the mix of posts in the establishment; the mix of employees in a post; the combination of skills available at a specific time; (...) or the combination of activities that comprise each role, rather than the combination of different job titles"* (Buchan et al. 2001, p. 233; Buchan et al. 2002, p. 575) (Figure 4).

Figure 4. Broad definition of skill-mix

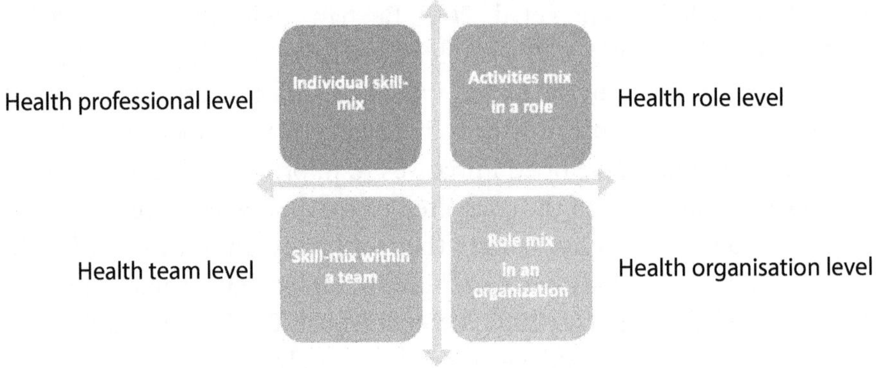

Source: Adapted from Buchan et al., 2000 a)

It can also be considered as the *"mix of skills or competencies possessed by an individual; ratio of senior to junior grade staff within a single discipline; or a combination of different types of staff within a multidisciplinary team"* (Sibbald et al. 2004, p. 28).

Some authors further argue that *"although the concepts of staff-mix and skill-mix are often used interchangeably, the four most prevalent conceptualisations are closer to the notion of staff-mix"* (Dubois et al. 2009, p. 3). That is *"the total number of workers in defined occupational groups", "the proportion of highly qualified staff members in the overall pool of professional resources", "the proportion of experienced staff members in health care teams"* and *"the mix of individuals from different professions and specialities in multidisciplinary teams"* (Dubois et al. 2009, p. 3-4).

In any case, the use of the term skill-mix should take into consideration that, in practice, academic qualifications, professional qualifications and years of experience are proxies for competencies (Dubois et al., 2009).

The concept of skill-mix is different from that of **task shifting** which is based on the redistribution of tasks between the elements of a work team. It translates the idea that, where appropriate and under specific conditions, specific tasks can be transferred from highly qualified professionals to others with shorter training and less specialisation, to achieve a more efficient use of the health workforce (WHO, 2008). Task shifting can be done in one of two ways: (i) transferring tasks from one group of workers to another already existing less qualified group; or (ii) transferring tasks from one group of workers to a newly established less qualified group (Bluestone, 2006). Consequently, task shifting is only one of the ways to change the skill-mix, which, in the taxonomy of Sibbald et al. (2004) corresponds to the substitution of professionals in the performance of certain roles.

A related concept is **advanced clinical practice** (ACP). Originally used in nursing, advanced practice is an umbrella term that covers a number of nursing roles, such as nurse practitioner and nurse specialist, whose titles are registerable in some countries (Buchan et al., 2004). According to the International Council of Nurses, an *"advanced practice nurse (APN) is a registered nurse who has acquired the expert knowledge base, complex decision-making skills, and clinical competencies for expanded practice, the characteristics of which are shaped by the context and/or country in which s/he is credentialed to practice. A Master's degree is recommended for entry"* (ICN, 2002).

Although the definition of advanced nursing varies from country to country, even within the same country as in the United Kingdom, nurses working at this level have autonomy to perform tasks traditionally considered to belong to the medical profession, namely, prescribing medications, ordering diagnostic tests and exams, discharging and referring patients to other health professionals or levels of care. A recent example of the introduction of this type of practice is the recognition of the *"exercice infirmier en pratique avancée"* in France (Ministre des Solidarités et de Santé et al., 2018).

Advanced nursing is a dynamic concept, characterised by the level of autonomy and not by the range of acts practiced (Department of Health, 2010). **Advanced clinical practice** has a broader scope than advanced practice nursing; it is *"characterised by a high degree of autonomy and complex decision making, underpinned by a master's level award or equivalent and that encompasses the four pillars of clinical practice, leadership, and management, education and research, with demonstration of core capabilities and area-specific clinical competence"* (NHS 2017, p. 8).

Advanced clinical practice enables practitioners to work to their full potential and to optimise their contribution to meet healthcare needs, yet, it is only one of the possible models of workforce skills-mix change to improve the performance of the healthcare system.

2.2 Skill-mix taxonomies

Often, skill-mix changes occur incrementally, as one professional group takes on new roles while another abandons them (Dubois et al., 2006). However, skill-mix changes can happen through strategies more or less structured. Sibbald et al. (2004, p. 28-29) theorise that skill-mix changes can happen:

i. *"within a given service, through enhancement (increasing the depth of a job by extending the role or skills of a particular group of workers), substitution (expanding the breadth of a job in particular by working across professional divides or exchanging one type of worker for another), delegation (moving a task up or down a traditional unidisciplinary ladder) or innovation (creating new jobs by introducing a new type of worker)* "; or

ii. *"between different services, through transfer (moving the provision of a service from one health care sector to another), relocation (shifting the venue from which a service is provided from one health care sector to another without changing the people who deliver the service) or liaison (using specialists in one healthcare sector to educate and support staff working in another sector)".*

Very close to this classification is that of Bourgeault et al. (2008, p. 1) that refers that **skill-mix changes** occur:

i. **directly**, by changing the professional roles through *"enhancement, substitution, delegation or innovation"*; or
ii. **indirectly**, by changing the interface between services, that is, the place where services are provided, through *"transfer, relocation or liaison"*.

Hyde et al. (2005, p. 704-705), referring to the English Changing Workforce Program, stated that the role redesign can happen through:

*i. "**skill-mix changes** - moving tasks or roles up or down an existing hierarchy, often through role substitution;*
*ii. **job widening** - the content of a role is expanded or enlarged, often by bringing together functions which may have been done by different individuals in the past;*
*iii. **job deepening** - the content of a role is enriched by giving the role more significant and substantial responsibilities, greater autonomy or opportunity for development; or*
*iv. **new role creation** - combining new and/or existing roles and functions in innovative ways introduction of a new professional role."*.

Finally, considering that competency management is the organisational capacity to optimise the use of the workforce, Dubois et al. (2009, p. 5-9) classified changes that occur at this level in:

i. "skill development" (workforce ability to play new roles and functions), then sub-classified in "role enhancement" ("vertical and upward expansion of work that alters authority, responsibility, level of complexity and assignment specificity; it occurs within a given full scope of practice") and in "role enlargement" ("horizontal accrual and diversification of employees skills; it expands workers' skill repertoires); or
ii. "skill flexibility" (highly skilled workforce ability to play different roles, mobilising different skills), also later sub-classified in "role substitution" ("extending practice scopes by encouraging the workforce to work across and beyond

professional divides to achieve a more efficient performance") and "role delegation" ("transferring certain responsibilities or tasks from one grade to another by breaking down traditional job demarcations and freeing up time from the former group that can devote more time to the interventions that only they can perform").

2.3. Assessment of the workforce skill-mix

The assessment of the level of skill-mix of the workforce can occur using either a quantitative approach by considering members of the same professional group (e.g. general practitioners and medical doctors, specialist and non-specialist nurses) or a qualitative approach by considering the different professional groups (e.g., doctors and nurses, nurses and auxiliaries) (Buchan et al., 2000 b). In both approaches, the detailed assessment of the available workforce skill-mix can be accomplished by using one of eight different techniques, each with advantages and disadvantages, and often used simultaneously (Buchan, 1999; Buchan et al., 2000 a, b) (Table 1).

Table 1. Techniques for assessing skill-mix

Techniques	Description
Task analysis	Analysis of the frequency, cost, and skills required for the tasks that form each job. Done by trained external observers and used to profile staff and identify gaps.
Activity analysis or activity sampling	Analysis, at predetermined intervals, of the time required for different activities. Done by trained external observers and used as a basis for re-allocation of activities or tasks to staff.
Daily diary or self-recording	Analysis, at predetermined intervals, of the time required for different activities. Done by staff but also used as a basis for re-allocation of activities or tasks to staff.
Case mix or patient dependency	Classification of patients in groups according to their diagnosis or dependency. Used to relate scores of healthcare needs to staff hours required
Re-profiling or re-engineering (zero-based)	Detailed analysis of the current mix, activity, skills, and costs of the workforce. Performed by working groups and considers the alternatives within the available resources to achieve an ideal mix.
Professional judgment	Assessment of the current activity and staffing. Performed by staff and managers Used to re-allocate work.
Job analysis interviews and role reviews	Detailed individual or group interviews to describe and to think critically about the work distribution.
Group discussion or brainstorming	Group or staff discussion to identify issues requiring change.

Source: Adapted from Buchan et al., 2000 a)

Any of these techniques faces complex practical difficulties. On the one hand, it is not easy to identify measurable indicators of patient care outcomes and to determine the impact of the performance of a professional group isolating it from the results of the performance of another. Thus, in this type of technique, quality of care indicators are usually used as proxies of the patient health status indicators (Buchan et al., 2000 b). On the other hand, it is not easy to obtain the exact costs of using each type of worker, taking into account direct and indirect costs, salary variations, amongst other aspects. Consequently, average wage costs are usually considered, and the costs of the additional training needs, inherent to the skill-mix modification process, should be incorporated (Buchan et al., 2000). Furthermore, even if such approach is useful for assessing the available skill-mix of the workforce, one should not forget that undertaking a skill-mix review is much more than a simple re-allocation of tasks (Temido et al., 2014).

2.4. Drivers for change

The drivers for skill-mix changes can vary depending on the service provider organisation, health system, and even on countries, and may therefore be of local or national origin (Buchan et al., 2001).

Commonly, the literature identifies skill-mix initiatives to be motivated by factors such as:

- shortages of certain health professionals;
- changes in the legal and regulatory framework of professions;
- improvement of career prospects of specific health professionals;
- increased demand for care and access constraints;
- reduction of health expenditure and search for cost-effectiveness care improvements;
- request for improvement of quality standards;
- provision of new services, programmes, technologies or procedures.

Often, these constraints coexist (Bougeault et al., 2008), and skill-mix changes are not the only possible response to these drivers.

In relation to shortages of certain health professionals to justify a modification of the available skill-mix, when insufficiently planned, this adjustment can cause imbalances in another occupational groups. Likewise, when considering the reduction of expenditure as a justificatory factor, replacing professionals with a higher cost with others with a lower one, savings are only obtained if the resources that they use are the same, and that. In addition, changes in the available skill-mix are initially an expense-inducing factor, due to the need for additional training (Bourgeault et al., 2008).

2.5. Barriers and facilitators

There are many contextual factors that can mediate changes in the health workforce skill-mix (Buchan et al., 2004; Dubois et al., 2006; Delamaire et al., 2010). Some of these factors work as obstacles, while others as levers, and sometimes the same factor works both ways.

The **lack of doctors** and the availability of nurses (Delamaire et al., 2010) is commonly the most invoked factor as a lever for reviewing the combination of roles between doctors and nurses, by broadening the field of exercise of the latter. Historically, the origin of nurse practitioners is associated with the lack of medical coverage in remote areas (Pulcini et al., undated; Kaasaleinen et al., 2010), though not all actors in this historical process share this perception. Loretta Ford, the co-founder of the first nurse practitioner program in the United States in 1965, wrote: *"the nurse practitioner (...) evolved from such societal needs and opportunities as nursing's development as a discipline and a profession, not because there was a shortage of physicians."* (Ford, 1986). However, it cannot be inferred that an adequate allocation of medical resources inhibits the expansion of professional nursing roles. This could be motivated by other reasons such as easier access to care or cost-effectiveness. Conversely, the unavailability of nurses can inhibit the possibility to initiate the process of broadening the nursing scope of practice, unless previous work is done with the aim to augment the size of the professional group. Otherwise, expanding the nursing role can result in work overload, professional demotivation or deterioration of the quality of care provided.

Nurses' technical competencies – a result of the increasing qualification that in recent years has characterised nursing education in many countries – is also one of the levers often mentioned (Buchan et al., 2004, Kroezen, 2014). In addition, there are the expectations of a more autonomous and stimulating profession(De Geest et al., 2008). The increasing technical quality of graduate nursing education does not, however, affect the need for additional training for the expansion of the nursing role. The consensus among professionals, employers, and regulators of the general contents of this additional training, as well as accepted criteria for the ownership of the new title, constitute themselves levers of skill-mix changes.

Payment methods can act as a barrier – as in the case of fee-for-service, in which the professional seeks to maximise his income by maintaining the highest number of remunerated acts within his jurisdiction – or as leverage – as in the case of salary in which the professional is more permeable to change as it does not result in loss of income. Capitation and pay for performance are theoretically more favourable to teamwork and to a more efficient skill-mix (Delamaire et al., 2010; Nelson et al., 2014).

Another critical lever is **leadership** at the macro, meso and micro levels (Nelson et al., 2014). At the macro level, leadership by political decision-makers contributes to mitigate resistance to changes in legal and regulatory frameworks, training curricula, remuneration, and financing models. At the meso level, leadership by organisations, ensures the necessary adjustments to the new models of care, in terms of information systems, working protocols, monitoring, and evaluation mechanisms. At the micro level, leadership by health teams ensures the effective implementation of the change strategy. The leadership of professionals who see their role expanded is itself determinant in ensuring that the team and service users recognise the added value of their performance in responding to unmet needs (Niezen et al., 2014).

Yet, in the same line of thought, the **level of centralisation/decentralisation of decisions** on management strategies can also act as a barrier or lever of skill-mix revision (Buchan et al., 2004). In health systems where the degree of managerial autonomy is greater, regional and institutional authorities may enjoy more flexibility in deciding which staff to hire and how to allocate the workload. In systems where this margin is smaller, or non-existent, it will be more difficult to adapt the distribution of labour to the concrete needs of services. Yet, in a centralised decision-making system, implementation of top-down strategies for reviewing the combination of available skills may be of easier implementation. This, however, does not inhibit the recognition that the effectiveness of any strategy in this area requires a combination of approaches where bottom-up initiatives are key.

The **legal and regulatory framework** can be an obstacle to the introduction of changes in the skill-mix and a barrier to innovation (Dubois et al., 2006; Delamaire et al., 2010), when it defines scopes of practice in a rigid manner. On the other hand, when it does not clarify the functions of the different occupations, their members may feel insecure if they consider that their legal responsibility is not clearly defined.

Weighting the barriers and levers specific to each health system is one of the most relevant exercises when considering a review of the skill-mix.

3. Evidence on skill-mix changes

3.1. Nurses and doctors

The combination of the medical and nursing (including midwives) professions is one of the most investigated areas in the field of skill-mix analysis (Buchan et al., 2002, Sibbald et al., 2004, Bourgeault et al., 2008; Dubois et al., 2009).

Initiatives to expand the field of exercise of the nursing profession extended from North America to other Anglo-Saxon countries, then to other European countries (Delamaire et al., 2010), and to low-income countries in Africa, Asia, and South America (WHO, 2008; All-Party Parliamentary Group on Global Health and the Africa All-Party Parliamentary Group, 2012). It is no surprise that most of the available evidence on the evaluation of the effectiveness of these initiatives results from literature reviews and meta-analyses of studies produced in a small number of high-income countries (Richardson et al., 1995; Horrocks et al., 2002; Sibbald et al., 2004; Laurant et al., 2010; Delamaire et al., 2010), though this trend is changing (Maier et al., 2017; Laurant et al., 2018).

In addition to the potential bias resulting from the characteristics of these countries and their health systems, the authors refer to several other limitations of the studies. These include the lack of robust evidence on the cost-effectiveness of the substitution of doctors by nurses (Richardson et al., 1995; Brown et al., 1995; Buchan et al., 2002; Sibbald et al., 2004; Hatem et al., 2008; Delamaire et al., 2010; Maier et al., 2017; Laurant et al., 2018). Some studies also present low capacity to measure the equivalence of care provided by doctors and nurses because of methodological limitations, namely a too short follow-up period of patients (Laurant et al., 2010).

Nonetheless, there is evidence that, in specific areas and conditions, nurses can provide care equivalent to doctors (Table 2).

Table 2. Main results and conclusions from reviews on skill-mix between nurses and doctors

Authors	Type of review	Main results and conclusions
Richardson et al., 1995	Narrative	Between 30% and 70% of the tasks performed by doctors could be carried out by nurses Evidence on the cost-effectiveness of substituting other health professionals for doctors or physicians is limited Feasibility of task transfer cannot be mistaken for its cost-effectiveness only on the basis that the costs with nursing staff were lower than with medical staff. It is necessary to evaluate the working time needed by each group, the need for medical supervision of nursing work and the qualitative performance of each of the professions.
Brown et al., 1995	Meta-analysis	Greater compliance to treatment in patients cared by nurse practitioners and nurse midwives compared to those cared by physicians, in primary care. Other indicators, such as quality of care, prescription of drugs, functional status, number of visits per patient and attendance to emergency services revealed similar performances. Nurses and midwives achieved neonatal outcomes equivalent to those of physicians with less technology and analgesia.
Horrocks et al., 2002	Systematic and metanalysis	Patients were more satisfied with care by a nurse practitioner. No differences in health status were found. Nurse practitioners had longer consultations and made more investigations than did doctors. No differences were found in prescriptions, return consultations, or referrals. Quality of care was in some ways better for nurse practitioner consultations however lack of data heterogeneity did not allow for solid conclusions.
Buchan et al., 2002	Systematic	In settings where there is actual or potential role overlap between registered nurses and doctors, there is scope for a cost-effective increase in the role and deployment of the former. Controlled clinical trials found that the care provided by nurse practitioners to patients with minor illness in general practice was effective, perceived as more satisfactory, providing more relevant information to patients and presenting identical prescription level. No cost differences found because nurses spent more time, on average, with each patient than did the doctors.

Authors	Type of review	Main results and conclusions
Sibbald et al., 2004	Systematic	Nurses generally achieve health outcomes as good as doctors and may have better interpersonal skills. Nurses had longer consultation times, carried out more investigations and often recalled patients at a higher rate thus eliminating net savings in salary costs. The evidence from doctor-nurse substitution in hospital care was weak not allowing for conclusions. Cost-effectiveness is generally not evaluated, nor is the wider impact of change on health care systems.
Hatem et al., 2008	Systematic	This review compared midwife-led care with models of doctor-led care and shared care. Midwife-led care was associated with several benefits and no identified adverse effects. The main benefits were a reduction in the use of regional analgesia, fewer episiotomies or instrumental births, increased chance of being cared for in labour by a known midwife, greater feeling of control during labour, greater chance of having a spontaneous vaginal birth and initiating breastfeeding. There was no difference in caesarean birth rates. Cost-effectiveness could not be evaluated as there was a lack of consistency in estimating costs.
Laurant et al., 2010	Systematic	Results showed that, at least in the short term, doctors and nurses provided similar health care though satisfaction was greater in the care provided by nurses. There were no significant differences in prescription, request for exams or referral but nurses' productivity in the first contact was lower due to longer consultations. However, while doctor-nurse substitution has the potential to reduce doctors' workload and direct healthcare cost, achieving such reductions depends on the particular context of care – whether nurses' work was used to fulfill previously unmet needs or if this would release medical time for more differentiated tasks that only doctors could guarantee. Savings in cost depend on the magnitude of the salary differential and may be offset by the lower productivity of nurses.
Delamaire et al., 2010	Review of the development of advanced practice nurses (APN) in 12 countries	With the proper education and training, APN can deliver the same quality of care as doctors for a range of services, such as routine follow-up of patients with chronic conditions or first contact for people with minor illness. No negative occurrences were identified, and most evaluations found a higher patient satisfaction rate. Most studies have not estimated the impact of APN on costs; but for those that have attempted to do so, most did not include education and training costs, productivity differences and long-term cost impacts. It is important to distinguishing between cases in which the expansion of the scope of the nursing profession is done by "substitution" of medical work, which is associated with reduction or neutrality in costs, and the one in which it is done by "supplementation" of the medical work, which is associated with increased costs.

Authors	Type of review	Main results and conclusions
Maier et al., 2017	Cross-country comparative research	Comparing nurses working in advanced roles to GP/physicians results in equivalent or improved quality of care. Nurse provided care generally leads to higher patient satisfaction. Evidence on the cost impacts and efficiency gains of these workforce innovations remains inconclusive. While some studies suggest cost savings due to lower salaries or reimbursement levels for nurses, others find mixed results, as nurses tend to have longer consultation times and request more return visits suggesting lower productivity.
Laurant et al., 2018	Systematic	Evaluation of the impact of nurses working as substitutes for doctors, involved in first contact care, ongoing care for physical complaints and follow-up of patients with a chronic condition Trained nurses probably provide equal or possibly even better quality of care and probably achieve equal or better health outcomes for patients. Nurses probably achieve higher levels of patient satisfaction, but their consultation length is probably longer and the frequency of attended return visits is probably slightly higher. Uncertainty of the effects of nurse-led care on the costs of care.

Source: Compilation by authors.

3.2. Other health professionals

In recent years, a growing number of studies explored the evidence resulting from redesigns of pharmacist and other paramedical roles, or even community health workers (CHW), *"selected, trained and working in the communities from which they come"*, and performing a *"wide range of different tasks that can be preventive, curative and/or developmental (...) or very specific interventions"* (Lehmann et al. 2010, p. v). (Table 3).

Table 3. Skill-mix between other health professionals

Authors	Type of study	Main results and conclusions
Lehmann et al., 2007	Narrative review	CHW can undertake actions that lead to improved health outcomes, especially, but not exclusively, in the field of child health. Although CHW can implement effective interventions, they do not consistently provide services likely to have substantial health impact and the quality of services they provide is sometimes poor. The largest and most successful programme in this regard is the Brazilian Family Health Programme.

Authors	Type of study	Main results and conclusions
Chilopora et al., 2007	Cohort study	Clinical officers performed 90% of all straight caesarean sections, 70% of those combined with subtotal hysterectomy, 60% of those combined with total hysterectomy and 89% of those combined with repair of uterine rupture. Postoperative outcomes (pyrexia, wound infection, wound dehiscence, need for re-operation, neonatal outcome or maternal death) in patients followed by clinical officers and medical officers were almost identical in the two groups.
Laurant et al., 2009	Systematic review	Non-physician clinicians (nurses, physician assistants, and pharmacists) working as substitutes or supplements for physicians in defined areas of care can maintain and often improve the quality of care and outcomes for patients. The effect on health care costs is mixed, with savings dependent on the context of care and specific nature of role revision. There is scarcity of research on pharmacists and physician assistants.
Dennis et al., 2009	Systematic review	Patients were more likely to comply with treatment regimens when managed by a pharmacist compared to a GP. The successful roles of pharmacists included review and change of medication or dose adjustment, medication compliance checks, screening for risk factors, and counseling. Task substitution did not result in reduced use of health services. Pharmacists identified additional problems and made referrals to other health professionals or back to the GP.
Fulton et al., 2011	Systematic review	In Kenya, no significant clinical differences were found between HIV/AIDS patients who received clinic-based antiretroviral therapy care versus primarily community-based care delivered by people living with HIV/AIDS who received pre-programmed personal digital assistants with decision support. In Mozambique surgically trained assistant medical officers produced similar patient outcomes as compared to physician obstetricians and gynaecologists, with surgery costs being one-quarter of physician specialists, and trained assistants providing over 90% of obstetric surgery.
Desmeules et al., 2013	Cross-sectional	The assessment of the diagnostic and treatment agreement, healthcare resource use and patient satisfaction between advanced practice physiotherapists (APP) and orthopaedic surgeons revealed that the diagnoses and triage recommendations for patients with hip and knee disorders made by the APP were similar to those of orthopaedic surgeons. Although not significant, the APP tended to order more imaging tests than surgeons. The APP tended to make certain recommendations more often than the orthopaedic surgeon. On average, it took the APP slightly more time to see the patients than the orthopaedic surgeon, but the patients reported being more satisfied with APP care.

Authors	Type of study	Main results and conclusions
Kredo et al., 2014	Systematic review	Moderate quality evidence from a single trial that when antiretroviral therapy was provided in the community, by trained field workers, there was probably no difference in death or losses to follow-up compared to doctor-led care.
Nkansah et al., 2011	Systematic review	There is not enough quality evidence available to conclude that pharmacists improve patient or health professional outcomes compared to other health professionals.
Dier et al., 2014	Systematic review	Authors assessed the effectiveness of dental auxiliaries compared with dentists in undertaking clinical tasks traditionally performed by a dentist. Only five studies were identified though none of them reported adverse effects. All were at high risk of bias.
Weeks et al., 2016	Systematic review	Non-medical prescribers, practicing with varying but high levels of prescribing autonomy, in a range of settings, were as effective as usual care medical prescribers. Non-medical prescribers can deliver comparable outcomes for systolic blood pressure, glycated haemoglobin, low-density lipoprotein, medication adherence, patient satisfaction, and health-related quality of life.
WHO, 2018	Several systematic reviews on specific questions regarding CHW	CHWs and other types of community-based health workers are effective in the delivery of a range of preventive, promotive and curative health services, and can contribute to reduce inequities in access to care.

Source: Compilation by authors.

4. Implementation approaches to skill-mix changes

4.1. Implementation cycle

Skill-mix changes can be driven by structured strategies (Dubois et al., 2006), that often occur incrementally. Bearing in mind that *"there is no common starting point for examining skill-mix"* (Buchan et al. 2002, p. 575), authors suggest that to revise the combination of professional roles and define their scope of practice, a set of steps should be considered (Buchan et al., 2000 a, b; Buchan et al., 2001; Buchan et al., 2002).

Step one (**evaluating the need for change**) involves the identification of the problems which the skill-mix revision aims at addressing and the appreciation of the capacity to do it. Step two (**identifying the opportunities and barriers**) requires the assessment of the margin of control over change. Step three (**planning for change**) considers the necessary resources and plans the change process. Step four (**making change happen**) involves choosing the appropriate approach to implementation.

Once the cycle ends, it returns to step one, evaluating the new skill-mix available and any new changes that may be necessary (Buchan et al., 2000 a) and b)) (Figure 5).

Figure 5. Skill-mix cycle

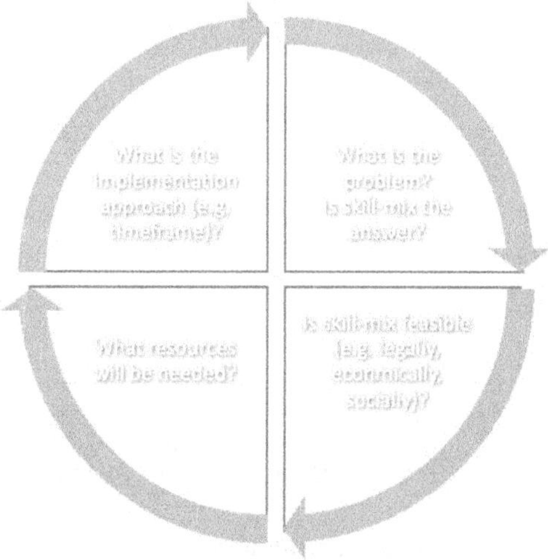

Source: Adapted from Buchan et al., 2000 b.

This approach to skill-mix review is not always as simple as it corresponds to an ideal technical model (Buchan et al., 2000 b). However, it provides a useful roadmap. Toolkits for skill-mix changes implementation identify similar major stages (Bryant-Lukosius et al., 2004; Canadian Nurse Practitioner Initiative, 2006); these stages are also implicit in reports of empirical experiences (Hyde et al., 2005; Berland et al., 2006).

Learning from foreign experiences in implementing skill-mix changes allows to identify the positive effects of policy entrepreneurs, strong leadership, local solutions, and pilot experiences, among other policy levers that promote change (Temido et al., 2015).

In sum, skill-mix approaches are more than just "a technical exercise" (WHO Regional Office for Europe 2018, p. 14); *"a long-term vision of the evolution of the healthcare system from the policy-makers, and a strong commitment from stakeholders is needed, since human resources for health strategy development require more than a short time perspective"* (Temido et al., 2015, p. 485).

4.2. Sociological approach to skill-mix implementation

For a thorough understanding of the cycle of implementation of skill-mix changes, it is important to stress that the evolution of professional roles is a dynamic process. The sociological theories of the professions address this subject.

Some approaches attribute the recognition of a profession to criteria of social legitimacy - as in the functionalist theories that emerged in the 1930s. Interactionists explain it by the negotiation and conflict relations through which an occupation becomes a profession. Critics of professionalism see health professions as monopolies, medicine being the most important, that limit access to some services to the benefit of occupational groups that succeeded in mobilizing political support to achieve control of an area of service provision. These explanatory models help understand the professions as evolutionary realities in historical and social terms (Rodrigues, 2002).

These sociological approaches also emphasise the role of power relations in the construction of boundaries between professions. Freidson (1986) shows that the division of labour is the result of a process of social negotiation in which a particular group claims to have certain competencies, acquired in formal educational institutions, that confers its members the privilege of controlling certain tasks.

Abbot's (1988) describes the history of professions as the struggle of certain occupational groups to claim jurisdiction over areas of activity that already exist and are under the dominance of other groups.

Skill-mix changes and workforce innovations occur in this macro scenario and involve *"negotiating jurisdiction in the workplace"* (Kroezen 2014, p. 1).

5. Conclusion

At a time of growing pressures on healthcare systems, achieving an optimal skill-mix offers promising paths to improve their performance.

It also involves challenges, in particular the need for more evidence about the cost-effectiveness of skill-mix changes and on their effects on health outcomes, and a better understanding of the process of their implementation. Above all, the communication of the expected results of change and engaging citizens and patients in the process of the workforce redesign is fundamental.

References

1. Abbot A. 1988. *The system of Professions. An essay on the division of expert labour.* The University of Chicago Press.
2. APPG All-Party Parliamentary Group on Global Health. 2012. *All the Talents Report. How new roles and better teamwork can release potential and improve health services.* http://www.who.int/workforcealliance/knowledge/resources/appggh_report2012resource/en/.
3. Berland Y, Bourgueil Y. 2006. *Rapport Cinq expérimentations de coopération et de délégation de tâches entre professions de santé* [Online]. Observatoire Nationale de la Démographie des Professions de Santé. https://solidarites-sante.gouv.fr/IMG/pdf/rapport_cinq_experim_juin2006.pdf.
4. Bluestone J. 2006. *Task shifting for a strategic Skill-mix* [Online]. Capacity Project Partnership. Chapel Hill: The Capacity Project. https://capacityproject.org/images/stories/files/techbrief_5.pdf.
5. Bourgeault IL, Kuhlmann E, Neiterman E, Wrede S. 2008. *How can optimal skill-mix be effectively implemented and why? Policy Brief* [Online]. Denmark: WHO Regional Office for Europe. http://www.euro.who.int/__data/assets/pdf_file/0005/75452/E93413.pdf.
6. Buchan J, O'May F. 2000 a). *Determining skill-mix: practical guidelines for managers and health professionals* [Online]. Human Resources Development Journal. 2000; 4(2). http://www.who.int.hrh/en/HRDJ_4_2_07.pdf.
7. Buchan J, O'May F. 2000 b). *Determining skill-mix: practical guidelines for managers and health professionals* [Online]. Issues in health service delivery paper 3. Department of Organization of Health Services Delivery. Geneva: World Health Organization. http://www.who.int/management/determining_skill_mix.pdf.
8. Buchan J, Ball J, O'May F. 2001. *If changing skill-mix is the answer, what is the question?* Journal of Health Services Research & Policy. 2001; 6(4): 233-238.
9. Buchan J, Dal Poz M. 2002. *Skill-mix in the health care workforce: reviewing the evidence.* Bulletin of the World Health Organization. 2002; 80 (7): 575-580. http://www.who.int/bulletin/archives/80(7)575.pdf.
10. Buchan J, Calman L. 2004. *Skill-mix and policy changes in the health workforce: nurses in advanced roles.* OECD Health Working Papers No. 17. OECD Publishing; 2004. http://www.oecd.org/health/health-systems/33857785.pdf.

11. Bryant-Lukosius D, DiCenso A. 2004. *A framework for the introduction and evaluation of advanced practice nursing role.* Journal of Advanced Nursing. 2004; 48: 530-540. https://onlinelibrary.wiley.com/doi/epdf/10.1111/j.1365-2648.2004.03235.x.
12. Brown SA, Grimes DE. 1995. *A meta-analysis of nurse practitioners and nurse midwives in primary care.* Nurs Res. 1995 Nov-Dec; 44(6):332-9.
13. Canadian Nurse Practitioner Initiative 2006. *Implementation and Evaluation Toolkit for Nurse Practitioners in Canada* [Online]. Canada Nurses Association. 2006. https://nurseone.ca/~/media/nurseone/files/en/toolkit_implementation_evaluation_np_e.pdf?la=en.
14. Chilopora, G, Pereira C, Kamwendo F, Chimbiri A, Malunga E, Bergstrom S. 2007. *Postoperative outcome of caesarean sections and other major emergency obstetric surgery by clinical officers and medical officers in Malawi* [Online]. Human Resources for Health20075:17. https://human-resources-health.biomedcentral.com/articles/10.1186/1478-4491-5-17.
15. De Geest S, Moons P, Callens B, Gut C, Lindpaintner L, Spirig R. 2008. *Introducing advanced practice nurses/nurse practitioners in health care systems: a framework for reflection and analysis.* Swiss Med WKLY 2008; 138 (43-44): 621-28. http://www.smw.ch/docs/pdf200x/2008/43/smw-12293.PDF.
16. Delamaire ML, Lafortune G. 2010. *Nurses in Advanced Roles: A description and evaluation of experiences in 12 developed countries* [Online]. OECD Health Working Papers No. 54. France: OECD Publishing. http://www.oecd.org/officialdocuments/publicdisplaydocumentpdf/?cote=delsa/hea/wd/hwp(2010)5&doclanguage=en.
17. Dennis S, May J, Perkins D, Zwar N, Sibbald B, Hasan I. 2009. *What evidence is there to support skill-mix changes between GPs, pharmacists and practice nurses in the care of elderly people living in the community?* [Online]. Aust New Zealand Health Policy. 2009; 6: 23. https://link.springer.com/article/10.1186/1743-8462-6-23.
18. Department of Health. 2010. *Advanced Level Nursing: a position statement.* https://www.gov.uk/government/uploads/system/uploads/attachment_data/file/215935/dh_121738.pdf.
19. Desmeules F, Toliopoulos P, Roy JS, Woodhouse L, Lacelle M, Leroux M, Girard S, Feldman D, Fernandes J. 2013. *Validation of an advanced practice physiotherapy model of care in an outpatient clinic.* BMC Musculoskeletal Disorders, 14: 162. https://bmcmusculoskeletdisord.biomedcentral.com/track/pdf/10.1186/1471-2474-14-162.
20. Dyer TA, Brocklehurst P, Glenny AM, Davies L, Tickle M, Issac A, Robinson PG. 2014. *Dental auxiliaries for dental care traditionally provided by dentists.* [Online]. Cochrane Database of Systematic Reviews 2014, Issue 8. Art. No.: CD010076. https://www.ncbi.nlm.nih.gov/pubmed/25140869.

21. Dubois CA, McKee, Nolte E. 2006. *Human resources for health in Europe*. European Observatory on Health Systems and Policies Series. Berkshire: Open University Press. http://www.euro.who.int/__data/assets/pdf_file/0006/98403/E87923.pdf.
22. Dubois CA, Singh D. 2009. *From staff-mix to skill-mix and beyond: towards a systematic approach to health workforce management*. Human Resources for Health. 2009; 7:87. http://www.human-resources-health.com/content/7/1/87.
23. Ford L. Nurses, Nurses Practitioners: The Evolution of Primary Care (Book Review). Journal of Nursing Scholarship. Volume 18, Number 4, Winter 1986:177-178.
24. Freidson E. 1986. Professional Powers. A study of the institutionalization of formal knowledge. Chicago, Univeristy of Chicago Press.
25. Fulton BD, Scheffler RM, Sparkes SP, Auh EY, Vujicic M, Soucat A. 2011. *Health workforce skill-mix and task shifting in low income countries: a review of recent evidence*. Human Resources for Health 2011, 9:1. https://link.springer.com/content/pdf/10.1186%2F1478-4491-9-1.pdf.
26. Hatem M, Sandall J, Devane D, Soltani H, Gates S. 2008. *Midwife-led versus other models of ca re for childbearing women (Review)*. The Cochrane Collaboration. https://www.cochranelibrary.com/cdsr/doi/10.1002/14651858.CD004667.pub2/epdf/full.
27. Hyde P, McBride A, Young R, Walshe K. 2005. *Role redesign: new ways of working in the NHS*. Personnel Review. 2005; 34 (6): 697-712. https://doi.org/10.1108/00483480510623475.
28. Horrocks S, Anderson E, Salisbury C. 2002. *Systematic review of whether nurse practitioners working in primary care can provide equivalent care to doctors*. BMJ 2002; 324;819-823.
29. International Council of Nurses. *ICN Nurse Practitioner/Advanced Practice Nursing Network*. https://international.aanp.org/Practice/APNRoles.
30. Kaasaleinen S, Martin-Misener R, Kilpatrick K, Harbman P, Bryant-Lukosius D, Donald T, Carter N, DiCenso A. 2010. *A historical overview of the development of advanced practice nursing roles in Canada*. Nursing Leadership. 2010; 23 (Special Issue) 35-60. http://www.longwoods.com/content/22268.
31. Kredo T, Adeniyi FB, Bateganya M, Pienaar ED. Task shifting from doctors to non-doctors for initiation and maintenance of antiretroviral therapy. Cochrane Database of Systematic Reviews 2014, Issue 7. Art. No.: CD007331. https://www.cochranelibrary.com/cdsr/doi/10.1002/14651858.CD007331.pub3/epdf/abstract.
32. Kroezen M. 2014. *Nurse prescribing: A study on task substitution and professional jurisdictions*. Utrecht: Wohrmann Print Service.

33. Laurant M, Harmsen M, Wollersheim H, Grol R, Faber M, Sibbald B. 2009. *The Impact of Nonphysician Clinicians: do they improve the quality and cost-effectiveness of health care services?. Medical Care Research and Review*. Vol 66, Issue 6_suppl, pp. 36S - 89S.
34. Laurant M, Reeves D, Hermens R, Braspenning J, Grol R, Sibbald B. 2010. *Substitution of doctors by nurses in primary care* [Online]. Cochrane Database of Systematic Reviews 2010, Issue 2. Art. No.: CD001271. https://www.cochranelibrary.com/cdsr/doi/10.1002/14651858.CD001271.pub2/epdf/full.
35. Laurant M, van der Biezen M, Wijers N, Watananirun K, Kontopantelis E, van Vught AJAH. 2018. *Nurses as substitutes for doctors in primary care (Review)*. Cochrane Database of Systematic Reviews 2018, Issue 7. Art. No.: CD001271. https://www.cochranelibrary.com/cdsr/doi/10.1002/14651858.CD001271.pub3/epdf/full.
36. Lehmann U, Sanders D. 2007. *Community health workers: What do we know about them? The state of the evidence on programmes, activities, costs and impact on health outcomes of using community health workers*. Evidence and Information for Policy, Department of Human Resources for Health Geneva, January 2007. http://www.who.int/hrh/documents/community_health_workers.pdf.
37. Maier C. B, Aiken L. H. 2017. *Task shifting from physicians to nurses in primary care in 39 countries: a cross-country comparative study*. The European Journal of Public Health, August 2016: 1–8. https://www.ncbi.nlm.nih.gov/pubmed/27485719.
38. Ministre des Solidarités et de la Santé, Ministre de l'Enseignement Supérieur, de la Recherche et de l'Innovation. 2018. *Communiqué de presse. Accès aux soins: Agnès BUZYN et Frédérique VIDAL saluent la reconnaissance officielle de la pratique avancée infirmière*. 19 de Juillet de 2018.
39. Nelson S, Turnbull J, Bainbridge L, Caufield T, Hudson G, Kendel D, Mowat D, Nasmith L, Postl B, Shamian J, Sketris I. 2014. *Optimizing scopes of practice. New models of care for a new health care system*. Canadian Academy of Health Sciences; Ottawa: 2014.
40. Nkansah N, Mostovetsky O, Yu C, Chheng T, Beney J, Bond CM, Bero L. 2010. *Effect of outpatient pharmacists' non-dispensing roles on patient outcomes and prescribing patterns* [Online]. Cochrane Database of Systematic Reviews 2010, Issue 7. Art. No.: CD000336. https://www.ncbi.nlm.nih.gov/pubmed/20614422.
41. NHS. *Multi-professional framework for advanced clinical practice in England* [Online]. https://www.hee.nhs.uk/sites/default/files/documents/Multi-professional%20framework%20for%20advanced%20clinical%20practice%20in%20England.pdf>.
42. Niezen MGH, Mathijssen JJP. 2014. *Reframing professional boundaries in healthcare: A systematic review of facilitators and barriers to task reallocation from the domain of medicine to the nursing domain* [Online]. Health Policy. 117 (2): 151–169. http://www.healthpolicyjrnl.com/article/S0168-8510(14)00115-8/abstract.

43. Pulcini J, Wagner M. Undated. *Nurse practitioner education in the United States* [Online]. Nurse Practitioner Education. http://international.aanp.org/pdf/pulciniarticle0305.pdf.
44. Richardson G, Maynard A. 1995. *Fewer Doctors? More Nurses? A review of knowledge base of doctor-nurse substitution.* The University of York. Centre for Health Economics. York Health Economics Consortium. NHS Centre for Reviews & Dissemination. Discussion paper 135.
45. Rodrigues M de L. 2002. *Sociologia das Profissões.* 2.ª Edição. Celta Editora. 2002.
46. Sibbald B, Shen J, Mc Bride A. 2004. *Changing the skill-mix of the health workforce.* Journal of Health Services Research & Policy. 2004; 9(1): 28-38.
47. Temido M, Dussault G. 2015. *How can a country learn from the experience of another? Expanding nurses' scope of practice in Portugal: Lessons from England* [Online]. Health Policy. 2015 Apr;119(4):475-87. https://www.ncbi.nlm.nih.gov/pubmed/25533548.
48. Weeks G, George J, Maclure K, Stewart D. 2016. *Non-medical prescribing versus medical prescribing for acute and chronic disease management in primary and secondary care.* Cochrane Database Syst Rev. 2016 Nov 22; 11: CD011227. https://www.ncbi.nlm.nih.gov/pubmed/27873322.
49. WHO. 2000. *The World Health Report 2000. Health Systems: Improving performance.* Geneva: World Health Organization. http://www.who.int/whr/2000/en/whr00_en.pdf.
50. WHO. 2006. *The World Health Report 2006 - Working together for health* Geneva: World Health Organization. http://www.who.int/whr/2006/en/
51. WHO. 2008. *Task shifting: rational redistribution of tasks among health workforce teams: global recommendations and guidelines.* Geneva, WHO Library Cataloguing-in-Publication Data. http://www.who.int/healthsystems/TTR-TaskShifting.pdf.
52. WHO. 2016. Global Strategy on Human Resources for Health: Workforce 2030. Disponível: http://www.who.int/hrh/resources/globstrathrh-2030/en/.
53. WHO Regional Office for Europe. 2018. *The toolkit for a sustainable health workforce in the WHO European Region.* http://www.euro.who.int/en/health-topics/HealthSystems/healthWorkforce/publications/2018/the-toolkit-for-a-sustainable-health-workforce-in-the-who-european-region-2018.
54. WHO guideline on health policy and system support to optimize community health worker programmes. Geneva: World Health Organization; 2018. Licence: CC BY-NC-SA 3.0 IGO. https://apps.who.int/iris/bitstream/handle/10665/275474/9789241550369-eng.pdf

Deployment, retention and mobility of health professionals

Marieke Kroezen

1. Introduction

Shortages of health workers are a critical issue in many countries. They prevent national health systems from meeting population needs and achieving the sustainable development goal of universal health coverage (Lopes et al., 2017). Apart from shortages, almost all countries are faced with imbalances in the geographical distribution of health professionals – mostly an undersupply in rural and sparsely populated areas and oversupply in some urban areas (Kroezen et al., 2015). According to estimates in 2015, 63 per cent of the rural population compared to 33 per cent of urban populations worldwide lacked access to health services (International Labour Organization, 2017). On top of already existing shortages and maldistributions, attrition rates among health professionals are high – defined broadly as exits from the workforce, which can be due to emigration, voluntary exits, illness, death or retirement (Lopes et al., 2017). Also, there is a high rate of intention to leave among health professionals. In a study in ten European countries in 2013, for example, one in ten nurses intended to leave their profession, with variations from 5 to 17% between countries (Heinen et al., 2013).

To respond to these challenges, it is important to recognize that all aspects of the professional working life should be taken into account, and that they should not be examined isolated from each other. One obvious connection is that deployment is often coupled with retention. Both are critical aspects of health workforce policy. Another is that retention is often also considered in the context of improving the geographical distribution of the health workforce (Buchan et al., 2018). Finally, mobility is connected to the factors which attract and retain health workers in certain areas, both nationally and internationally. Therefore, deployment, retention and mobility are fundamental aspects to be taken into account for developing a sustainable health workforce. This chapter provides an introduction to these dimensions and discusses what they encompass, how they can be measured and what the current evidence on each dimension is.

2. Deployment

2.1. What is deployment?

Deployment is the process of distributing the health workforce in such a way that a sufficient number of staff is available to operate healthcare facilities. In other words, adequate deployment should ensure that health workers are assigned to the worksites where their knowledge, skills and competencies are most needed (Necochea et al., 2013). For a long time already, optimal deployment of staff has been recognized as a way to effectively deal with shortages in human resources for health (Kazanjian et al., 1992).

2.2. Types of deployment models

Generally, there are two ways to deploy or distribute health staff:

- Top-down deployment (push mechanism): this consists of sending health staff to pre-determined locations identified in the planning process in a mandatory way.
- Bottom-up deployment (pull-down): in which the local or facility level plays an active role in trying to attract the type of staff it needs.

Top-down deployment

Top-down deployment is used in several countries. There are Ministries of Health that specify that health professionals who were educated with government support, have to fulfil a limited period of service after their graduation in locations determined by the government. Some of the shortcomings of this approach are that the periods of service are usually quite limited, only two or three years, and that it is often not adequately enforced. If this method is continuously and effectively implemented, in theory it can contribute to alleviate critical deployment gaps. However, it does not offer a permanent solution to long-term staffing inequities. Only indirectly – through the fact that initial placements can positively influence final settlement decisions – can top-down deployment contribute to long-term solutions (Necochea et al., 2013).

Another way in which the top-down mechanism is implemented is by the regulation of transfers. Ministries of Health or other bodies may establish conditions for leaving posts that are considered high priority, or they may delay decisions on transfer of staff in these positions. Employers, on the other hand, may facilitate transfers to difficult or critical areas (Necochea et al., 2013).

Finally, some countries faced with critical shortages in certain occupations sign bilateral agreements with other countries to "import" staff. The international medical staff that is available through these agreements often serve for limited periods of time and are usually distributed through a top-down mechanism (Necochea et al., 2013).

Bottom-up deployment

Bottom-up deployment has become increasingly important over the last years. This is mainly due to the fact that many countries are introducing decentralization schemes (i.e. administrative restructuring by central governments). In this way, local level governments, and sometimes even individual health facilities, have more resources and decision-making powers. For example Ethiopia started a decentralization process in 2002 with the stated goal of improving deployment of health professionals, by increasing local authority and introducing flexibility in hiring practices (Michael et al., 2010). Also in the private sector, bottom-up deployment forms the main method of recruiting staff. Under this modality, institutions have to develop a staffing plan that includes attractive employment packages and a process for the successful recruitment of staff (Necochea et al., 2013).

2.3. Measuring deployment

Deployment is usually measured through the deployment rate, e.g. the number of health workers recruited and assigned for a job in specified period of time as numerator, and the available health workforce at the end of the same period as denominator (Michael et al., 2010). In 2007, Bossert et al. (2007) developed two primary indicators to measure deployment:

1. Guidelines exist for forms and procedures for approving recruitment, promotions and transfers.
2. Guidelines exist for forms and procedures for discipline, grievances and termination.

Both indicators can be assessed through document review or key informant interviews at national or subnational levels.

2.4. Evidence on the deployment of health professionals

There is a scarcity of evidence on the effectiveness of deployment of health professionals. Also, while countries at all levels of socioeconomic development face difficulties in deployment of their health workforce, albeit to varying degrees (World Health Organization, 2016), the majority of the limited evidence seems to focus on African and Asian countries (Kanchanachitra et al., 2011). One of the most important tasks to ensure successful deployment is ensuring that staff are placed in the correct positions, according to their competencies and job descriptions (Necochea et al., 2013). However, the evidence shows that this is not always done successfully. In Mozambique, for example, it has been found that nurses are often placed in positions that do not match their competencies (Necochea et al., 2013). Also in Botswana, the appropriate deployment of staff has been reported as a problem, as staff preparation for initial posting and transfer are not always taken into account (Seitio-Kgokgwe et al., 2016). This is especially true for nurse specialists, who are sometimes placed in areas which are not of their expertise. This results in inappropriate placements of specialist staff and hence ineffective deployment. Concerns have also been raised about the deployment of doctors to management positions, despite clinical shortages in hospitals (Seitio-Kgokgwe et al., 2016). This is a common practice in African countries. Another example is Kenya, where the deployment process has been termed 'outdated'. However, in 2005, a fast-track hiring and deployment model was implemented, which shows positive effects (Adano, 2008). In general though, there are still significant gaps in the evidence base with respect to how best to address deployment challenges in human resources for health (Kanchanachitra et al., 2011).

3. Retention

3.1. What is retention?

Retention is a central aspect in the overall health labour market, and fundamental for developing a sustainable health workforce. Retention can be defined as the capacity to maintain health workers in the health care system, limiting unjustified ("voluntary") losses to other organizations, sectors or geographical areas, within and out of the country (Barriball et al., 2015). However, there is not one definition of retention commonly agreed upon in the literature. Many definitions tend to confine themselves to stating that health workers stay in their present job. A more comprehensive definition is "the continued employment of skilled and productive staff" (Dieleman and Harnmeijer, 2006). In this definition, attention is specifically drawn to the activities and productivity of staff. This is important, as health staff may remain in the health system (and hence become part of the retained health workforce) whilst being inactive or active but not practising.

3.2. Types of retention interventions

Interventions to retain health workers can have different targets, for example focusing on the education of health professionals or working conditions (Barriball et al., 2015, Kroezen et al., 2015). Generally, retention interventions can be classified – based on WHO's 'Global policy recommendations on increasing access to health workers in remote and rural areas through improved retention' (WHO, 2010) – in the following categories:

- Education: this includes a variety of strategies including clinical rotations; placements in rural regions; coaching or mentoring of students; adaptation of curricula for rural health workers and decentralisation of education institutions or programmes and scholarships in exchange to commitment to work in a rural or remote setting or in certain fields of practice (Barriball et al., 2015).
- Regulatory: interventions under this category can be defined broadly to encompass any government control exercised through legislative, administrative, legal or policy tools. Hence, these are policy

levers. They are less commonly used to retain healthcare staff as they are more demanding, politically and economically. Examples are changes in the status of nurses or of family physicians, in the revision of scopes of practice, in the management structure, in employment contracts or in remuneration mechanisms (Barriball et al., 2015, WHO, 2010).

- Financial incentives: this category includes all additional benefits paid or provided to health workers to (recruit or) retain them. These include salary increases, financial incentives, in-kind benefits (free accommodation or transport), but also the provision of good working tools such as information and communication technologies, and training opportunities (Barriball et al., 2015, WHO, 2010).
- Professional and personal support: this category includes measures at personal level – such as the availability of a good infrastructure, opportunities for social interaction, schooling for children and employment for spouses – and measures at professional level – including opportunities to advance careers and to communicate and consult with peers through networks, telehealth or other approaches (WHO, 2010).

3.3. Measuring retention

Retention can be measured prospectively and retrospectively and by various indicators:

- Turnover (synonyms: attrition, wastage): this is the most commonly used measure of retention. It refers to the percentage of staff of a particular workplace or system who have left the organisation (or have moved jobs) within the last 12 months (Buchan et al., 2018).
- Intention to leave: with this measure, health workers are asked how likely it is that they will remain in their job within the next X years or, vice versa, how likely it is that they will leave their job within the next X years.
- Stability: this measure calculates the percentage of staff of a particular workplace or system who were in substantive posts at the beginning of year one and who are still in substantive posts a year later (Buchan et al., 2018).

- The overall duration of the occupational career of a health worker: a measure of, or one element in the measurement of, retention (Lehmann et al., 2015).

3.4. Evidence on the retention of health professionals

In general, there is little evidence about the effectiveness of retention interventions for health professionals. It is clear that single recruitment and retention interventions have little impact and that packages are more effective, but the successfulness of retention interventions is to a large extent dependent on their context-sensitivity (Kroezen et al., 2015). Despite these limitations, a few general conclusions can be drawn. Dissatisfaction with employment and working conditions – including low salaries, work overload, long hours and weak career prospects – has been reported as one of the main causes for the high turnover and attrition rates of health workers in many countries (International Labour Organization, 2017). Hence, the work environment – the place, conditions and surrounding influences in which people carry out an activity – constitutes an important factor in the retention of health professionals (Wiskow et al., 2010). The International Labour Organization (ILO) has developed the following model to depict the quality of the work environment (Table 4).

Table 4. ILO model on quality of the work environment

Quality of the work environment	
Dimension	**Elements**
Employment quality	Wages Type of contract Working hours, including work schedules and family-work balance Social benefits Participation Professional development (training and skill development)
Work quality	Work autonomy Work organization (including division of work and staffing) Organizational culture and trust Safety and health Pace of work Social work environment

Source: International Labour Organization (2017)

Employment quality

One of the major elements affecting the attractiveness of the work environment for health workers, and a major retention and worker motivation factor, is payment (International Labour Organization, 2017). An overview of 33 reviews found that compensation was the most effective intervention in terms of health workforce outcomes, including retention, recruitment, turnover and intent to leave (Misfeldt et al., 2014). However, it has also been found that financial incentives alone are unlikely to achieve their goals and are more effective if combined with other types of measures (Kroezen et al., 2015). Misfeldt et al., in their overview of reviews, also found that health professionals respond positively to incentives linked to the quality of the working environment, including opportunities for professional development, interprofessional collaboration, professional autonomy and improved work-life balance. A family-friendly work environment is deemed especially important in the health sector because of its gender dimension (Misfeldt et al., 2014), and many retention interventions currently applied in Europe focus on family-friendly practices and on promoting a healthy work-life balance (Kroezen et al., 2015).

Work quality

Overall, there is more limited evidence for the impact of elements of work quality – such as job demands, restructured staffing models, re-engineered work designs, ward practices or staff skills-mix – on retention (Misfeldt et al., 2014) .

Recently, Buchan et al. (2018) specifically summarized the evidence on nurse retention by merging the evidence from systematic reviews on this topic. This resulted in a number of key points:

- Most of the evidence for nurse retention is focused on hospital-based nurses in high income countries.
- The factors that contribute to nurse retention are complex and multi-dimensional but are usually influenced both by organizational and individual / demographic factors.
- There is a range of factors impacting nurse retention, including: work environment, working relationships, and working conditions; pay, other financial and non-financial incentives; flexibility and so

called "family-friendly" policies; career opportunities and access to education; productive working relationships with other staff and teams; responsive management, effective supervision and focused mentoring; and job mobility and relative job opportunities in different organizations, sectors, regions and countries.

4. Mobility

4.1. What is mobility?

There is not one commonly accepted definition of health professional mobility. Some attempts have been made to overcome this deficit. One proposed definition of health professional mobility is "any intentional change of country after graduation with the purpose and effect of delivering health-related services, including during training periods" (Wismar et al., 2011). However, this definition is not in common use yet.

4.2. Types of mobility

Regardless of the definition used, it is important to recognize that health professional mobility is not a homogeneous phenomenon. Rather, there are different types of mobile health professionals, with different motives and behaviours, who also differ in terms of their purpose of migration, length of stay, personal profile and direction of movement. Glinos and Buchan (2014) distinguish six types of mobile health professionals :

1. The livelihood migrant: moves to earn a (better) living.
2. The career-oriented migrant: travels to develop his or her career (e.g. through training and/or education or to specialize).
3. The backpacker migrant: works to travel (i.e. may try to work in several countries to experience other countries and health systems).
4. The commuter migrant: commutes across borders to work.
5. The undocumented migrant: is migrating for work, like the livelihood migrant, but unofficially (e.g. by being employed by a care-recipient and working in his/her private home).
6. The returner migrant: migrates in reverse (i.e. migrates back to the home country).

Circular mobility

Most of the time, when health professionals migrate, there is a net migration loss of health workers from low to high-income countries. This usually results in a so-called 'brain drain' for the country of origin and in a 'brain gain' for the destination country, which benefits from health workers' skills and experience. Naturally, the extent of brain drain depends on where health workers are trained and whether the country of origin has a deficit. This is usually the case though. Hence, brain drain increases existing inequalities, while further weakening already weak health systems (HealthWorkers4All, 2013).

An alternative to the brain drain - brain gain dichotomy is presented by circular migration. There is no common definition of circular migration, but the concept has been defined by the European Commission (MEMO 07/197) as *"A form of migration that is managed in a way that it allows migrants some degree of legal mobility back and forth between two countries"*. Circular migration is generally expected to open up the potential of brain sharing or brain circulation (Kroezen, 2016). Table 5 summarizes the advantages and disadvantages of circular migration of health professionals.

Table 5. Commonly cited advantages and disadvantages in the debate on circular migration of health professionals

	Destination country	Source country	Migrant worker
Advantages	Health worker shortages handled in a flexible and timely way Savings in training of health professionals Part of a development friendly national migration policy Limited integration costs Can meet health worker shortages in rural and remote areas Enhanced links with origin country	Benefit from inflow of remittances Brain drain human capital loss not as great Health workers return with greater skills and enhanced networks and ideas Contribution to health of the nation Enhanced links with destination country	Enhances income, skills and experience Able to contribute to health of homeland population Children can gain experience of growing up in both countries Easier return to a workplace and family in the home country Retain traditional and family associations
Disadvantages	Workers not available on a permanent basis Complications of organisation health system at destination Governance challenges Difficulties for immigration policy	Loss of skills for part of the time Difficulty of organising health system with personnel only in the country for a limited time Governance challenges	Disruption and costs of moving Social cost of separation from family for part of the time Difficulties of adjusting to two work contexts Restricted rights and entitlements (e.g. pension benefits, health insurance)

Source: Kroezen, 2016

4.3. Measuring mobility

In lack of a commonly accepted definition of health professional mobility, three indicators are used to describe and measure the mobility of health workers: "foreign-trained" (place of education/training), "foreign-born" (place of birth) and "foreign-national" (nationality) (Glinos and Buchan, 2014). None of these indicators is perfect though. The nationality--indicator has the disadvantage that foreigners disappear from the statistics once they are naturalized. Also, in many countries, people who were born and raised in the country nonetheless hold a different nationality. There is, therefore, no systematic link between migration and nationality (OECD, 2016). The indicator related to the place of birth gives some useful information on the country of origin, but tells nothing about the time of migration (which may have taken place at a very young age) or where health workers pursued their education. The place of education/training therefore seems to be a more reliable indicator, although it should account for the growing internationalization of medical and nursing education (OECD, 2016).

With no clear definition and not one indicator able to capture all facets of mobility, the general understanding of health professional mobility is bound to be an approximation. This is illustrated in countries where data for all three indicators are available. Comparisons between the three indicators show large differences in their numbers. For example, in 2009, Poland identified 858 foreign-national medical doctors, but three times as many foreign-trained (2.868) and four times as many foreign-born (3.887). This discrepancy shows that the three indicators cannot tell the full story of a mobile health professional's journey, and different indicators will tell different stories. This has consequences for data collection, research and policy (Glinos and Buchan, 2014).

4.4. Evidence on health professional mobility

In general, health workforce research is hampered by a lack of data. A specific challenge in this regard is formed by the lack of data on cross-border and cross-sectoral mobility of health professionals; to quantify where health workers go, how long they stay away and whether they come back or not. Accurate data about the migration of health workforce is not available in many countries. This deficit is partly explained and at the same time compounded by the fact that there is no single definition of health professional mobility (Kroezen et al., 2018). Nonetheless, some general trends can be observed, especially for European countries.

Overview of health workforce migration

The 'International Migration Outlook 2015' (OECD, 2015) shows the scale of health workforce migration flows and recent trends, the dependence of host countries' health system on foreign practitioners and how this impacts host countries and countries of origin. Foreign-born doctors and nurses account for a significant and growing share of the healthcare professionals working in the OECD area. Doctors' share grew in most countries between 2000/01 and 2010/11 from an average (across 22 countries) of 19.5% to more than 22%, while that of nurses rose from 11% to 14.5% (Figure 6 and Figure 7). In most OECD countries, the proportion of health workers trained abroad is lower than that of health workers born abroad, which points to the fact that host countries provide part of migrants' training and education. In most OECD countries that supplied data, the proportion of nurses trained abroad tends to be much lower than that of doctors.

When looking at the countries of origin of foreign-born doctors and nurses who work in OECD countries, increases from the South East Asia region between 2000/01 and 2010/11 mainly came from doctors born in India (Figure 8). In Europe, Romania stands out for its high volume of

Figure 6. Percentage of foreign-born doctors in 29 OECD countries, 2010/11

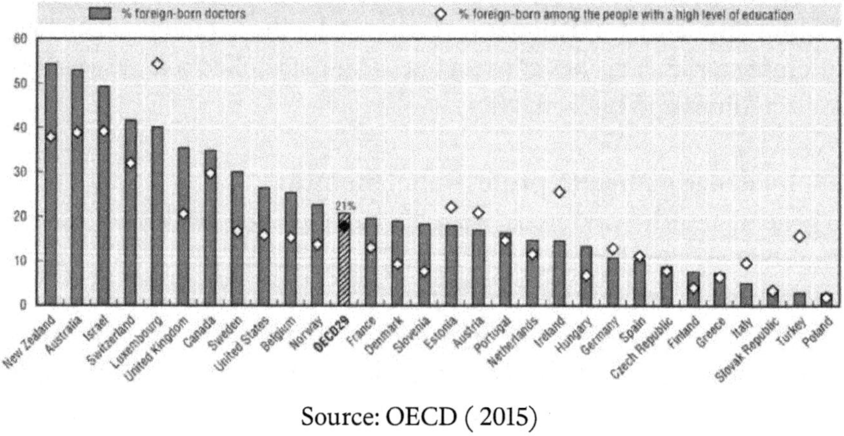

Source: OECD (2015)

Figure 7. Percentage of foreign-born nurses in 28 OECD countries, 2010/11

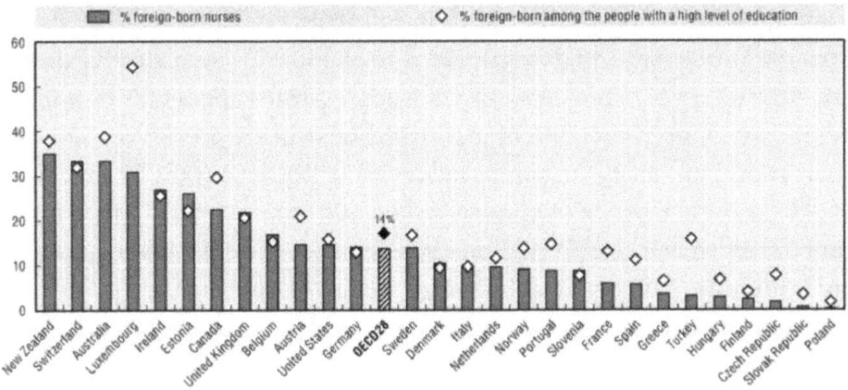

Source: OECD (2015)

Figure 8. Foreign-born doctors and nurses in OECD countries by 25 main countries of origin, 2000/01 and 2010/11

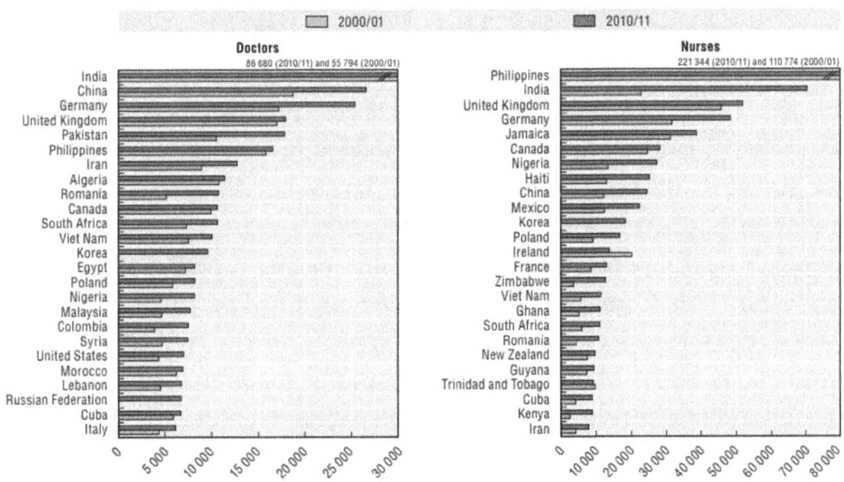

Source: OECD (2015)

emigration. In the Eastern Mediterranean and the Western Pacific regions, Pakistan and China accounted for the highest shares of foreign-born doctors in the OECD area, while the Philippines sent the largest proportion of nurses. Germany and the United Kingdom were the main countries of origin among OECD countries.

The OECD report also shows a growing negative impact of these emigration patterns on health systems in countries of origin. In 2010/11, doctors and nurses who had immigrated to the OECD area from countries affected by severe shortages of healthcare professionals (as defined by WHO) accounted for 20% of estimated healthcare workforce needs in their countries of origin, compared to 9% in 2000/01 (OECD, 2015).

There is an absence of empirical data and research on circular migration of health workers. While much is claimed, little is known about circular migration in any field, including health (Kroezen, 2016).

5. Conclusion

Shortages and maldistribution of health workers are a critical issue in many countries. Therefore, whilst policy efforts must focus on the production of new staff, there also needs to be a policy emphasis on retention and distribution (Buchan et al., 2018). In this regard, deployment, retention and mobility are fundamental aspects to be taken into account for developing a sustainable health workforce. This chapter provided an overview on these three dimensions and how they can be measured and showed that the evidence base for all three dimensions is still limited. As a prerequisite for improving the knowledge on what works and what doesn't work, better health workforce data is needed. Also, most of the evidence that is available to date is related to doctors, and much less data for other health professionals such as nurses and especially lower qualified staff. This is problematic for obtaining a full picture of the health workforce in terms of its deployment, retention and mobility. Furthermore, it has been noted that efforts should be made to standardize definitions and measurements, in order to enable a clearer evidence base on these issues. This is especially true for health professional mobility. Once these improvements have been made, policies on deployment, retention and mobility of health professionals can be adapted and attuned to those interventions that have the most proven effectiveness in improving the sustainability of the health workforce.

References

1. ADANO, U. 2008. The health worker recruitment and deployment process in Kenya: an emergency hiring program. *Human Resources for Health*, 6, 19.

2. BARRIBALL, L., BREMNER, J., BUCHAN, J., CRAVEIRO, I., DIELEMAN, M., DIX, O., DUSSAULT, G., JANSEN, C., KROEZEN, M. & RAFFERTY, A. M. 2015. Recruitment and retention of the health workforce in Europe. Luxembourg: Publications Office of the European Union.
3. BOSSERT, T., BÄRNIGHAUSSEN, T. & MITCHELL, A. 2007. *Assessing financing, education, management and policy context for estrategic planning of human resourses for health*, Geneva: World Health Organization.
4. BUCHAN, J., SCHAFFER, F. A. & CATTON, H. 2018. Policy Brief: Nurse Retention. Philadelphia: International Centre on Nurse Migration. https://www.icn.ch/sites/default/files/inline-files/2018_ICNM%20Nurse%20retention.pdf
5. DIELEMAN, M. & HARNMEIJER, J. W. 2006. Improving health worker performance: in search of promising practices. *Geneva: World Health Organization*, 5-34.
6. GLINOS, I. & BUCHAN, J. 2014. Health professionals crossing the EU's internal and external borders: a typology of health professional mobility and migration. *Health Professional Mobility in a Changing Europe. New dynamic, mobile individuals and diverse responses. Observatory Studies Series*, 32, 129.
7. HEALTHWORKERS4ALL 2013. One billion people world-wide will never see a health worker
8. HEINEN, M. M., VAN ACHTERBERG, T., SCHWENDIMANN, R., ZANDER, B., MATTHEWS, A., KÓZKA, M., ENSIO, A., SJETNE, I. S., CASBAS, T. M. & BALL, J. 2013. Nurses' intention to leave their profession: a cross sectional observational study in 10 European countries. *International Journal of Nursing Studies*, 50, 174-184.
9. INTERNATIONAL LABOUR ORGANIZATION 2017. Improving employment and working conditions in health services. Geneva: International Labour Organization.
10. KANCHANACHITRA, C., LINDELOW, M., JOHNSTON, T., HANVORAVONGCHAI, P., LORENZO, F. M., HUONG, N. L., WILOPO, S. A. & DELA ROSA, J. F. 2011. Human resources for health in southeast Asia: shortages, distributional challenges, and international trade in health services. *The Lancet*, 377, 769-781.
11. KAZANJIAN, A., PULCINS, I. R. & KERLUKE, K. 1992. A human resources decision support model: nurse deployment patterns in one Canadian system. *Journal of Healthcare Management*, 37, 303.
12. KROEZEN, M. 2016. Circular Migration of the Health Workforce. Report as part of the Joint Action on Health Workforce Planning and Forecasting.
13. KROEZEN, M., DUSSAULT, G., CRAVEIRO, I., DIELEMAN, M., JANSEN, C., BUCHAN, J., BARRIBALL, L., RAFFERTY, A. M., BREMNER, J.

& SERMEUS, W. 2015. Recruitment and retention of health professionals across Europe: a literature review and multiple case study research. *Health Policy,* 119, 1517-1528.

14. KROEZEN, M., VAN HOEGAERDEN, M. & BATENBURG, R. 2018. The Joint Action on Health Workforce Planning and Forecasting: Results of a European programme to improve health workforce policies. *Health Policy,* 122, 87-93.
15. LEHMANN, P., MEYSTRE, N. R. & MAMBOURY, N. 2015. Factors for lifelong job retention among Swiss radiographers. *Radiography,* 21, 181-187.
16. LOPES, S. C., GUERRA-ARIAS, M., BUCHAN, J., POZO-MARTIN, F. & NOVE, A. 2017. A rapid review of the rate of attrition from the health workforce. *Human resources for health,* 15, 21.
17. MICHAEL, Y., JIRA, C., GIRMA, B. & TUSHUNE, K. 2010. Health workforce deployment, attrition and density in East Wollega zone, Western Ethiopia. *Ethiopian Journal of Health Sciences,* 20.
18. MISFELDT, R., LINDER, J., LAIT, J., HEPP, S., ARMITAGE, G., JACKSON, K. & SUTER, E. 2014. Incentives for improving human resource outcomes in health care: overview of reviews. *Journal of health services research & policy,* 19, 52-61.
19. NECOCHEA, E., BADLANI, M. & BOSSEMEYER, D. 2013. Systematic Management of Human Resources for Health: An Introduction for Health Managers. Baltimore: Jhpiego Corporation - John Hopkins University.
20. OECD 2015. *International Migration Outlook 2015,* Paris, OECD Publishing.
21. OECD 2016. *Health Workforce Policies in OECD Countries: Right Jobs, Right Skills, Right Places,* Paris, OECD Publishing.
22. SEITIO-KGOKGWE, O. S., GAULD, R., HILL, P. C. & BARNETT, P. 2016. Understanding human resource management practices in Botswana's public health sector. *Journal of health organization and management,* 30, 1284-1300.
23. WHO 2010. Increasing access to health workers in remote and rural areas through improved retention: Global policy recommendations. Geneva: WHO.
24. WISKOW, C., ALBREHT, T. & DE PIETRO, C. 2010. *How to create an attractive and supportive working environment for health professionals,* World Health Organization Geneva.
25. WISMAR, M., MAIER, C. B., GLINOS, I. A., BREMNER, J., DUSSAULT, G. & FIGUERAS, J. 2011. Health professional mobility and health systems in Europe: an introduction. *Health Professional Mobility and Health Systems,* 23, 1.
26. WORLD HEALTH ORGANIZATION 2016. Global strategy on human resources for health: workforce 2030. Geneva: World Health Organization.

The economic impact of human resources in health systems

PEDRO PITA BARROS, EDUARDO COSTA

1. Why should we be concerned about human resources in healthcare?

When a gunshot-wound patient enters the emergency room of a central hospital, a team of doctors, nurses and other staff is immediately mobilized to stabilize the patient and restore her condition. The interaction between these different professionals is key to achieving good outcomes in the healthcare system. Additionally, the interaction between these human resources (HR) and non-human resources (such as technology, facilities, drugs...) is also essential for the success of such endeavour.

As each of these inputs is scarce and expensive, when designing the healthcare system, a policy maker needs to consider their economic impact. In other words, when deciding the reference skill-mix, one needs to select the optimal allocation of inputs and their quantity, such that a desired level of care is assured, at the minimum possible cost. Such decision must be made at the level of each organization, which can differ from the country average level.

In this chapter, we provide an assessment of the efficiency of health services systems, using an aggregate production function as a representation of the broad features and characteristics of the health system, to highlight the role of doctors and nurses. We find that inefficiencies, in the sense of waste of resources, do not seem to be a result of different HR policies, here captured as varying nurses to doctor ratios; these lead to different costs. Here, we estimate the excess cost faced by the system associated with non-optimal nurses to doctor ratios.

Increasing health expenditures, as well as a fragile economic outlook, are raising legitimate concerns about the financial sustainability of health systems.

In our sample of OECD countries, health expenditures have been increasing over time as a percentage of GDP, signalling that countries are devoting relatively more resources to healthcare. If in 2000 the average spending on health was around 7,2% of GDP, in 2015 it was close to 9%. Moreover, this increasing pattern is consistent across countries. Apart from Turkey and Iceland, all other countries increased the share of national resources devoted to healthcare between 2000 and 2015.

Such increase in per capita health spending was followed by an improvement in health outcomes. In 2000, at the age of 80, individuals would live on average 8,6 additional years. In 2015, life expectancy at the age of 80 had increased by more than one year, to 9,8. This positive effect was common to all countries analysed, suggesting that health spending can contribute to the improvement of health (Hadley 1982). However, health spending only explains part of the gains in life expectancy over time (OECD, 2017). Moreover, not all investments in healthcare contribute uniformly to better health outcomes. In fact, Cutler (2004) estimates that only 40% of life expectancy gains from 1950 to 2000 were due to medical improvements in low-weight infant care and cardiovascular disease treatment.

There are several reasons at the roots of this increasing trend in healthcare spending. On one hand, the aging of societies imposes an additional burden on health systems (Schneider & Guralnik, 1990), though with much smaller impact than expected(Stearns & Norton, 2004; Zweifel, Felder, & Meiers, 1999). Also, the increase in disposable income augments the demand for health services (Gerdtham, Jonsson 2000). On the other hand, technologies and drugs are becoming more expensive, and health systems are using them more intensively (Okunade, Murthy 2002).

Additionally, despite significant investments in technology over the last decades, HR expenditure in healthcare does not seem to decrease in absolute terms. It may be the case that technology-driven savings are lower in healthcare when compared to other sectors, an effect known as the Baumol disease (1993), that suggests that productivity in healthcare increases at a slower pace than in other sectors and leads to expenditure (and HRH) growth (Atanda, Menclova, Reed 2018).

It is difficult to obtain a very precise measure of HR spending in healthcare across countries given the lack of comparable data on the number of doctors and nurses, as well as on their respective wages. Based on available OECD data, we estimate that core HR expenditure, including only physicians and nurse's wages, amounts to at least one fourth of total healthcare expenditure. If we include all other staff, this share would increase significantly. Estimates point that in high-income countries, HR expenditure amounts to 38% of total spending (Hernandez-Peña et al., 2013). In Portugal, this ranges between 32 to 34% (OPSS, 2018), representing the largest spending category in the hospital sector (Costa, Santana, & Lopes, 2013). This proportion should even be larger in primary care, since it is more labour intensive than hospital care.

In 2015, more than 10% of the OCED labour force was employed in the health and social work sector. Nordic countries, such as Norway or Denmark, were at the top of this ranking, with around 20% of their labour force working in the health sector. The proportion of workers employed has increased by 42% since 2000 (OECD, 2017). Therefore, when discussing policies that aim to slow down the growth in health spending, it is difficult to ignore policies that deal with HR.

Taking a closer look at HR evolution in healthcare, and focusing on physicians and nurses, one notices that the increase in health spending is partially a result of the increase of the sector's workforce. On average, from 2000 to 2015 in OECD countries, the number of doctors per 1000 population increased by 23% from 2,6 to 3,1, while the number of nurses per 1000 population increased by 20% from 7,0 to 8,5. These increases are common across the majority of countries with the exception the UK and Israel with a reduction on the number of nurses.

Countries like Austria or Norway exhibit a very high proportion of doctors per 1000 people (5,1 and 4,7 respectively), while Switzerland and Norway, again, have more than 17 nurses per 1000 people. However, lower income countries like China, Turkey, South Africa or India have still less than 2 doctors per 1000 people and less than 3 nurses per 1000 people.

Figure 9. Relation between efficiency estimates and nurses to doctor ratio

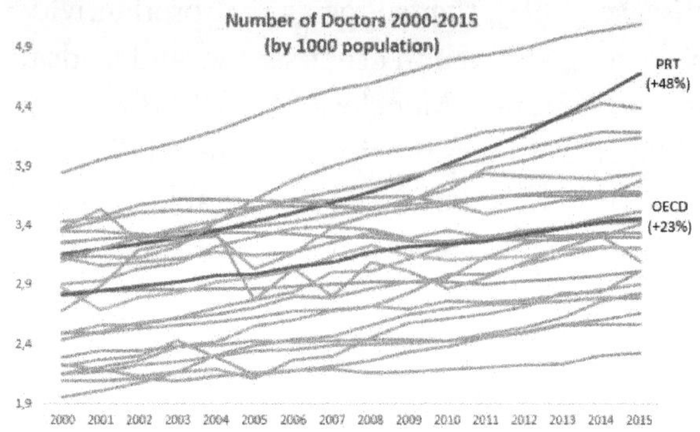

(OECD; 2000-2015)

The significant increase in both professional categories, did not change the relative number of nurses per doctor substantially. In 2000, it was on average 2,7 nurses per doctor and 2,8 in 2015. Japan, Finland, Denmark or the USA are the countries with more nurses per doctor (between 4,4 and 4,6), while Spain, China, Mexico or Turkey rank among the countries with less nurses per doctor (a ratio close to one). Countries with a high gap between doctors' and nurses' wages, are usually countries with a higher ratio of nurses to doctor (Figure 9).

The striking differences among the nurses to doctor ratio suggest that the role of doctors and nurses varies across countries. This raises immediate questions: what is the optimal combination between nurses and doctors? Is such optimal combination common to all countries?

Folland, Goodman and Stano (2013) note that health professionals often recognize only one correct way of treating a given illness, meaning a fixed ratio of nurses to doctors, which is seldom true. Such restrictive approach prevents policy-makers from achieving cost-savings substitutions without impacting the quality of care provided. Instead, if there is some flexibility in the way HR are combined in treating a given illness, namely in terms of who treats and how teams are composed, then cost-saving improvements might be possible without sacrificing outcomes or quality of care.

To understand if the healthcare sector has such flexibility, we need to consider questions such as whether nurses can substitute some of the functions currently performed by physicians. This discussion has become more frequent given the shortage of physicians, strong economic constraints, and the need for high-quality care.

Typical proposals range from nurses managing chronic patients or following low-risk pregnancies, to providing follow-up care to patients with chronic diseases. These grey areas are usually very controversial. On one side, doctors argue that patients will be harmed and overall quality reduced. On the other side, nurses claim that their training has prepared them for those responsibilities. Regardless of the legal and political barriers, this substitution is already a reality.

Such substitution between nurses and doctors can have two important effects: to generate immediate cost savings for the system, since a nurse is usually cheaper to employ than a doctor; and, to reduce physicians' workload.

The substitution idea is not limited to the doctor versus nurse example. There is also the substitution between nurses and auxiliary staff, doctors and administrative staff, or even HR and technology. At each of these levels, a decision must be made to determine the input allocation compatible, not only with no waste of resources, but also with achieving the lowest possible cost.

The next section sheds some light on the impact on health outcomes of having different nurses to doctor ratio. Then we discuss the efficient allocation of nurses to doctor and map the cost associated to such inefficiencies. Finally, the last section summarizes the key messages one should bear in mind when thinking about the economic impact of HR in healthcare.

2. Do HR policies impact health outcomes?

The increase in spending threatens health systems' financial sustainability, as it has typically outpaced economic growth in most OECD countries. Any attempt to control or mitigate this growth must address HR spending. Therefore, it is important to consider the impacts of adjusting the number of doctors and nurses in a country.

From a hospital administrator perspective, both doctors and nurses, as well as the remaining staff, contribute to the same output (healthcare), although with different productivities and costs. If hiring a nurse is cheaper than hiring a doctor, we do not expect that a nurse will provide the same full range of services. However, we can expect some degree of substitution between them. There are some tasks that both doctors and nurses can perform equally well. Based on these, one can determine the efficient combination of doctors and nurses.

Before proceeding, it is important to define this concept of *efficiency*, which in turn leads us to introduce the idea of a *production function for healthcare*. In this context, we consider that different staff, drugs, beds, and technology, among other factors, interact to produce healthcare services.

If each hospital produces the maximum possible amount of healthcare, with the set of inputs it has, we say that this unit is technically efficient. In other words, this hospital does not waste resources and cannot increase its production given the inputs it has. **Technical efficiency** implies that teams are cooperating, machines are working properly and at full capacity, in a word that the hospital is operating at its maximum.

However, if the hospital administrator has also room to choose the quantity of each input, then there might be room for improvement. This is the idea behind the concept of **allocative efficiency**: the hospital selects the optimal amount of inputs, such that a certain healthcare production level is achieved at the minimum cost. This definition is stricter than the technical efficiency, since it introduces the idea of optimizing input choices given input prices. For instance, a hospital administrator may decide to increase the proportion of nurses relative to the number of doctors, if the cost of hiring a nurse is significantly lower than the one of a doctor and the production remains the same.

Production functions estimation, using classic linear regression models, implies the assumption that different countries are equally efficient in the production of health care. Any difference, positive or negative, between the true production and the one predicted by a linear model, would be captured by an error term. A stochastic frontier analysis approach, whose methods have been extensively developed, among others by Kumbhakar and Lovell (2000), allows to deviate from such strong assumption. Instead, when estimating the production function of healthcare, we allow countries to be efficient (on the frontier) or not (below the frontier).

These methods are particularly useful in healthare (Jacobs, Smith, Street 2006; Ferrier 2014). Existing literature provides us with different statistical models for stochastic frontier analysis. All these models hinge on the same principle: the error component will be based on two elements.

A non-positive element capturing inefficient allocations, and a stochastic (random) error to capture exogenous factors. This allows to control for situations in which a country, or a hospital, is operating efficiently, but is subject to an exogenous environmental factor, that affects its output. In such case, the country's best possible practice, the production frontier, will be randomly shifted regardless of its inputs.

The inefficiency term captures wasteful allocations of inputs, which can capture effects such as lack of team work among staff, incorrect proportion of doctors and nurses, or poor management practices. This inefficiency is usually associated with lower health outcomes (Deily, McKay 2008). To illustrate this type of the analysis, we use data from 2000 to 2015 for 25 OECD countries, although we do not have all time periods available for all countries. We are considering North-American countries, European countries, as well as Australia and New Zealand. For each country, data on life expectancies, nurses, doctors, beds, transplants, wages, and other health-related controls was collected (www.oecd.org/els/health-systems/health-data.htm and http://www.transplant-observatory.org/)

In our production function estimation, both inputs and outputs need to be specified. Measuring health output is not obvious. It is difficult to choose simultaneously a measure of population health status that captures healthcare related aspects, and that can be measured accurately (Folland, Goodman, Stano 2013),. Considering the goals of a health system, we use life expectancy as the output of the production function. If a country uses its inputs correctly, its population can achieve a longer life expectancy.

Life expectancy is affected, not only by the healthcare system, but also by the population lifestyle. If two countries have the same health system, but the population of one country has a high smoking prevalence, one should expect life expectancy to be lower in that country(Fuchs 1974).

Estimations were performed using life expectancy at birth, at the age of 65, and at the age of 80. Using these different measures allows to test the robustness of the estimation, as well as to understand how the impact of certain variables changes depending on the indicator.

Usually, economists tend to think about production as a function of an aggregate technology level, which transforms labour and capital inputs into an output. In this context, as labour inputs we consider the proportion of doctors and nurses in the population. As a proxy for capital, we use the proportion of beds in the population, as it signals the investment made. Finally, the technology level is proxied by the proportion of complex transplants (heart and lungs) in the population.

To capture health behaviours, we tested for smoking habits, alcohol consumption and obesity. Finally, we also tested for demographics characteristics, namely the proportion of elderly individuals in the population, as well as for environmental factors, such as air pollution, as suggested by Cropper et al. (1997). Other tests were performed, and some variables were dropped due to collinearity, time stability and data availability. Variables are listed in Table 6.

Table 6. List of variables

Variable	Definition	Units
Doctors	Number of physicians	Per 1000 population
Nurses	Number of nurses	Per 1000 population
Beds	Number of beds	Per 1000 population
Transplants	Number of heart and lung transplants	Per million population
Air Pollution	Emissions of carbon dioxide	Tonnes per capita
Alcohol consumption	Consumption for individuals with more than 15 years	Litres per capita

For countries with low ratios of doctors and nurses, an increase in the number of doctors contributes to the increase in life expectancy. However, this impact declines with the number of doctors . Conversely, changes in the number of nurses seem to have a close to zero impact on life expectancy (Figure 10).

Figure 10. Relation between nurses to doctor ratio and relative wages (average values from 2000-2015)

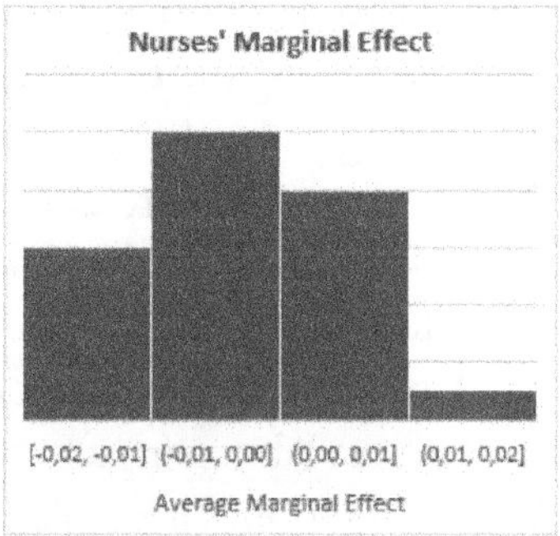

If we consider life expectancy at birth, we also observe that countries that perform more complex transplants, indicating a higher level of technological sophistication, also achieve better health outcomes. However, this does not seem to be relevant for improving life expectancy at the age of 65 or 80.

The same happens with the number of beds in most periods considered. An increase in the number of beds, capturing the investment and capacity of the health system, leads to a significant increase in life expectancy. The number of beds was analysed in each year, comparing with the baseline year 2000, to isolate the time trend. Throughout time, the number of beds has been decreasing to increase efficiency and reduce hospitalization durations. The interaction between the number of beds and each year allows to control for this effect, capturing only the contribution of beds in life expectancy. Also, the reduction in the number of beds has a different impact in each year due to changes in technology. Everything else being constant, to achieve the same output in both 2015 and 2005, it would have been necessary to have three times more beds in 2005.

Finally, air pollution and alcohol consumption, capturing environmental and lifestyle, seems to negatively impact life expectancy.

These estimates represent the set of allocations compatible with a technically efficient use of inputs. However, not all countries are equally efficient in the production of life expectancy. Some countries, with the same inputs, achieve lower life expectancies, even after controlling for country specific characteristics. Such deviations from the estimated frontier are partially due to inefficiencies at the country level, such as poor management practices, under-utilized equipment, lack of team cooperation, and others. We can estimate efficiency scores for each of the 25 countries analysed, as shown below, in Table 7.

Table 7. Efficiency estimates

Dependent Variable	Min	Max	Average
Life Expectancy at Birth	91%	100%	98%
Life Expectancy at 65	80%	100%	95%
Life Expectancy at 80	74%	99%	92%

Our efficiency estimates are time-invariant and country specific. Conditional on the dependent variable considered, efficiency ranges from 74%-91% up to 100%, depending on the countries. In all cases, we have countries close to an efficient allocation, as well as countries which are relatively far from such benchmark. In fact, regardless of the variable considered, if we rank countries according to their efficiency scores, we achieve similar results.

Eastern European countries, such as Hungary, Czech Republic, Latvia or Poland, are typically the countries with higher inefficiencies. Conversely, countries such as Luxembourg, Australia, Canada or Italy are ranked consistently as countries with efficient allocations. Using life expectancy at birth, we estimate that Portugal has inefficiencies of about 3%. However, using life expectancy at the age of 65, or 80, we estimate higher inefficiencies (8% and 15%, respectively).

There are multiple factors that might explain the inefficiency pattern. However, different nurses to doctor ratio do not seem to be a relevant one. Although we might expect that countries with higher nurses to doctor ratio yield higher efficiency, this relation is not statistically significant at 5%.

This suggests that, although not all countries are efficient in the production of life expectancy, different HR policies (and specifically, different nurses to doctor ratio) are not causing such inefficiencies.

3. Do HR policies impact health costs?

Different nurses to doctor ratios do not seem to impact the efficient production of life expectancy. However, this does not mean that any nurses to doctor ratio is optimal. Given that doctors usually receive higher wages than nurses, a lower proportion of nurses to doctor may signal a higher cost for the production of the same healthcare services.

The degree to which costs are affected by different nurses and doctor ratios, depends on the substitutability between these two inputs. Multiple studies have already identified the substitution effect between doctors and other staff. Brown (1988) shows that office-based physicians underutilize their aides; Martínez-Gonzaléz et al. (2015) Embase, CINAHL and The Cochrane Library for all available dates up to August 2012 and updated in February 2014. We selected and critically appraised published randomised controlled trials (RCT). Laurant et al. (2004) found that specially trained nurses can provide primary care management of chronic diseases yielding some improvements in outcomes. Jensen and Morrisey (1986a, 1986b) explore substitution effects in teaching hospitals and Okunade and Murthy (2008) investigate the substitution or complement effect on mental health professionals. Research shows that one physician extender, for instance nurses or physicians aides, could substitute 25% to 50% of a doctor's services (Brown, 1988; Deb, Holmes, 1998; Liang, Ogur, 1987; Okunade, Suraratdecha, 1998).

Regardless of the actual spectrum of action for nurses, we can observe some substitution already in place. Following the usual cost minimization problem, which is derived below under a Constant Elasticity of Substitution (CES) production function, an increase in the relative wage of doctors implies a reduction in the proportion of doctors (relative to nurses). Conversely, if the relative wage of doctors decreases, the nurses to doctor ratio should also decrease.

Using the same dataset as above, despite less data for wages is available, we observe this effect. For instance, Canada, Germany and Luxembourg show large gaps between the wage paid to doctors and nurses, leading to high nurses to doctor ratio. Conversely, countries such Spain or Poland, where the wage difference is not as significant, tend to have lower nurses to doctor ratios.

A policy maker wants to minimize costs, while ensuring that the production of health services is efficient and does not go below a certain threshold. This definition is stricter than the technical efficiency presented before, which only requires that production is maximized given the set of available inputs. Since the policy maker considers now the input cost (doctors and nurses' wages), a solution for this problem must be allocative efficient (Barros 2005; Gouveia, Pereira 1997).

According to our data, the elasticity of substitution between doctors and nurses is close to 0.2. This means that a 1% change in the relative nurses to doctor wages, leads to a 0,2% change in the nurses to doctor ratio. This elasticity of substitution is aligned with common estimates from the literature. For instance, such elasticity is in-between the estimates from Jensen and Morrisey (1986b) between nurses and doctors for teaching hospitals (0,55) and non-teaching hospitals (0,16).

The optimal ratio ranges from 3,5 to 4,0 nurses to doctor, depending on the country. New Zealand, Canada, Australia and Luxembourg have nurses to doctor ratios close to their optimum levels. On the other hand, countries such Spain, Estonia, Poland and Czech Republic display nurses-to-doctor ratios significantly lower than the optimal ones. On average, the countries considered are 16% below their optimal level.

Not surprisingly, countries close to their optimal ratio are also countries with a close to zero excessive cost. This shows that countries with a non-optimal ratio face a higher cost, failing to achieve the cost minimization solution.

On average, the excess cost associated with non-optimal ratios accounted for 7% of HR expenditures across the countries in our sample (Table 8). However, this changes significantly depending on how far each country is from the optimal ratio. For instance, Spain has a cost up to 40% higher than the one it would have, should it converge to the optimal ratio, to achieve the same output for the aggregate contribution of nurses and doctors. Similar results are obtained for Portugal, with an estimated HR excess cost of 35%.

Table 8. Optimal ratios and excess costs estimates

Country	Current ratio (N/D)	Relative wage (N/D)	Optimal ratio (N/D)	Deviation	Excess Cost
Australia	3,5	0,5	3,6	-4%	0%
Belgium	3,2	0,4	3,8	-15%	2%
Canada	3,9	0,4	3,9	2%	0%
Czech Republic	2,2	0,4	3,9	-42%	16%
Estonia	1,9	0,5	3,6	-48%	19%
Germany	3,3	0,3	4,0	-19%	2%
Ireland	4,4	0,5	3,7	21%	2%
Luxembourg	4,0	0,4	3,9	3%	0%
Netherlands	4,1	0,4	3,8	8%	0%
New Zealand	3,8	0,5	3,7	2%	0%
Poland	2,3	0,6	3,5	-35%	9%
Slovenia	3,2	0,4	3,8	-15%	1%
Spain	1,3	0,6	3,6	-63%	43%
Portugal[1]	1,4	0,6	3,5	-60%	35%

[1] Data for wages obtained from Pordata and from the 2017 financial statements *of Centro Hospitalar de Lisboa Norte*

Hence, improvements of HR practices might result in significant savings in healthcare systems' budgets. Promoting efficiency in HR allocation might contribute to slow down the growth of health expenditure.

4. What have we learned?

Health expenditures are rising across countries. On average, OECD countries spend 9% of their GDP in health, ranging from 4% in Turkey to 17% in the USA. Since 2000, there was a significant increase of more than 40% in the employment in the health and social work sector, representing over 10% of total labour force.

The increase in the health workforce, reflected in the increase in the number of doctors and nurses, imposes a significant burden on health expenditures.

Fragile economic conditions, shortage of physicians and increasing needs of an ageing population, have raised concerns regarding whether nurses can replace doctors in some functions.

Using a stochastic frontier model, we confirm that, on average, countries that devote more resources to healthcare (beds, doctors, nurses) and have better technology, achieve better health outcomes – here captured by life expectancy. We also find that air quality and alcohol consumption may impact negatively life expectancy. Still, not all countries are technically efficient, in the sense that they are not always producing the maximum possible life expectancy given the resources they have.

Inefficiencies range from 26% to 0% depending on the country and on the variables considered. However, we do not find evidence that different nurses to doctor ratios explain such inefficiencies. However, regardless of being able to achieve the same outcomes, different nurses to doctor ratios lead to different costs.

Using a constant elasticity of substitution production function, we observe that the substitution between nurses and doctors is already a reality. Countries where the wage gap between nurses and doctors is larger are also countries that use nurses more intensively.

Finally, we investigated whereas non-optimal nurses to doctor ratio lead to higher costs if the optimal production were to be achieved. We estimated that countries face, on average, a 7% excess cost due to non-optimal nurses to doctor ratio. Our results suggest that ignoring substitution effects between nurses and doctor increases the inefficiency of the health system and leads to higher costs.

References

1. Atanda, A., Menclova, A. K., & Reed, W. R. (2018). Is health care infected by Baumol's cost disease? Test of a new model. *Health Economics, 27*(5), 832–849. https://doi.org/10.1002/hec.3641
2. Barros, P. P. (2005). *Economia da Saúde: conceitos e comportamentos* (1.ª ed.). Coimbra: Almedina.
3. Baumol, W. J. (1993). Health Care, Education and the Cost Disease: A Looming Crisis for Public Choice. *Public Choice, 77*(1), 17–28.
4. Brown, D. M. (1988). Do Physicians Underutilize Aides? *The Journal of Human Resources, 23*(3), 342. https://doi.org/10.2307/145833
5. Costa, C., Santana, R., & Lopes, S. (2013). *Custos e preços na saúde: passado, presente e futuro.* Fundação Francisco Manuel dos Santos. https://www.ffms.pt/publicacoes/detalhe/843/custos-e-precos-na-saude
6. Cropper, M. L., Simon, N. B., Alberini, A., Arora, S., & Sharma, P. K. (1997). The Health Benefits of Air Pollution Control in Delhi. *American Journal of Agricultural Economics, 79*(5), 1625. https://doi.org/10.2307/1244393
7. Cutler, D. M. (2004). *Your money or your life: strong medicine for America's Health Care System*, Oxford, Oxford University Press.
8. Deb, P., & Holmes, A. M. (1998). Substitution of physicians and other providers in outpatient mental health care. *Health Economics, 7*, 347–361. https://doi.org/10.1002/(SICI)1099-1050(199806)7:4<347::AID-HEC354>3.0.CO;2-L
9. Ferrier, G. D. (2014). The «usefulness» of stochastic frontier analysis for health care. *Economics and Business Letters, 3 (1)*(27–34), 8.
10. Folland, S., Goodman, A. C., & Stano, M. (2013). *The Economics of Health and Health Care* (7.ª ed.). Pearson.
11. Fuchs, V. R. (1974). *Who Shall Live?: Health, Economics and Social Choice.* World Scientific Publishing Co. Pte. Ltd.
12. Gerdtham, U.-G., & Jonsson, B. (2000). International comparisons of health expenditure: Theory, data and econometric analysis. In Culyer AJ, Newhouse JP (eds) *Handbook of Health Economics*, v. 1: 11-53; Elsevier.
13. Hadley, J. (1982). *More medical care, better health?* Washington, DC: The Urban Institute Press.
14. Hernandez-Peña, P., Poullier, J., Van Mosseveld, C., Van de Maele, N., Cherilova, V., Indikadahena, C., ... Evans, D. B. (2013). Health worker remunera-

tion in WHO Member States. *Bulletin of the World Health Organization, 91*(11), 808–815. https://doi.org/10.2471/BLT.13.120840

15. Jacobs, R., Smith, P. C., & Street, A. (2006). *Measuring Efficiency in Health Care: Analytic Techniques and Health Policy*. Cambridge University Press.
16. Jensen, G. A., & Morrisey, M. A. (1986a). Medical staff specialty mix and hospital production. *Journal of Health Economics, 5*(3), 253–276. https://doi.org/10.1016/0167-6296(86)90017-2
17. Jensen, G. A., & Morrisey, M. A. (1986b). The Role of Physicians in Hospital Production. *The Review of Economics and Statistics, 68*(3), 432. https://doi.org/10.2307/1926020
18. Kumbhakar, S. C., & Lovell, C. A. K. (2000). *Stochastic Frontier Analysis*. Cambridge University Press.
19. Laurant, M., Reeves, D., Hermens, R., Braspenning, J., Grol, R., & Sibbald, B. (2004). Substitution of doctors by nurses in primary care. *Cochrane Database of Systematic Reviews*, (4), 40. https://doi.org/10.1002/14651858.CD001271.pub2
20. Liang, N. J., & Ogur, J. D. (1987). Restrictions on dental auxiliaries: an economic policy analysis. Washington D.C. Federal Trade Commission, https://www.ftc.gov/reports/restrictions-dental-auxiliaries
21. Martínez-González, N., Rosemann, T., Tandjung, R., & Djalali, S. (2015). The effect of physician-nurse substitution in primary care in chronic diseases: a systematic review. *Swiss Medical Weekly*. https://doi.org/10.4414/smw.2015.14031
22. McKay, N. L., & Deily, M. E. (2008). Cost inefficiency and hospital health outcomes. *Health Economics, 17*(7), 833–848.
23. OECD (Ed.). (2017). *Health at a glance 2017: OECD indicators*. Paris: OECD.
24. Okunade, A. A., & Murthy, V. N. R. (2002). Technology as a 'major driver' of health care costs: a cointegration analysis of the Newhouse conjecture. *Journal of Health Economics*, pp. 147–159.
25. Okunade, A. A., & Murthy, V. N. R. (2008). Are physician and non-physician providers of outpatient mental healthcare substitutes or complements? a conceptual clarification. *Health Care Management Science, 11*(4), 393–398. https://doi.org/10.1007/s10729-007-9044-5
26. Okunade, A. A., & Suraratdecha, C. (1998). Cost efficiency, factor interchange, and technical progress in US specialized hospital pharmacies. *Health Economics, 7*, 363–371.
27. OPSS. (2018). Meio caminho andado: Relatório Primavera 2018. OPSS. http://opss.pt/relatorio-primavera/
28. Pereira, A., & Gouveia, M. (1997). *Estratégias de Reforma do Estado Providência – Saúde e Pensões de Reforma*, Lisbon. Forum de Administradores de Empresas.

29. Schneider, E. L., & Guralnik, J. M. (1990). The Aging of America: Impact on Health Care Costs. *Journal of the American Medical Association, 263*(17), 6.
30. Stearns, S. C., & Norton, E. C. (2004). Time to include time to death? The future of health care expenditure predictions. *Health Economics, 13.4,* 315–327.
31. Vita, M. G. (1990). Exploring Hospital production relationships with flexible functional forms. *Journal of Health Economics,* (9), 1–21.
32. Zweifel, P., Felder, S., & Meiers, M. (1999). Aging of population and health care expenditure: a red herring? *Health Economics, 8.6,* 485–496.

Appendix

Key variables descriptive statistics

Variable	Units	Mean	Standard Deviation	Minimum	Maximum
Life Expectancy at birth	Years	78,8	3,0	70,1	83,3
Life Expectancy at 65	Years	20,2	1,5	16,6	24,0
Life Expectancy at 80	Years	9,2	0,9	6,9	12,0
Doctors	Per 1000 citizens	3,1	0,6	2,0	5,1
Nurses	Per 1000 citizens	9,2	3,4	2,8	18,0
Beds	Per 1000 citizens	5,2	1,8	2,4	9,1
Transplants	Per million citizens	7,0	5,1	0,0	23,6
Air Pollution	Tonnes per capita	8,9	4,3	2,9	24,6
Alcohol consumption	Litres per capita	10,2	2,0	5,5	15,2

Stochastic Frontier Estimation (variables in logs)

Life expectancy	At birth	At 65	At 80
Constant	4,252* (0,027)	2,687* (0,072)	1,600* (0,129)
Doctors	0,186* (0,032)	0,501* (0,086)	0,856* (0,152)
Nurses	0,047* (0,015)	0,170* (0,039)	0,309* (0,069)
Doctors^2	-0,029* (0,009)	-0,070* (0,023)	-0,038 (0,041)
Nurses^2	0,002 (0,006)	0,002 (0,016)	0,031 (0,027)
Doctors x Nurses	-0,044*(0,015)	-0,138* (0,042)	-0,360* (0,072)
Transplants	0,003*(0,001)	0,002(0,002)	0,002(0,004)
Beds 2001	0,001(0,001)	0,004(0,002)	0,003(0,003)
Beds 2002	0,001(0,001)	0,000(0,002)	-0,007 (0,003)
Beds 2003	0,002 (0,001)	0,000 (0,002)	-0,013* (0,004)
Beds 2004	0,005* (0,001)	0,014* (0,002)	0,011* (0,004)
Beds 2005	0,007* (0,001)	0,016* (0,002)	0,013* (0,004)
Beds 2006	0,009* (0,001)	0,026* (0,002)	0,033* (0,004)
Beds 2007	0,010* (0,001)	0,029* (0,002)	0,040* (0,004)
Beds 2008	0,012* (0,001)	0,034* (0,002)	0,049* (0,004)
Beds 2009	0,013* (0,001)	0,037* (0,002)	0,054* (0,004)
Beds 2010	0,015* (0,001)	0,042* (0,003)	0,063* (0,005)
Beds 2011	0,018* (0,001)	0,048* (0,003)	0,076* (0,005)
Beds 2012	0,018* (0,001)	0,043* (0,003)	0,064* (0,005)
Beds 2013	0,019* (0,001)	0,048* (0,003)	0,073* (0,005)
Beds 2014	0,022* (0,001)	0,056* (0,003)	0,088* (0,005)
Beds 2015	0,021* (0,001)	0,049* (0,003)	0,071* (0,004)
Air Pollution	-0,005 (0,004)	-0,037* (0,006)	-0,053* (0,011)
Alcohol consumption	-0,017* (0,004)	-0,028* (0,009)	-0,025 (0,015)

*Significant at 1% **Significant at 5% Note: standard errors within brackets

PART II

INVESTMENT IN HRH AND FUTURE NEEDS OF POPULATION AND HEALTH SYSTEMS

Economic development, investment in health and the health market

Jim Campbell, Pascal Zurn, Michelle McIsaac

1. Introduction

There is a growing recognition that the health sector contributes to direct and indirect employment, productivity gains, inclusive economic growth in addition to progress towards achieving universal health coverage (UHC) and to the attainment of the Sustainable Development Goals (SDGs). The positive spill-over effects from the health market go well beyond the health sector; they have important impacts on other economic sectors and on sustainable and equitable development. The heath market is broadly defined to include a wide range of activities: pharmaceuticals, health technologies, diagnostics, hospitals and primary care facilities, nursing homes, insurance providers, biotechnology, management and administration, and some life sciences. The health market comprises a large part of many countries' economies, accounting for an average of 9% of GDP in OECD countries (OECD, 2018). Even in low and middle-income countries (LMICs) such as India, health care has become one of the largest sectors in terms of employment (as the fifth largest employment sector in the country with over 5 million jobs) and contribution to GDP (KPMG, 2015).

There are an estimated 92 million jobs in health and social work globally, comprising around 3% of global employment (ILO, 2018). In high-income countries, the proportion of employment in health and social work is much higher, with 1 in every 10 jobs in OECD countries (OECD, 2016).

The importance of employment in health and social work is predicted to be one of the fastest in the coming 15 years (OECD, 2016). In recent years, employment growth in the health sector has been superior to that of all other sectors. In 15 countries of the European Union (EU-15), employment in this sector rose by 5.9 million between 2000 and 2014, an increase of 39%, or almost double the rate of growth observed in the service sector (22%) (Hofmarcher et al., 2016). In contrast, over the same period, employment in industry went down as a whole almost everywhere, generating job losses in the order of 6.9 million. Consequently, the share of employed persons in the health and social care sector in total employment rose across the EU-15 from 9.5% to 12.1% between 2000 and 2014 (Hofmarcher et al., 2016).

Employment in the health sector is also resilient, as previous experiences with recession have shown that employment in the health sector tends to be less sensitive to cyclical fluctuations than employment in other sectors (James, 2016).

Health has long been thought of as a pre-requisite for development, as unhealthy populations can lead to significant GDP loss. However, the health market is now also considered a strategic investment area for achieving sustainable development, apart from its contribution to health and quality of life. As such, the health sector provides not just the pre-requisites for productivity and growth, but generates inclusive economic growth by its very nature.

This emerging shift towards full consideration of the economic potential of the health sector has been highlighted by the recent work of the UN High Level Commission on Health Employment and Economic Growth (WHO, 2016a) which shows that the health markets contribute to countries' economic growth and labour market performance.

Building on the recent work of the UN High Level Commission and on the *Global Strategy on Human Resources for Health: Workforce 2030* (WHO, 2016b) this chapter presents and discusses the key contributions that the health market and notably employment in this sector makes to the economy and to the achievement of wider social goals. Firstly, it discusses the rise of the health economy as a central job and growth sector. It then examines the fundamental links between the health economy and economic, social and development goals. It then discusses some of politics and policies that are influencing the health market, and the opportunities it presents to policy makers.

2. The rise of the health economy

Improving health care and increasing access to quality health services is a key developmental goal. However, even in rapidly growing economies, there has been difficulty in raising sufficient funds to increase spending on health care to the levels needed to ensure quality universal health coverage. In LMICs, this is driven in part by austerity policies imposed by lenders, which frequently places limits on the fiscal space for public spending, and in part by many governments inability to raise sufficient tax revenues required to meet domestic budget requirements.

With evidence increasing that fiscal multipliers are substantially higher than has been assumed, meaning that fiscal consolidation has been associated with lower growth than expected (Blanchard and Leigh, 2013). The prevailing view that wide sweeping fiscal consolidation is necessary for inducing economic growth is losing favour amongst growing evidence that fiscal austerity and cuts to government spending have held back growth (Krugman, 2012). This is particularly true for essential services such as education and health care, where it is clear that lenders who have imposed austerity measures have grossly underestimated the harm that spending cuts in these areas inflict on weak economies. It has been suggested that the high fiscal multiplier attributed to the health care sector is a direct result of the fact that the health sector is labour intensive and many employees have a high propensity to consume their income, therefore contraction in this sector can have a negative impact on consumption and GDP (Darvas et al., 2018). In addition, a decline in employment resulting from health-care spending cuts can result in a feedback effect on public finances through higher unemployment and lower tax revenue (Darvas et al., 2018). Therefore spending in the health sector can have a stabilizing effect on the economy.

Fortunately in the health sector, the "austeritarian" ideology seems to be fading everywhere and a paradigm shift from looking at the health sector as having negative fiscal budget implications to a sector ripe for strategic investment is occurring, with many economies looking to diversify the health market as a sector capable of boosting economic growth and creating decent jobs.

3. Health economy's contribution to economic growth

The health market is one of the world's largest and fastest-growing ones. The health economy is estimated at US$ 6.5 trillion per year in OECD countries (Lauer et al., 2017). The health sector is labour-intensive, and thus growth in this sector leads to employment growth, in a manner that is not always observed in other sectors, and increasingly plays a critical role in propelling economic growth. In addition, pharmaceutical, biotechnologies, and health care equipment are responsible for over US$ 170 billion of research and development (R&D) investment worldwide, representing almost 20% of all R&D investment in the world (European Commission, 2016).

A framework was developed in the context of the UN High Level Commission on Health Employment and Economic Growth which presents six pathways from the health system to economic growth: (1) health pathway;

Figure 11. Pathways to economic growth

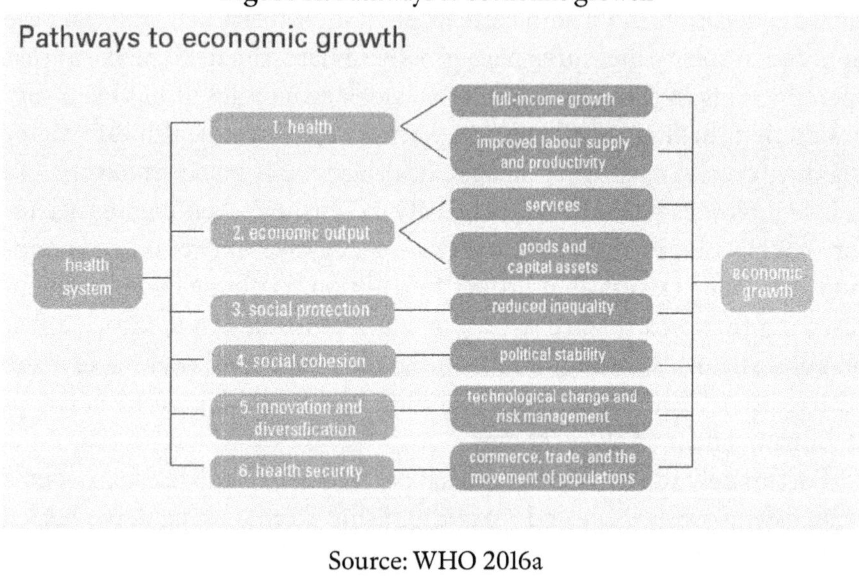

Source: WHO 2016a

(2) economic output pathway; (3) social protection pathway; (4) social cohesion pathway; (5) the innovation and diversification pathway; and (6) the health security pathway (Figure 11).

First, labour supply decisions depend on an individual's health status. Better health through longer life expectancy and better quality of life allow citizens to engage in higher level of activities for longer periods which increases labour supply and productivity. Healthy workers have lower absenteeism and are more productive, and productivity of the workforce underpins economic growth.

Secondly, the economic output of the health sector is large and increasing, a trend that is expected to grow further in the future. The direct and indirect benefits related to economic outputs from health employment have been found to be particularly effective for rural economic development. The health market impacts the local economy, creating indirect jobs and income in other support sectors. It has been estimated that one frontline health worker is supported by 5 support staff (KPMG, 2015), and on average, a physician supported 17 jobs (IQVIA, 2018).

The direct and secondary impacts on community employment and income often account for 15 to 20 percent of the total community's employment and income. In addition, the literature strongly supports the conclusion that a viable health sector is needed if a community wants to attract industries, businesses, etc. (Doeksen et al., 1997).

Eilrich et al. (2007) showed that in rural areas in the United States the economic contributions of health care services are as equally important as the medical contributions. They estimate that a rural physician generates approximately US$ 1.5 million in revenue, US$ 0.9 million in payroll (wages, salaries and benefits) and creates 22 jobs. Avery et al. (2014) showed that a family physician practicing obstetrics in a rural Alabama in the United States adds an additional US$ 488,560 in economic benefit to the community; this is in addition to the US$ 1,000,000 from practicing family medicine, for a total annual benefit of US$ 1,488,560 per physician. They estimate that of the US$ 616,385 invested by the Alabama Family Practice Rural Health Board, each dollar resulted in a US$ 399 benefit to the community.

The significant economic impact of health employment in rural areas is not limited to physicians. Physician assistants and nurse practitioners were also found to have an economic effect on the local community. The situation in rural areas differs significantly in low-income countries, notably in terms of infrastructure, health and education. Nonetheless, similar factors are recognized as key elements for rural economic development in LMICs (Proctor, 2015).

Third, formal health employment offers a range of social protection benefits. These benefits reduce economic and social vulnerabilities to poverty and deprivation. In addition, health systems offering protection against the financial consequences of illness present important positive spill-over benefits which contribute to economic growth (Lauer et al., 2017).

Fourth, societies are more cohesive when they have the capacity to manage collective decision making peacefully. Jobs contribute to social cohesion by nurturing trust in others and reinforcing social capital. Decent jobs are needed for economic growth and decent work contributes the most to societal goals. Jobs in health are clearly contributing to societal goals. Investing in health employment also provides opportunities to increase women's participation in the labour market and reduce youth unemployment or underemployment. Currently, the female labour force participation rate is consistently lower than for men, and integrating women and youth into the labour force is an opportunity to promote gender equity and transform it into social and economic progress (World Bank, 2013).

Fifth, the health sector can be used to diversify the economy and some countries have invested in their health sector specifically to promote economic growth, e.g. medical tourism. Also, the role of technological innovation is important in the health market and is a driver for economic growth (European Union, 2016).

Sixth, the health workforce contributes to reducing vulnerabilities to acute public health events that endanger the collective health of populations, both national and international. The protection from threats to health is recognised as one of the most important non-traditional security issues (Heyman et al., 2015). Countries better insulated from disease threats provide safer environments for economic activities. Pandemic disease threats and ineffective responses can have devastating impact on public health and the global economy. For instance, output forgone due to Ebola in Guinea, Liberia and Sierra Leone in 2015 is estimated to be more than US$ 1.6 billion, that is over 12 percent of their combined GDP (World Bank, 2015).

If the economic and employment impact of the health market are ignored, it could lead sub-optimal public expenditure. Education and health are widely recognised as the two most significant building blocks of human capital. It is well understood that a healthy educated workforce enjoys higher human capital and allows for greater productivity. For this reason, the leading monetary benefit from investing in the health workforce is the potential gain in GDP per capita. However, there is a growing global consensus that GDP does not provide a good measure of overall economic performance (Stiglitz et al., 2009).

4. Health economy's contribution to social development

The global economy will be shaped by global health challenges such as non-communicable diseases, population ageing, global health security, and more generally by policies aimed at achieving universal health coverage and the Sustainable Development Goals (SDGs) adopted by the 70th UN General Assembly in 2015. There are many social benefits which are identified as pathways from health workforce investments to inclusive growth. These include employment creation, greater social cohesion, greater income redistribution as well as their indirect effects. In addition, the health sector provides an opportunity for investment in decent jobs, particularly important for women and youth, with higher unemployment rates.

The health workforce is a main contributor to achieving improvements in health outcomes and population wellbeing. Moving towards the Sustainable Development Goals (SDGs) brings an opportunity to the health market and health employment. The health workforce is the largest sub-component of resources needed to achieve the health-related SDG (SDG3), comprising over a third of the health sector investments (Stenberg et al., 2017). In addition, investing in the health workforce also contributes to SDGs 4 "Quality education", 5 "Gender equality", 8 " Decent work and economic growth" and 10 "Reduced inequalities".

The training and employment of health workers fosters greater gender and intergenerational equity. Some health services such as family planning help to promote gender equity (Stenberg et al. 2014). In turn, women in good health can improve their lot, as well as the welfare of their children, when it comes to redistributing resources within the household (Drèze and Sen, 1989).

The structure of employment in lower income economies is such that work often relies on strength and endurance, and therefore on good health. Adults in poorer economies are more likely to be afflicted with health problems, some of which stem from early childhood. The functional consequences of poor health act to exclude workers from participating in the labour market and thus entail economic deprivations that are felt throughout the life cycle (Strauss, Thomas, 1998). Healthcare delivery helps to reduce this early life inequalities, helps to sustain human capital building as well as its equitable distribution across socio-economic groups. Such healthcare interventions are crucial for reducing income inequality and persistent poverty. Clearly, the delivery of healthcare services is an essential component for channelling improvements in maternal and child health. Equitable healthcare delivery via additional health workforce investments helps to reduce socio-economic and regional inequalities in health.

Compared to other sectors, the health sector is in a unique position to support the development agenda. Firstly, health workers are essential in ensuring access to high quality health services. Access to health care is essential for populations to reach their productivity potential. The health workforce plays a vital role in building the resilience of communities and health systems able to respond to public health risks and crises.

5. Policy context

Despite the clear potential economic and social benefits brought by the health sector, many countries are still grappling with major health workforce challenges. Critical shortages in the supply of workers, an inadequate mix of skills in the workforce, and an inequitable distribution of health workers--as well as gaps in their capacity, motivation, and performance--will seriously affect the future performance of health systems if not addressed by bold new measures. Moreover, the dramatic projection of increased demand for new health worker jobs needs to be understood in the context of projected supply shortages of as many as 18 million health workers, primarily, but not only, in LMICs (Cometto et al., 2017). Reaching an adequate number of jobs--and creating the right type of jobs--requires not only political and social will, but also requires significant financial investment. This raises the issue of the return on such investment.

The health workforce is a central factor in the overall health of a population, it is a critical factor given its role in service delivery. Its importance is also evident in the large share of total health expenditure made in employing the health workforce. The remuneration of all salaried health workers in the public and private sectors combined was estimated to represent between 35% and 55% of total health expenditure (Lauer et al., 2017; Hernandez-Pena et al., 2013)

Addressing population needs for the SDGs and UHC requires making the best possible use of limited resources. The SDG Health Price Tag estimates the costs and benefits of progressively expanding health services in order to reach 16 Sustainable Development Goal (SDG) health targets in 67 low- and middle-income countries that account for 75% of the world's population. Under the "ambitious" scenario, achieving the SDG health targets would require new investments increasing over time from an initial US$ 134 billion annually to US$ 371 billion, or US$ 58 per person, by 2030. The model includes adding more than 23 million health workers, and building more than 415 000 new health facilities, 91% of which would be primary health care centres (Stenberg et al., 2017).

It is important to align investment in the health market with the current and future needs of the population and health systems, taking account of labour market dynamics and education policies, to address shortages and enable maximum improvements in health outcomes, social welfare, employment creation and economic growth. Investing in health employment is instrumental for robust economic growth, since it contributes to decreasing inequalities and is inclusive. Reducing health inequalities not only improves population health, but it also leads to additional social benefits.

6. Conclusions

Focus on HRH as costs to be contained is misplaced and could lead to lower economic output. The health market represents an increasing economic force, and the health workforce is one of its most important resources. The health workforce represents a large and growing share of the total labour force in many countries. Evidence suggests that rather than being only a cost, strengthening the health workforce, if well done, can be a wise investment .

References

1. Avery, DM., Hooper, DE., McDonald JT., Love, MW., Tucker, MT., and Parton, JM."The Economic Impact of Rural Family Physicians Practicing Obstetrics. *Journal of the American Board of Family Medicine* 27 : 602-610.
2. Blanchard O. & Leigh D. (2013) Growth Forecast Errors and Fiscal Multipliers. *IMF Working Paper WP/13/1.* https://www.imf.org/external/pubs/ft/wp/2013/wp1301.pdf
3. Cometto et al., (2017) Health Workforce Needs, Demand and Shortages to 2030: An Overview of Forecasted Trends in the Global Health Labour Market. In ed. Buchan J, Dhillon IS, Campbell J, editors. *Health Employment and Economic Growth: An Evidence Base,* Geneva: World Health Organization; 2017.
4. Darvas Z., Moes N., Myachenkova Y. & Pichler D. (2018) *The Macroeconomic Implications of Healthcare.* http://bruegel.org/wp-content/uploads/2018/08/PC-11_2018_cover.pdf
5. Doeksen, GA., Johnsonn, T. and Willoughby C. Measuring the Economic Importance of the Health Sector on a Local Economy : A Brief Literature Review and Procedures to Measure Local Impact. Southern Rural Development Center, 1997. http://srdc.msstate.edu/publications/archive/202.pdf
6. Drèze, J. & Sen A. (1989) *Hunger and Public Action.* Oxford: Clarendon Press.
7. Eilrich, FC., Doeksen, GA & St. Clair, CF. (2007) The Economic Impact of a Rural Primary Care Physician and the Potential Health Dollars Lost to Out-migrating Health Services. National Center for Rural Health Works, Oklahoma State University. https://ruralwellness.files.wordpress.com/2007/03/impact_rural_physician1.pdf
8. European Commission (2016) *EU R&D Scoreboard.* http://iri.jrc.ec.europa.eu/scoreboard16.html#close
9. Hernandez-Pena, P., Poullier JP.,Van Mosseveld, CJM., Van de Maele, N., Cherilova, V., Indikadahena, C., Lie, G., Tan-Torres, T. & Evans DB. (2013) Health Worker Remuneration in WHO Member States. *Bulletin of the World Health Organization* 91: 808-15.
10. Heymann, David L., Lincoln Chen, Keizo Takemi, David P Fidler, Jordan W Tappero, Mathew J Thomas, et al. (2015) Global Health Security: the Wider Lessons from the West African Ebola Virus Disease Epidemic. *The Lancet* 385: 1884–1901
11. Hofmarcher M., Festl, E. & Bishop-Traver. (2016) Health Sector Employment Growth Calls for Improvements in Labour Productivity. *Health Policy.* 120(8), 894-902.

12. ILO (2018) *Care work and care jobs for the future of decent work.* https://www.ilo.org/wcmsp5/groups/public/---dgreports/---dcomm/---publ/documents/publication/wcms_633135.pdf
13. IQVIA (2018) *The National Economic Impact of Physicians.* https://www.ama-assn.org/sites/default/files/media-browser/public/2018-ama-economic-impact-study.pdf
14. James C. (2016) *Health and Inclusive Growth: Changing the Dialogue.* http://www.who.int/hrh/com-heeg/Health_inclusive_growth_online.pdf
15. KPMG (2015) *Healthcare: The neglected GDP driver.* https://assets.kpmg.com/content/dam/kpmg/pdf/2016/03/Healthcare-the-neglected-GDP-driver-2015.pdf
16. Krugman P. (2012) The Austerity Agenda, *The New York Times,* 1 June 2012 p. A27.
17. Lauer JA., Soucat A., Araujo E. & Weakliam D. Pathways: the health system, health employment, and economic growth. In ed. Buchan J, Dhillon IS, Campbell J, editors. *Health Employment and Economic Growth: An Evidence Base.* Geneva: World Health Organization; 2017.
18. OECD (2016) *Health Workforce Policies in OECD Countries: Right Jobs, Right Skills, Right Places, OECD Health Policy Studies,* OECD Publishing, Paris. doi.org/10.1787/9789264239517-en.
19. OECD (2018) *Spending on Health Latest Trends.* http://www.oecd.org/health/health-systems/Health-Spending-Latest-Trends-Brief.pdf
20. Proctor, J (2014). Rural Economic Diversification in Sub-Saharan Africa. International Institute for Environment and Development. 2014. http://pubs.iied.org/pdfs/14632IIED.pdf
21. Stenberg, K., Hanssen, O., Tan-Torres Edejer, T., Bertram, M., Brindley, C., Meshreky, A., Rosen, JE., Stover, J., Verboom, P., Sanders, R. & Soucat A. (2017) Financing transformative health systems towards achievement of the health Sustainable Development Goals: a model for projected resource needs in 67 low-income and middle-income countries. *Lancet Global Health* 5: e874-878.
22. Stiglitz, JE., Sen, A. & Fitoussi, JP. (2009) Report by the Commission on the Measurement of Economic Performance and Social Progress. https://ec.europa.eu/eurostat/documents/118025/118123/Fitoussi+Commission+report
23. Strauss, J. & Thomas, D. (1998) Health, Nutrition, and Economic Development. *Journal of Economic Literature.* 36(2): 766-817.
24. WHO 2016a) UN High-Level Commission on Health Employment and Economic Growth. *Working for health and growth: Investing in the health workforce.* Geneva: World Health Organization.

25. WHO (2016b) *Global Strategy on Human Resources for Health: Workforce 2030.* Geneva: World Health Organization. http://www.who.int/hrh/resources/global_strategy_workforce2030_14_print.pdf?ua=1
26. World Bank (2013) World Development Report 2013: Jobs. Washington: World Bank. DOI:10.1596/978-0-8213-9575-2
27. World Bank (2015) Ebola: Most African Countries Avoid Major Economic Loss but Impact on Guinea, Liberia, Sierra Leone Remains Crippling. Washington: The World Bank, 2015. https://www.worldbank.org/en/news/press-release/2015/01/20/ebola-most-african-countries-avoid-major-economic-loss-but-impact-on-guinea-liberia-sierra-leone-remains-crippling

Planning the future health workforce

Diana Lopes, Eduardo Castro, Jorge Simões

1. Introduction

Given that the quantity and the quality of health care depends on the quality and quantity of workers employed, health workforce planning is an activity of public interest (Michelutti, 2015). The planning process aims to streamline decision-making to ensure that the right number of health workers is available at the right time and in the right places to meet the needs of the population, and to guarantee their equitable access to high quality services (Dussault, 2015b). Much research has been devoted to health workforce planning, however it remains a major challenge worldwide, with several countries reporting gaps between need, demand and supply of HRH, which may lead to negative consequences. On one hand, the undersupply or shortage of HRH potentiates underservicing and unmet healthcare needs, overworked practitioners, unfilled public positions and higher costs. On the other hand, the oversupply or surplus of certain categories of health workers involves a waste of human resources (unemployment or underemployment) and declining average practitioner incomes (Ono et al., 2013). Understanding HRH imbalances is therefore essential for the improvement of many outcomes, such as equity of access to health care services, as targeted by the United Nations Sustainable Development Goals (SGDs) for 2016-2030 (WHO, 2016). Health workforce planning is even more critical in the context of limited resources and of the hard-to-predict changes in the roles and responsibilities of different health providers, in the structure and organization of health service delivery, and in the demand for health services (Ono et al., 2013).

Although health workforce planning has been present on the public health agenda, as it has been advocated by the World Health Organization (WHO, 2010a), the Organisation for Economic Co-operation and Development (OECD) (Ono et al., 2013), and the Joint Action on European Health Workforce Planning and Forecasting (Malgieri, A. et al., 2015), there is no agreement among researchers on how to forecast HRH (Cruz-Gomes et al., 2018). Moreover, despite the leveraging efforts to encompass two or more health professions (Liu et al., 2017; Murphy and Birch, 2016; Segal et al., 2018; ten Hoope-Bender et al., 2017), the great majority of studies in the field is focused on a single profession. This is the case in the Portuguese context. This chapter considers two health professions and addresses the following research questions: What are the future needs of physicians and nurses in Portugal until 2040? What are the medical and nursing training needs in the medium and long term? How should vacancies for the medical and nursing schools be managed? How should the *numerus clausus* (the quantitative limits on the number of students entering the medical and nursing schools) be defined: population needs versus training capacity? What public policies might help ensure a sustainable evolution? We developed the HEALTH2040 model that follows a sociotechnical approach to answer such questions.

The chapter is structured as follows: Section 2 presents a brief review of related literature. Section 3 presents the Portuguese context of the health workforce, including public policies implemented in this field. Section 4 describes the proposed methodology. Section 5 shows the results of the application of the model. Finally, section 6 discusses the results and points out to future research.

2. Review of the literature

Workforce planning is essential in every organization as it aims to fit the best combination of HRH by addressing critical staffing issues as effectively and efficiently as possible (Bechet, 2008). Records of using this planning process can be traced back to at least 50 years ago (O'Brien-Pallas et al., 2001; Sinclair, 2004). However, just over the past twenty years there has been a dramatic growth in this field (Dussault, 2015a). A confluence of forces contributed to this evolution. In general, great advances in information and technology led to more efficient and simpler ways to gather and process data. In addition, health systems suffered high cost containment pressures, requiring an increasing accountability in healthcare professions and facilities. In the health sector, in particular, this topic has gained momentum given: (i) the labour-intensive character of the sector; (ii) the time and cost involved in training new HRH; and (iii) the Millennium Development Goals targeted for 2015 that had been established at the United Nations in 2000 (Dussault, 2015a; WHO, 2005). There is a growing literature that aims at understanding and modelling the HRH planning, being the main conceptual approaches highlighted by Lopes et al. (2015).

Regarding the supply side, these approaches can be decomposed as follows (Lopes et al., 2015): (i) training, (ii) productivity, (iii) skills-mix and (iv) worker-to-population ratios. In the supply – training approach the availability of HRH is determined by the current stock, the training process, migration flows, attritions and retirement rates, disregarding whether the service delivery patterns are optimal or adequate. The demand is assumed to remain constant, which may be a strong assumption. In the supply – productivity approach, there is a reformulation of health services and/or establishment of economic incentives aiming to achieve a higher productivity level. Enhancing the productivity does not require a change in the number of HRH, but may be not sufficient to fill significant gaps in the supply of health workers. The supply – skills-mix approach considers a redefinition of roles and tasks assigned to HRH. As a result, horizontal and/or vertical substitution between professionals can occur. The former refers to shifts of activities between HRH of the same professional level (e.g. different medical specialists), and the latter to shifts between HRH of different occupational levels (e.g. physicians and nurses) (Van Greuningen et al., 2013). Typically, the number of HRH is not modified and, consequently, gaps in the supply may not be solved. The supply – worker-to-population ratios approach defines references of good practices based on direct comparison with another region or country. However, the productivity and skills-mix of the HRH, as well as differences between countries or regions are typically disregarded (Kinsella and Kiersey, 2016; Lopes et al., 2015).

In what concerns the demand side, approaches can be decomposed as follows (Lopes et al., 2015): (i) economic, (ii) needs and (iii) service targets. In the demand – economic approach future demand for HRH is estimated by projecting the effect of demographic and socioeconomic aspects (e.g. GDP growth and income) on the current level of service. Typically, there is no critical assessment of the appropriateness of service delivery patterns, including skills-mix and HRH distribution. The demand – service targets approach specifies normative goals for the provision of services. These goals (e.g. number of occupied beds, number of inpatients and outpatients, number of consultations, among others) are then translated to HRH requirements, assuming that service targets are attainable, which may be not true. The demand – needs approach, or epidemiological approach, estimates health workforce requirements by assessing the extent that the existing HRH meets healthcare needs, by analysing the relationship between a country's health workforce and its health outcomes (Kinsella and Kiersey, 2016). Typically, this approach projects age- and gender-specific needs based on epidemiological trends and evidence about adequate care delivery patterns, which are commonly acquired by experts' knowledge. However, the term need for HRH is normative with no economic and financial issues that might limit what is feasible (Dussault and Vujicic, 2008). Typically, a huge amount of data is required to determine the needs for a specific specialty, which may make this approach unpractical whenever evaluating the needs for a wide range of health providers. This is even more critical in the context of limited epidemiological data, making other demand-related approaches the easiest, least time-consuming and least expensive proxies for the needs.

Previous forecasting studies usually entail more than one of the approaches aforementioned. This conceptualization denotes the need for more integration in the process of the health workforce planning and that there is no approach capable of estimating accurate HRH requirements without considerable weaknesses. As a result, several studies report the need for a comprehensive approach to aid government structures and policy-makers to take more informed decisions (Dussault, 2015b; Lopes et al., 2015).

3. The medical and nursing workforce

The starting point of a sound HRH planning consists in assessing the current health workforce situation (Dussault and Fronteira, 2010). This section presents this basis, from which decision-makers can evaluate the impact of previous policies and exploit the need for new interventions.

3.1. Evolution of the Portuguese physicians and nurses workforce

The Portuguese HRH have been increasing over time. Nurses are the professional group with the highest number of individuals, followed by physicians (WHO, 2018). Portuguese physicians numbers grew from 0.95 per 1 000 inhabitants in 1970 to 2.83 in 1990. Afterwards, this trend has been maintained, reaching 4.4 per 1 000 inhabitants in 2014 - higher than the EU average of 3.5 (Simões et al., 2017). A similar trend is observed in the nurse to population ratio. In 2000, there were 3.54 nurses per 1 000 inhabitants and in 2014 there were 6.1 (OECD, 2016). However, the nurse to physician ratio of 1.4 is below the EU and OCDE averages of 2.5 and 2.8, respectively. Thus, Portugal is located in the lower right quadrant of Figure 12, in the group of countries with a ratio of physicians to population higher than the EU average, and lower on nurses to population ratio. Portugal is the third country of the EU with the lowest ratio, preceded only by Greece and Spain. Denmark, located in the first quadrant (higher right quadrant), is the country with the highest ratio, with 4.56 nurses per physician, followed by Finland (4.45), Ireland (4.39) and Iceland (4.25). According to Simões et al. (2017), the Portuguese ratio of nurses to physicians suggests the need for a redefinition of tasks for HRH. Notwithstanding, this issue is not yet translated into policy actions and it is not even present on the public agenda, although the international evidence points to an expansion of nurses' role (Buchan and Seccombe, 2012; Delamaire and Lafortune, 2010; Dussault, 2014).

Given the long periods of training, the supply adjustment of HRH is not immediate. Typically, medical students undertake a six-year programme of undergraduate studies. After finishing their medical degree, they proceed to a national examination and to a year of general internship as non-specialist physicians. Afterwards, to become a specialist, medical graduates are placed in their postgraduate training positions, filling slots allocated in accordance to the grade obtained in a national exam. The duration of

Figure 12. Number of physicians and nurses per thousand inhabitants in 2014 (adapted from (WHO, 2018)).

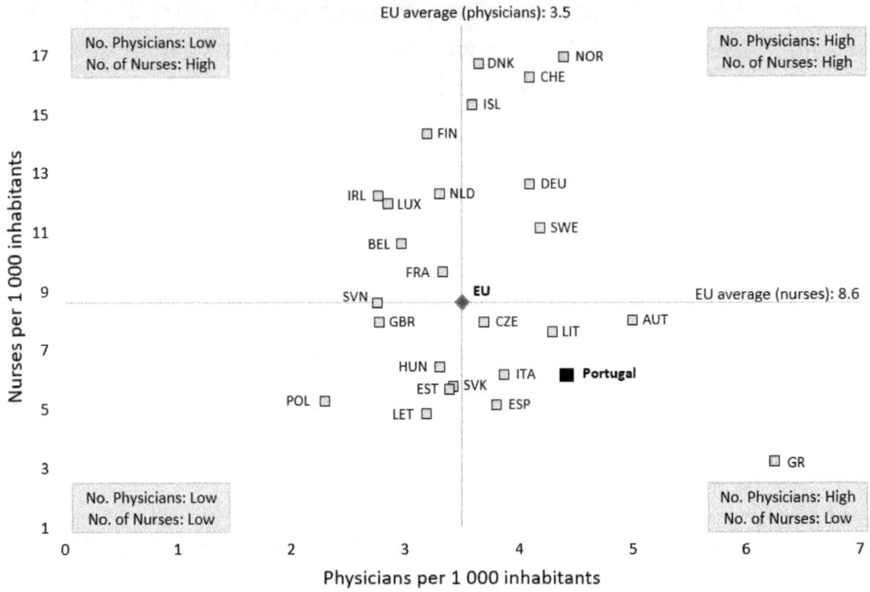

this post-graduation varies between 4 and 6 years. Nursing students take at least 4 years to complete the undergraduate studies, which prepare them to provide general nursing care. The nursing specialization requires 2 years of practice as well as a specialization course (Simões et al., 2017). Registration by the Medical and Nursing Councils is mandatory (Simões et al., 2017) and is a pre-requisite to work in the public or private services.

3.2. A roadmap of public policies for human resources for health in Portugal

Workforce planning is an important tool for monitoring and guaranteeing an even balance between demand and supply of HRH. Before 1977, there was no record of strategic thinking for planning the HRH in Portugal. The first steps in this field can be traced back to 1977, when *numeri clausi* were introduced with the aim of limiting the number of entries in medical schools, given a perceived surplus of physicians after the revolution in 1974 (Celestino da Costa, 1990). The *numerus clausus* decreased from approximately 1 000 in 1977 to 190 in 1986, to 1 400 in 2007 and 1 704 in 2014 (Celestino da Costa, 1990; EDULOG, 2018; Leone et al., 2013). Similar restrictions were also implemented in nursing schools, and led to the recruitment of foreign HRH (Barros et al., 2011). This situation was gradually reverted with the creation of new medical schools and of a special regimen (integrated Master of Medicine with a 4-year programme) totally and exclusively organized for students with a first cycle degree (available at the University of Algarve), contributing to the increasing number of new medical students. There were five medical schools in 1995 and presently there are eight. The number of nurses has also increased thanks to a 1998 policy of opening at least one publicly funded nursing school per district. Currently there are forty-one nursing schools, of which twenty-one are public and twenty are private. The number of entries has increased more than 200% between 1995 and 2005, passing from 1 364 to 4 167 students, and then this number has gradually been reduced to 2 823 in 2014 (Figure 13).

These policies were basically *ad hoc* rather than part of a strategy (Leone et al., 2013). Problems such as an insufficient number of nurses, a lack of physicians in some regions and specialties, and an uneven distribution of HRH between primary and hospital care persisted (Barros et al., 2011). In reaction to the difficulty to attract health personnel in rural areas, the Ministry of Health has recruited physicians and nurses through bilateral agreements with some Latin American countries (e.g. Uruguay, Cuba, Colombia and Costa Rica) to fill positions that national workers disregarded (Leone et al., 2013).

Currently, Portugal is facing critical HRH challenges: there are shortages of HRH in specific medical specialties, in particular in family medicine. Internship places have been augmented, but healthcare institutions are at the limit of their training capacity (Simões et al., 2017). In 2017, 2 300 new graduates did the national entry examination to specialty training, but only 1 758 vacancies were opened which left around 500 individuals unable to proceed to post-graduation (ACSS, 2017). Although the WHO (WHO, 2010b) recognized advances in the period 2012-2016, it emphasized the absence of a strategic approach for developing the health workforce. Actually, the Portuguese National Health Plan has been based on numerical targets of HRH *per capita* over the years.

Figure 13. Evolution of the numeri clausi in the Portuguese medical and nursing schools. Important marks are also highlighted over time.

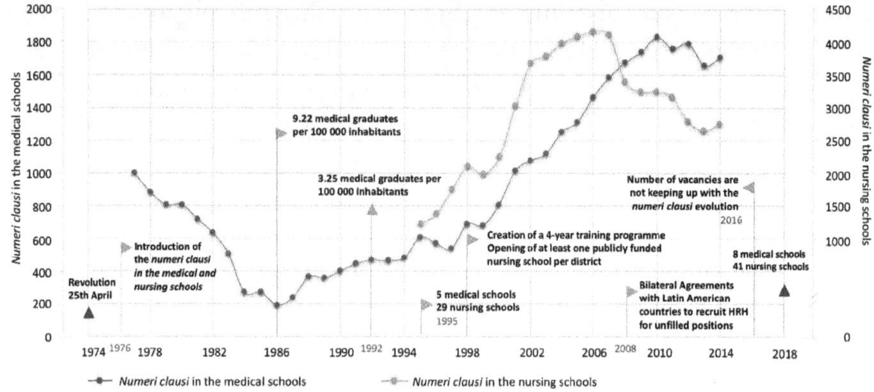

4. Method

The construction of the HEALTH2040 model aimed: (i) to estimate the future needs of physicians and nurses till 2040; (ii) to calculate the training needs to meet the number of physicians and nurses obtained in the previous step; and (iii) to determine the number of students that should enter medical and nursing schools. The main activities in developing the model are presented in Figure 14.

In the structuring phase, we started by providing a rapid review of the related literature, followed by the identification of the driving forces involved in the health workforce planning process, and the data collection to characterize the past and current situation. Regarding the driving forces, on the demand side we identified: (i) population's wages or GDP; (ii) morbidity or epidemiology, as different pathologies put a different burden on the health system; and (iii) the demographic evolution of the population as more people require more HRH. The latter has already been modelled and estimated in a previous project, DEMOSPIN - Economically sustainable demography – Reverting the decline in peripheral areas (de Castro et al., 2015). On the supply side, we identified: (i) the demographic evolution of the health workforce; (ii) HRH competencies; and (iii) wages. Organizational factors and technological evolution are drivers of both supply and demand for HRH.

Figure 14. Activities developed for forecasting the Portuguese health workforce.

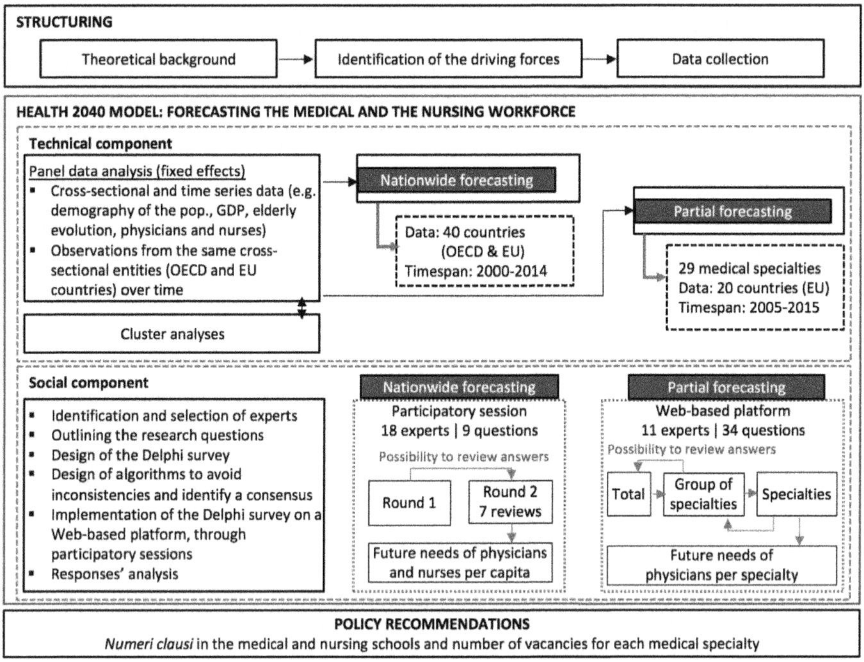

The existence of reliable and accurate data on all these components is crucial to characterize the current situation. We observed a deficit of valid and updated data and that different sources provide data according to different criteria. For instance, the OECD database, the Portuguese medical and nursing councils, and the Central Administration of the Health System (ACSS, Portuguese acronym) produce data on the number of physicians and nurses per thousand inhabitants. The latter refers to staff working in the NHS, whereas the two other databases include all the physicians and nurses licensed to practice, which may over-estimate the number of practising physicians. OECD evaluates this over-estimation at about 30%. These databases do not provide information about emigration, type of activity (in the case of the medical councils), and sector of activity (private and/or public) (Ribeiro et al., 2014). This lack of data is transversal to other areas which are essential to health workforce planning. For instance, there is no or only scarce information on the technological impact, organizational factors or the relationship between healthcare services' consumption and population age groups.

Given the difficulties to obtain data, we applied a methodology that included not only Portuguese but also international information, with a view to integrating more variability and enriching the analysis. Data from forty countries from OECD (35) and EU, covering the period between 2000 and 2014 were used:

- Number of physicians per thousand inhabitants (OECD, 2017a);
- Number of physicians per thousand inhabitants, by specialty (Eurostat, 2017);
- Number of nurses per thousand inhabitants (OECD, 2017c);
- Percentage of elderly population (i.e., individuals over 65 years old) (OECD, 2017b);
- GDP *per capita* (constant 2010 US dollars) (World Bank, 2017);

Based on this information, the HEALTH2040 model was applied to forecast the medical and the nursing workforce. The model follows a socio-technical approach grounded based in the following premises: (i) in principle, health workforce planning should adopt an integrated perspective of the whole workforce; (ii) there is a global evolution trend of the *per capita* number of HRH; and (iii) this trend must be corrected by specific values for each country, concerning the demography, GDP and technology (see the Technical annex for a detailed description). Also, alternative scenarios were considered to compare results, being highlighted in this chapter the scenario where the *numeri clausi* are kept steady and a null migration flow of professionals.

5. Results

5.1. Physicians and nurses

Figure 15 presents the results regarding the evolution of the number of physicians and nurses per 1 000 inhabitants to 2040. A low growth of the number of physicians per population is expected until 2020, followed by a negative evolution until 2040, with 4.24 physicians per 1 000 inhabitants estimated in 2040. As to nursing, the results point out to a steady growth rate (26% between 2014 and 2040), reaching 7.72 nurses per thousand

Figure 15. Evolution of the total physicians and nurses per 1 000 inhabitants until 2040

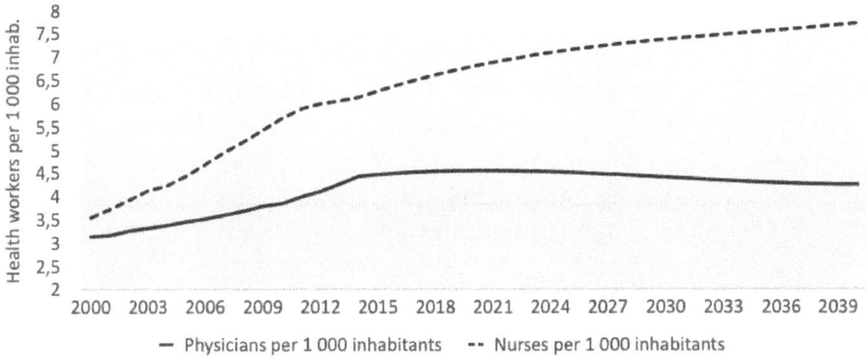

inhabitants in 2040. Hence, an increasing evolution of the nurses to physician ratio is expected, from 1.38 in 2014 to a 1.82 in 2040.

Once the future needs of physicians and nurses are obtained, it is possible to infer the *numerus clausus*. Figure 16 represents data for the period 1996-2014 for: (i) the total number of physicians, (ii) *numerus clausus*, and (iii) new medical graduates. The completion rate of the medical 6-year programme is almost 100%. For this reason, we assumed that in the period 2015-2020 the number of medical graduates is equal to the number of entries with a lag of 6 years (2009-2014). The exits due to retirement (at 70 years old) and deaths were estimated according to the demographic profile of physicians and the mortality rates (age group 25-69) estimated in the scope of a previous research project called DEMOSPIN - Economically sustainable demography – Reverting the decline in peripheral areas (de Castro et al., 2015).

Considering these assumptions and a null migration flow of professionals, the number of medical graduates in year , needed to achieve the number of physicians estimated above (Figure 15), was given by the difference between the stock of physicians between year and the previous year, plus the exits (retirement or death) in the year . As a result, a striking reduction is expected in the medical *numeri clausi* in the period 2015-2030, being estimated 654 entries in the medical schools in 2030 (Figure 16). The number of retired physicians follows a sinusoidal trend given the strong restrictions on the *numeri clausi* in the 80's and 90's. However, these estimates should be thoroughly analysed as they result from an automatic adjustment and may represent a very specific context given the inherent assumptions. A broader discussion is provided in the next section. Given the significant reduction of the *numeri clausi* aforementioned, an alternative scenario characterized by keeping steady the *numeri clausi* was considered. Within this scenario, the number of physicians will grow by more than 25% between 2014 and 2040, passing from 46 035 to 58 127 physicians.

Figure 16. Results of the HEALTH2040 model regarding the evolution of physicians, respective numeri clausi, medical graduates and exits till 2040. All the variables should be read by the left axis, with the exception of the physicians' ones.

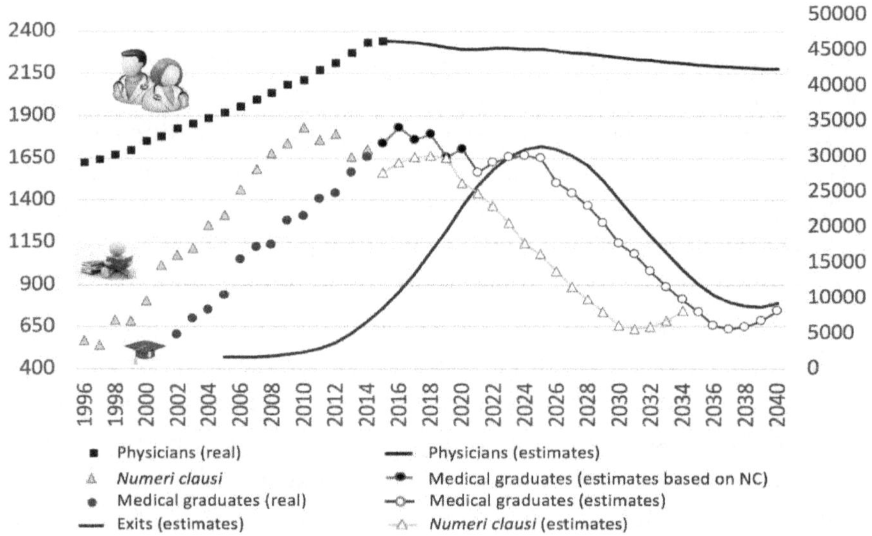

Figure 17 shows the results regarding the nursing profession. The real data corresponds to the total number of nurses for the period 2000-2014, *numerus clausus* for 1996-2014 and nursing graduates (completion of the nursing 4-year programme) for 2002-2014. The number of nursing graduates was determined by the number of entries plus four years, assuming a 90% completion rate. A reduction on the number of students entering nursing schools is expected. In 2014, there were 2 823 entries, and an

Figure 17. Results of the HEALTH2040 model regarding the evolution of nurses, respective numeri clausi, nursing graduates and exits until 2040. All the variables should be read by the left axis, with the exception of the nurses' ones.

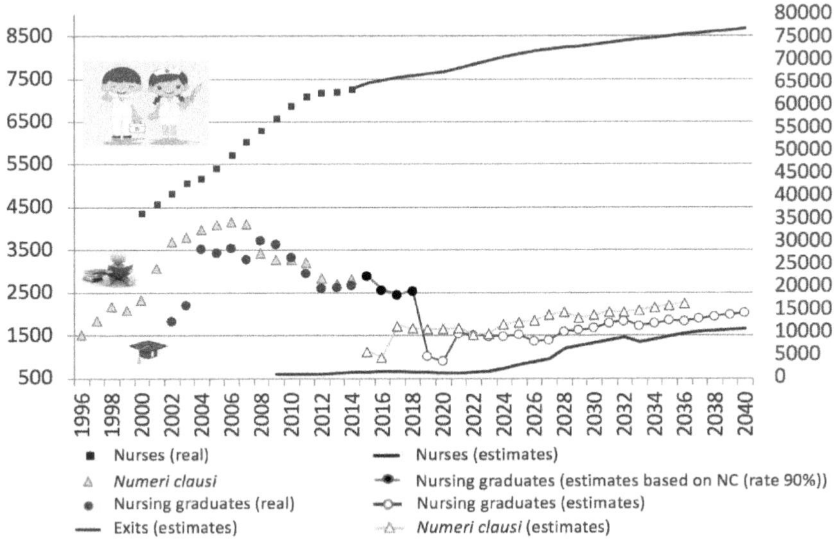

estimate of 1 656 and 2 253 in 2020 and 2036, respectively. The number of entries in the system exceeds the number of exits for the period 2015-2040.

Alternatively, considering the scenario where the *numeri clausi* are kept constant for the medical schools and the nurses to physician ratio gathered from the group of experts (1,82), the number of nurses would have to adjust accordingly and increase from 63 758 to 105 789 nurses in 2014 and 2040, respectively. This would require: (a) an increase of 58% in the *numeri clausi* for the nursing schools between 2014 and 2035 (from 2 823 to 4,457 entries in 2014 and 2035, respectively); and (b) an extension of the training capacity to accommodate all the students. The application of 3 120 annual entries from 2015 to 2035 would be enough for the target determined by 2040 (105 789 nurses).

5.2. Medical specialists

Even though there are 48 medical specialties, we considered only 29 according to the ISCO-08, so it was possible to integrate in the model not only Portuguese data, but also international information (Table 9).

Among medical specialties with a positive growth, we can highlight Anaesthesiology and Intensive Medicine, General and Paediatric Surgery, Dermatovenereology, Gynaecology and Obstetrics, Medical and Physical Rehabilitation, Neurological surgery, Psychiatry and Orthopedics. Allergology and Immunology, Gastroenterology, Clinical Haematology and Otorhinolaryngology are specialties with a negative growth.

Table 9. Expected evolution of the number of physicians per thousand inhabitants by each (group of) specialty. The real data corresponds to the years 2005 and 2015.

(Group of) Speciality	2005	2015	2040	(Group of) Speciality	2005	2015	2040
Group of medical specialties	1,292	1,763	1,541	***General and Family Medicine***	1,246	1,486	1,353
Allergology and Immunology	0,056	0,075	0,057	***Group of surgical specialties***	0,238	0,309	0,326
Cardiology	0,091	0,120	0,102	*Angiology and Vascular Surgery*	0,015	0,022	0,018
Endocrinology e Nutrition	0,020	0,028	0,027	*General and Paediatric Surgery*	0,171	0,219	0,238
Clinical Pharmacology	0,002	0,005	0,008	*Neurological Surgery*	0,018	0,025	0,030
Internal Med. Tropical & Infectious Diseases	0,209	0,315	0,225	*Plastic, Recons. & Aesthetic Surg.*	0,022	0,028	0,026
Clinical Haematology	0,020	0,028	0,022	*Thoracic Surgery*	0,012	0,015	0,015
Medical and Physical Rehab.	0,066	0,090	0,101	***Group of hybrid specialties***	0,672	0,905	1,022
Gastroenterology	0,048	0,064	0,050	*Anaesthesiology and Int. Med.*	0,154	0,224	0,392
Occup. Med. & Public Health	0,143	0,180	0,143	*Dermatovenereology*	0,032	0,046	0,060
Neurology	0,040	0,058	0,057	*Gynaecology and Obstetrics*	0,168	0,211	0,217
Medical Oncology	0,023	0,036	0,031	*Ophthalmology*	0,093	0,123	0,097
Pathology and Legal Med.	0,119	0,136	0,111	*Otorhinolaryngology*	0,104	0,137	0,106
Paediatrics	0,165	0,242	0,237	*Orthopedy*	0,060	0,076	0,078
Pneumology	0,056	0,074	0,068	*Urology*	0,060	0,088	0,072
Psychiatry	0,117	0,152	0,153				
Radiology and Nuclear Med.	0,117	0,160	0,151	**Total**	**3,448**	**4,463**	**4,242**

6. Conclusions and further research

Portugal, compared to other countries, presents one of the lowest nurses to physician ratio, affecting not only Government spending but also the tasks' distribution among the HRH in healthcare facilities. Our forecasting model allows a comprehensive vision, by focusing on more than a single profession (physicians and nurses). The results anticipate challenges in health workforce planning, however they should be thoroughly analysed given the exploratory nature of this study. Although the methodology is innovative and contributes to the literature, the lack of data and the assumptions considered (e.g. null migration flow of professionals), may lead to results associated with a very particular context. As such, this study does not allow the drawing of definitive conclusions about how many physicians and nurses should exist in Portugal in the future. Rather, this study is a starting point for further analysis and to expand the debate on public policy and research work, so that more informed policy decisions can be made contributing to a greater system's stability, without disregarding the quality of education and healthcare services.

Thus, a broader and more robust discussion is needed on what policy decisions should be taken, considering the future retirement rates, physical investment, educational capacity and quality of education systems. The following points highlight the sequential aspects that should be considered to analyse the results:

1. The results point to a significant reduction in *numeri clausi* in both courses (to less than half of the current value for the medical profession). However, this reduction is temporary, given the estimated sinusoidal trend of medical and nursing retirements, with considerable amplitude in the case of the medical profession, thanks to the up and down strategy that has been applied to student intakes over time.
2. In the case of the medical profession, the results suggest an increase in *numeri clausi* from the year 2031 to anticipate the number of exits. Although there is room to reduce the number of entries to some medical schools that are receiving students beyond their capacity, it is unreasonable to reduce *numeri clausi* to less than half of the present value.
3. The reduction suggested for *numeri clausi* is therefore not recommended, as it would lead to the destruction of training capacity, which involves not only human but also physical investments. Thus, it is important to adopt policies, aiming to correct the up and down strategy that has been applied to student intakes, through a more balanced distribution of professionals among age groups.

In addition to the previous points, it should be noticed that the results were based on *numeri clausi* as an instrument to ensure the reference values obtained through the HEALTH2040 model. However, it is increasingly recognized that the education system not merely is more than a means to reach a certain number of health professionals in the future, but a goal in itself. The focus on education and research in these professions is therefore essential in the strategy of regional development and geographically balanced distribution of health research provision. This contributes not only to the strengthening of the education system but also to the development of scientific research in key areas such as biotechnology and biomedicine.

These questions led us to the analysis of an alternative scenario characterized by the maintenance of the *numeri clausi* at 2014 level, in which a growth rate of 25% is expected on the number of physicians between 2014 and 2040. Taking the nurses to physician ratio gathered from the group of experts, the number of nurses would have to adjust accordingly and increase about 65% between 2014 and 2040. Therefore, the *numeri clausi* for the nursing schools should increase, passing from 2 823 to 4 457 entries in 2014 and 2035, respectively. This would require an extension of the training capacity to accommodate all the students.

In brief terms, if we consider *numeri clausi* as a tool to achieve the medical and nursing forecasts, there is a problem of instability created by the significant reduction in *numeri clausi*, leading to a waste of physical resources. This situation is critical, given the prospective sinusoidal nature of entries thanks to the period of restrictions on access to medical and nursing schools in the 80s and 90s.

On the other hand, despite the decreasing trend in the Portuguese population, previous studies show that Portugal will present an increasingly ageing demographic structure (de Castro et al., 2015). The increase in average life expectancy has been reflected in the increasing number of individuals with chronic diseases and disabilities, which require higher medical attention. Within this context, there are reasons to think that the number of physicians should increase. Given the scarcity of data and the uncertainty surrounding many of the constraints on the demand for health professionals, it is not possible to advocate the exact number of physicians and nurses that the country should train. Several aspects that require data and research need to be further investigated.

We trust that the experience from designing the HEALTH2040 model and applying it to the Portuguese context (with data from other countries) provides valuable insights for future policies. However, several challenges emerged as in need of future research:

1. To improve the quality and quantity of HRH databases, as a requirement for any sound health workforce projection (Dussault and Fronteira, 2010);
2. To extend research to other health professions, namely diagnosis and therapy technicians and psychologists (Ono et al., 2013);
3. To study the territorial distribution of HRH, with methods and tools to:
   - Characterize future population's needs regarding the various typologies of health services. Such tools are dependent of epidemiological data, that should be available at a territorial level;
   - Evaluate the territorial equity of access to healthcare and other public services (e.g. schools) and identify policy options to overcome the difficulties in attracting and retaining HRH in underserved areas as current monetary-based incentives to attract HRH in deprived areas have been insufficient.

Acknowledgments
The project "HEALTH 2040 – Future needs of human health resources in Portugal till 2040" was funded by the Calouste Gulbenkian Foundation. The authors are grateful to experts for their collaboration.

References

1. ACSS. (2017). Mapa de vagas do Concurso Internato Médico – Ingresso na área de especialização. http://www2.acss.min-saude.pt/DepartamentoseUnidades/DepartamentoGestãoePlaneamentoRH/InternatoMédico/Arquivoanosanteriores/tabid/1238/language/pt-PT/Default.aspx
2. Barros, P. P., Machado, S. R., and Simões, J. A. (2011). Portugal: Health Systems in Transition. *Health Systems in Transition, 13*(4), 1–156.
3. Bechet, T. (2008). *Strategic Staffing: A Comprehensive System for Effective Workforce Planning.* New York, NY: American Management Association.

4. Buchan, J. and Seccombe, I. (2012). Overstretched. Under-resourced. The UK nursing labour market review 2012. https://eresearch.qmu.ac.uk/handle/20.500.12289/3127
5. Celestino da Costa, J. (1990). Evolução do ensino no ciclo clínico na faculdade de medicina de Lisboa (2ª parte). *Acta Médica Portuguesa, 3,* 171–178.
6. Cruz-Gomes, S., Lopes, M. A., and Almada-Lobo, B. (2018). A labor requirements function for sizing the health workforce. *Human Resources for Health, 16*(67). https://doi.org/https://doi.org/10.1186/s12960-018-0334-4
7. de Castro, E. A., Martins, J. M., and Silva, C. J. (2015). *A demografia e o país: previsões cristalinas sem bola de cristal* (junho de 2). Lisboa: Gradiva.
8. Delamaire, M. L. and Lafortune, G. (2010). Nurses in advanced roles: a description and evaluation of experiences in 12 developed countries, OECD Health Working Papers No. 54; Paris: OECD; https://www.oecd-ilibrary.org/social-issues-migration-health/nurses-in-advanced-roles_5kmbrcfms5g7-en
9. Dussault, G. (2014). Plano Nacional de Saúde 2012-2016: Roteiro de intervenção recursos humanos em saúde (RHS). https://pns.dgs.pt/roteiros-de-intervencao-do-plano-nacional-de-saude/
10. Dussault, G. (2015a). Bringing the Health Workforce Challenge to the Policy Agenda. In Kuhlmann, E., Blank, R. H., Bourgeault, I. L., & Wendt, C. (Eds.), *The Palgrave International Handbook of Healthcare Policy and Governance* (pp. 273–288). Palgrave, Basingstoke.
11. Dussault, G. (2015b). Planning capacity evaluation. In Michelutti, P. & Van Hoegaerden, M. (Eds.), *Handbook on health workforce planning methodologies across EU countries* (pp. 273–277). Bratislava: Ministry of Health of the Slovak Republic.
12. Dussault, G. and Fronteira, I. (2010). *Human resources for health (HRH) plan component of national health plan 2011-15 (Portugal).*
13. Dussault, G. and Vujicic, M. (2008). Demand and supply of human resources for health. *International Encyclopedia of Public Health*, 77–84. https://doi.org/10.1016/B978-012373960-5.00162-3
14. EDULOG. (2018). Produção de diplomados em medicina em Portugal. https://edulog.pt/publicacao/22?
15. Eurostat. (2017). Health care staff - Physicians by medical specialty. https://ec.europa.eu/eurostat/web/health/health-care
16. IHS Global Inc. (2017). EViews. http://www.eviews.com/general/about_us.html
17. Kinsella, S. and Kiersey, R. A. (2016). Models, tools and processes in five countries: An evidence review. https://www.hrb.ie/fileadmin/publications_files/Health_Workforce_Planning_Models_2016.pdf
18. Leone, C., Conceição, C., and Dussault, G. (2013). Trends of cross-border mobility of physicians and nurses between Portugal and Spain. *Human*

Resources for Health, 11(36), 1–11. https://doi.org/https://doi.org/10.1186/1478--4491-11-36
19. Liu, J. X., Goryakin, Y., Maeda, A., et al. (2017). Global health workforce labor market projections for 2030. *Human Resources for Health, 15*(11), 1–12. https://doi.org/10.1186/s12960-017-0187-2
20. Lopes, M. A., Almeida, Á. S., and Almada-Lobo, B. (2015). Handling healthcare workforce planning with care: where do we stand? *Human Resources for Health, 13*(1), 38. https://doi.org/https://doi.org/10.1186/s12960-015-0028-0
21. Malgieri, A., Michelutti, P., and Van Hoegaerden, M. (Editors). (2015). *Handbook on Health Workforce Planning Methodologies across EU Countries* (Funded by). Bratislava: Ministry of Health of the Slovak Republic.
22. Michelutti, P. (2015). Health workforce planning in EU. In Malgieri, A., Michelutti, P., & Van Hoegaerden, M. (Eds.), *Handbook on health workforce planning methodologies across EU countries* (pp. 27–30). Bratislava: Ministry of Health of the Slovak Republic.
23. Murphy, G. T. and Birch, S. (2016). Simulating future supply of and requirements for human resources for health in high-income OECD countries. *Human Resources for Health, 14*(77), 1–18. https://doi.org/10.1186/s12960-016-0168-x
24. O'Brien-Pallas, L., Baumann, A., Donner, G., et al. (2001). Forecasting models for human resources in helth care. *Journal of Advanced Nursing, 33*(1), 120--129. https://doi.org/https://doi.org/10.1046/j.1365-2648.2001.01645.x
25. OECD. (2016). OECD Health Statistics 2016 - Frequently Requested Data.
26. OECD. (2017a). Doctors (indicator). https://data.oecd.org/healthres/doctors.htm#indicator-chart
27. OECD. (2017b). Elderly population (indicator). https://data.oecd.org/pop/elderly-population.htm
28. OECD. (2017c). Nurses (indicator). https://data.oecd.org/healthres/nurses.htm#indicator-chart
29. Ono, T., Lafortune G., and Schoenstein M. (2013). Health workforce planning in OECD countries: A review of 26 projection models from 18 countries, OECD Health Working Papers No. 52; Paris: OECD; https://www.oecd-ilibrary.org/social-issues-migration-health/health-workforce-planning-in-oecd-countries_5k44t787zcwb-en
30. Ribeiro, J. S., Conceição, C., Pereira, J., et al. (2014). Health professionals moving to...and fom Portugal. *Health Policy, 114*(2–3), 97–108. https://doi.org/https://doi.org/10.1016/j.healthpol.2013.05.009
31. Segal, L., Guy, S., Leach, M., et al. (2018). A needs-based workforce model to deliver tertiary-level community menatl health care for distressed infants, children, and adolescents in South Australia: a mixed-methods study. *Lancet Public Health, 3*(6), e296–e303. https://doi.org/10.1016/S2468-2667(18)30075-6

32. Simões, J., Augusto, G. F., Fronteira, I., et al. (2017). Portugal: Health system review. *Health Systems in Transition, 19*(2), 1–184.
33. Sinclair, A. (2004). *Workforce planning: A literature review*. Brighton, UK: Institute for Employment Studies.
34. ten Hoope-Bender, P., Nove, A., Sochas, L., et al. (2017). The 'Dream Team' for sexual, reproductive, maternal, newborn and adolescent health: an adjusted service target model to estimate the ideal mix of health care professionals to cover population need. *Human Resources for Health, 15*(1), 46. https://doi.org/10.1186/s12960-017-0221-4
35. Van Greuningen, M., Batenburg, R. S., and Van der Velden L.F. (2013). The accuracy of general practitioner workforce projections. *Human Resources for Health, 11*(1), 1. https://doi.org/https://doi.org/10.1186/1478-4491-11-31
36. WHO. (2005). Health and the Millennium Development Goals. https://www.who.int/hdp/publications/mdg_en.pdf
37. WHO. (2010a). Models and tools for health workforce planning and projections. https://www.who.int/hrh/resources/observer3/en/
38. WHO. (2010b). WHO evaluation of the national health plan of Portugal (2004-2010). http://pns.dgs.pt/ava-ext-who/
39. WHO. (2016). Global strategy on human resources for health: Workforce 2030. https://www.who.int/hrh/resources/globstrathrh-2030/en/
40. WHO. (2018). Health System Review: Portugal (Phase I, Final Report). https://www.sns.gov.pt
41. World Bank. (2017). GDP per capita (constant 2010 US dollars). https://data.worldbank.org/indicator/NY.GDP.PCAP.KD

Technical Annex

HEALTH2040 model: Technical component

The technical component integrates several interconnected steps:

I. Implementation of panel unit root tests to analyse the (non-) stationarity of the time series in analysis, through the use of EVIEWS 9.5 Student Version Lite (IHS Global Inc., 2017). Results have shown that all the time series are stationary at the first differences, being thus integrated of first order;
II. Determination of the relationship between HRH and the remaining variables, by using the respective first differences of the

variables (to remove the trend), through the following mathematical expressions:

$$\frac{\Delta P_i}{P_i} = \beta_0 + \beta_i + \beta_1 \times P_{it_0} + \beta_2 \times \frac{\Delta N_i}{N_i} + \beta_3 \times \frac{\Delta GDP_i}{GDP_i} + \beta_4 \times \frac{\Delta E_i}{E_i} \quad (1)$$

$$\frac{\Delta N_i}{N_i} = \gamma_0 + \gamma_i + \gamma_1 \times N_{it_0} + \gamma_2 \times \frac{\Delta P_i}{P_i} + \gamma_3 \times \frac{\Delta GDP_i}{GDP_i} + \gamma_4 \times \frac{\Delta E_i}{E_i} \quad (2)$$

Where $\Delta P_i/P_i$ corresponds to the growth rate of physicians from country *i*, β_0 (and γ_0), to a constant, β_i (and γ_i, to a specific constant for each country *i* (*dummy*), β_1 (γ_1), to the coefficient of the number of physicians (nurses) from country *i*, at the initial instant t_0; β_2 (γ_3), to the coefficient of the growth rate of the number of nurses (physicians), $\Delta N_i/N_i$; β_3 (γ_3), to the coefficient of the growth rate of GDP *per capita* from country *i*, $\Delta GDP_i/GDP_i$; and β_4 (γ_4), to the coefficient of the growth rate of the elderly population's percentage from country *i*, $\Delta E_i/E_i$. The software *R* was used to perform this analysis, considering two growth rates, from 2000 to 2007 and from 2007 and 2014 (the full timespan would lead to a higher number of variables than equations);

III. Cluster analyses of the dummies obtained in the previous steps for each country β_i and γ_i) with the aim to group countries together according to their similarities and in a meaningful manner. This step was developed in the statistical software *SPSS* by using the *Ward* and the *K-means* methods.

IV. Integration of the previous information in Eqs. (1) and (2). Determination of the relationship between the variables in analysis considering at this moment growth rates between 2000 and 2014. In the Portuguese case, we obtained the following regressions to estimate the number of physicians and nurses:

$$\left(\frac{\Delta P}{P}\right)_{t-(t-1)} = 1{,}12 - 0{,}28 \times P_{t-1} + 0{,}15 \times \left(\frac{\Delta N}{N}\right)_{t-(t-1)} - 0{,}096 \times \left(\frac{\Delta GDP}{GDP}\right)_{t-(t-1)} + 0{,}27 \times \left(\frac{\Delta E}{E}\right)_{t-(t-1)} \quad (3)$$

$$\left(\frac{\Delta N}{N}\right)_{t-(t-1)} = 0{,}72 - 0{,}095 \times N_{t-1} + 0{,}27 \times \left(\frac{\Delta P}{P}\right)_{t-(t-1)} + 0{,}014 \times \left(\frac{\Delta GDP}{GDP}\right)_{t-(t-1)} + 0{,}2 \times \left(\frac{\Delta E}{E}\right)_{t-(t-1)} \quad (4)$$

Where $\left(\frac{\Delta P}{P}\right)_{t-(t-1)}$, $\left(\frac{\Delta N}{N}\right)_{t-(t-1)}$, $\left(\frac{\Delta GDP}{GDP}\right)_{t-(t-1)}$, $\left(\frac{\Delta E}{E}\right)_{t-(t-1)}$ refers to the growth rate of the number of physicians, nurses, GDP *per capita*, elderly population, respectively, between the years t and $t-1$; and P_{t-1} corresponds to the number of physicians at the year $t-1$.

A similar process was used to estimate the relationship between physicians per medical specialty (29 medical specialties defined by the International standard Classification of Occupations (ISCO-08) from the International Labour Organization) and variables such as elderly population and GDP.

Considering the regressions obtained and the estimates for the future Portuguese elderly population and GDP *per capita* from a previous research project called DEMOSPIN - Economically sustainable demography – Reverting the decline in peripheral areas (de Castro et al., 2015), we determined the nationwide number of physicians and nurses as well as the number of physicians per medical specialty till 2040.

HEALTH2040 model: Social component

The consultation of experts on the health workforce needs and on policy objectives is determinant for the success of any tool to predict the future needs of HRH (Dussault and Fronteira, 2010). The social component of our model involved two participatory sessions with experts with a web-based platform to acquire their knowledge and experience regarding the population's needs on HRH, considering different scenarios and the results from the technical component. The group of experts was heterogeneous as it was composed by physicians (from different medical specialties), nurses, hospital administrators, clinical directors, and academics with relevant research in this field.

In general, the first participatory session involved a 2-round online questionnaire and feedback regarding the future needs of the nationwide physicians and nurses. The expected evolution of physicians and nurses till 2040, that resulted from the technical component (described above) served as a basis for experts to answer the questionnaire composed by nine questions (e.g. what should be the desirable number of physicians (nurses and nurses per physician) per thousand of inhabitants in 2020,

2030 and 2040, considering the expected evolution of GDP *per capita* and elderly population?). The experts answered individually and anonymously these questions by reacting to our technical component estimates. The web-based platform was able to detect inconsistencies on the experts' answers so they could review them in a valid and coherent manner. Once finished the first round, each expert was confronted with a summary of the answers, being possible to compare the answers' average coming from all experts with their own. Then, in the second round, the experts were able to review their answers, by confirming or adjusting their previous ones.

The data processing considered the average and the variance (*var*) of the experts' responses, regarding three variables: physicians per thousand inhabitants (P), nurses per thousand inhabitants (N) and nurses to physician ratio (R). Based on this information, the system verifies if the average of nurses divided by the average of physicians is equal to the average of nurses per physician. If so, the three averages are validated, otherwise an optimization process is implemented in order to minimize the changes present in Eq. (5), to ensure the equality expression in Eq. (6), through the use of the *R* software. Then, an automatic adjustment was performed by using the three data points (related to 2020, 2030 and 2040) from each variable.

$$Objective\ function\colon Min(|x_1 \times var_1| + |x_2 \times var_2| + |x_3 \times var_3|) \tag{5}$$

$$subject\ to\colon \frac{\overline{N_t} + x_1}{\overline{P_t} + x_2} = \overline{R_t} + x_3 \tag{6}$$

The second participatory session was also supported by a web-based platform, in which the experts were invited to answer 34 questions regarding the desirable level of physicians per medical specialty.

As a result, we determined the total number of physicians and nurses needed in Portugal until 2040, as well as the number physicians per medical specialty. Based on these achievements, we inferred about the training needs and the number of vacancies that should be available for each medical specialty until 2040.

In particular, the medical graduates until 2040 were determined by the following equation:

$$P_i = P_{i-1} + P_{(Medical\ graduates)i} - E_i \qquad (7)$$

In which, P_i and P_{i-1} corresponds to the total number of physicians in the years i and $i-1$, respectively; $P_{(Medical\ graduates)i}$ to the number of recently medical graduates (that complete the first 6-year medical programme) in the year i; and E_i to the medical exits (retirement or death) in the year i.

PART III

EFFECTIVE PUBLIC POLICY STEWARDSHIP, LEADERSHIP AND GOVERNANCE

Governance issues in the development of the health workforce

Ellen Kuhlmann

1. Introduction

Governance reform is a key to stronger health systems and universal health-care coverage for the population. International organisations and national governments have taken action to develop sector- and disease specific tools and intervention strategies for better governance. A recent high-level meeting in Europe, for instance, called for 'stronger governance arrangement in relation to health system stewardship for non-communicable diseases (NCDs) in order to ensure coherence across the different settings' (WHO, 2018: 3). Added to this, the European Observatory on Health Systems and Policies, on behalf of WHO Regional Office of Europe, has developed a comprehensive framework and methodological tool for strengthening health system governance and better performance (Greer et al., 2016a). However, the governance of the health workforce has received little attention of health policymakers and researchers so far, despite an urgent need for action. Dieleman and colleagues have argued that neglecting governance issues in the field of human resources for health (HRH) 'could be an important reason why HRH policy formulation and implementation is often poor' (2011: 1).

A governance approach moves far beyond 'outcomes' and 'the workforce crises' (Cometto and Campbell, 2016). Moreover, it brings intersections between health workforce development, health systems and leadership into view. Buchan, with regard to shortages of nurses, reminded us, that if we do not understand the importance for health system-based solutions and 'make better use of the available evidence, we are doomed to endlessly repeat a cycle of inadequate, uncoordinated, obsolete and often inappropriate policy responses' (2006: 458). The Lancet Commission on health professional education also stressed the importance of a systems-based approach (Frenk et al., 2010). Bodenheimer and Sinsky added, that a compass to optimise health system performance should include the goal of improving the work life of healthcare providers and reminded us, 'that care of the patient requires care of the provider' (Bodenheimer and Sinsky, 2014: 573).

Growing awareness of the critical relevance of human resources for the health system and the health of the population (Campbell et al., 2013; Dussault et al., 2010; Frenk et al., 2010; OECD, 2016; WHO, 2016; UN, 2016) has not led to comprehensive and systematic changes in the institutions of the healthcare sector and society at large, however. Moreover, policy support for the building of a people-centred health workforce is still weak, and appropriate funding and research programmes are lacking (Kuhlmann et al., 2018a). As Dussault (2015: 286) put it, 'action on the ground has yet to follow'.

This chapter contributes to the 'rethinking of HRH' by applying a governance lens and exploring contemporary developments in the health workforce in the context of changing health systems and professions. With a focus on Europe, the chapter seeks to contribute to our knowledge on what works, how and why in the building of a future health workforce that is sustainable and people-centred. Some clarification of terms may be useful: The concept of 'HRH' refers to an approach developed by WHO (Campbell et al., 2013; WHO, 2016), while the term 'health workforce' (or health human resources) is broader and not linked to a specific approach, yet for the purpose of this chapter the two terms are used interchangeably. In terms of methods, the chapter draws on published research and other secondary sources. It has three main objectives:

- to provide a synthesis of approaches from the realm of the sociology of professions (Dent et al., 2016) and governance studies (Greer et al., 2016a) with a focus on the healthcare sector;

- to introduce a comprehensive framework for researching governance and health workforce developments in order to improve empirical research, which may inform evidence-based decision-making and policy;
- to illustrate the capacity of a comparative governance approach by using an empirical case study of selected EU healthcare systems.

Finally, some conclusions will be drawn on how innovation in governance may contribute to the rethinking of HRH to serve better the changing population needs.

2. Making connections between governance and the health workforce

There is growing agreement on the importance of stronger governance in healthcare and the wider public sector. Despite an elaborate theoretical debate since the 1990s, no uniform definition is available, however. This is especially true for the governance of HRH. It is not sufficiently clear, how governance can be used to transform the health workforce and build capacity for more integrated and people-centred approaches, and how governance reforms could be implemented in different national and regional contexts. We also do not understand well, how to overcome 'professional silo' approaches and involve diverse stakeholder groups to support the 'rethinking of HRH' and make 'action on the ground' (Dussault, 2015) happen, called for by the editors of his book.

This section introduces the concept of governance (Greer et al., 2016b; WHO, 2018) and discusses how governance approaches may be connected to health workforce issues. Especially relevant are two strands of the literature: approaches from the sociology of professions (also taking social policy and organisation studies into account) (Bertilsson, 1990; Dent et al., 2016; Johnson, 1995; Kirkpatrick et al., 2016; Kuhlmann et al., 2016) and the debates into HRH and governance (Dieleman et al., 2011; Hastings et al., 2016; Kuhlmann et al., 2015; Maier, 2015).

2.1. The concept of governance

Following a broad definition of governance as suggested, for instance, by Greer and colleagues (2016b) and WHO, governance is understood as a framework for 'navigating complex relationships' (WHO, 2018: 4) and negotiating policy interventions. When applied to health workforce development, a particular benefit of governance is its focus on coordination and integration, which makes it possible to overcome the traditional 'silo approaches' of professions and the fragmentation of the healthcare sector (Dieleman et al., 2011; Kuhlmann et al., 2018a).

Governance is relevant as a conceptual framework and as a tool to facilitate policy implementation and capacity building (Kuhlmann et al., 2016). It is important to recall that growing attention to governance was closely connected to the introduction of new public management in the public sector. These developments were characterised through an overall shift of regulatory power from the macro-level of 'government' towards the meso-level of organisations and professions. This, in turn, broadens the scope of stakeholders as well as the tools of policymaking and governing, for instance, the new mechanism of performance management.

Governance theory may help to assess in more detail the connections between various dimensions or 'sets' of governance. This includes, for instance, the relationships between and within systems and sectors (Greer et al., 2015, 2017) as well as actor-centred dimensions and stakeholder involvement (Burau et al., 2017). A governance approach may also address dimensions of culture and discourse (e.g. ethics, professional identities). This makes it possible to explore the processes of policy-making more systematically as a result of intersecting conditions of institutions, actors and ideas (Blank et al., 2018).

Greer and colleagues (2016a), in their framework developed for WHO, identified five major dimensions of governance – Transparency, Accountability, Participation, Integrity and Capacity building. These five dimensions form the 'TAPIC' framework for the analysis of governance (Greer et al., 2016b). The approach certainly contributes to standardisation, definition and operationalisation of governance as an important tool of policy implementation. Yet further investigation is necessary to specify the health workforce connections and the role of professions and professionalism (Kuhlmann et al., 2016).

A major benefit of governance analysis is that it helps us to move beyond the silo approaches and interest-based strategies of professional groups. As discussed elsewhere, these silo approaches 'are strongly embedded in the education and organisation of the health workforce. Moreover, occupational categories based on silos inform health workforce governance and planning as well as research' (Kuhlmann et al., 2018a). Another important issue is that a governance approach, initially connected to 'government' and national health systems, may be extended to include globalisation (Frenk and Moon, 2013). Taking a global approach might, for instance, improve our knowledge of health workforce mobility and migration issues (Buchan et al., 2014) and identify potential threats of 'health system draining' and growing inequality in Europe and globally.

2.2. Professions, professionalism and organisations

Connections between professions and governance matter on various levels of governance, as several authors explained from different theoretical perspectives (Bertilsson, 1990; Johnson, 1995; see for an overview, Dent et al., 2016). To begin with the state/government (macro- level), Moran has argued that 'the welfare state was a professional state; it depended on professionals both for the expertise needed to formulate policy and to deliver that policy' (2004: 31). This approach brings a 'collective momentum' and the embeddedness of professions and professionalism in public sector services into view. The connectedness has been described in various ways. For instance, the metaphor of an 'officer and servant' (Bertilsson, 1990) highlights the double role of professions as key stakeholders in the governance process as well as being the target groups of governance interventions. The metaphor of 'citizen professional' sets the focus on the intersections between expert status and embeddedness of professionals in society as citizen, while the 'mediator' role of professions highlights intersections between the state and the citizens (for an overview, see Kuhlmann, 2006).

The close connections between professions and governance call for a critical review of contemporary developments in healthcare systems and society at large. 'On the edge of the postmodern era' the collective momentum of professions and the expert role of a professional are facing a number of challenges and transformations. One important development has been the establishment of new public management policies targeting professions as key group of better performance (Kirkpatrick et al., 2016).

Another important and more serious issue is the growing populist movements and their attacks on expert knowledge and their views on professionals as opposed to 'the people'. This may be illustrated by the so-called 'Anti Vax' movement in Italy and growing resistance against life-saving vaccination programmes in several other countries. An increase in physical attacks on healthcare and emergency staff provides another illustrative examples of a 'collective momentum' of health professionals. Attacks against an emergency nurse or doctor are not primarily an individual issue, but a serious threat to public health and healthcare. Within the scope of governance of global networks and nation states, the capacity of professionals to legitimise political decisions and to maintain trust in social services is needed more than ever in times of leaner budgets, more demanding customers, and growing populist movements (Pavolini et al., 2018).

Close connections between professions and organisations are also obvious when looking at the operational dimensions (meso-levels) of governance. As Muzio and Kirkpatrick (2011: 390) have highlighted, professions and organisations are 'collective agents' that have distributed responsibility for public sector services. Some authors have discussed these developments as 'hybridisation' of medicine and management, or more generally, of professionalism and managerialism (see for an overview, Kirkpatrick et al, 2016). Denis and colleagues found that the 'traditional view of professional practice as self-regulating and based on "peer group control" is supplemented with bureaucratic measures for professional production that push toward a greater embodiment of professions within organized settings and the development of strategies to better control risks' (2016: 215).

A comparison of hospital management in European countries identified different forms of embodiment. In all countries, doctors increasingly incorporated new forms of performance management in medical professionalism, yet organisational settings create different patterns of 'control' and governing doctors (Kuhlmann et al., 2013). Similarly, when looking at leadership, a comparison of developments in Canada and the Netherlands illustrated different policy experiences regarding the engagement and leadership of medical doctors, despite similar policy challenges: 'Achieving alignment between soft (trust, collaboration) and hard (financial incentives) levers may require facilitative conditions at the level of the health system, like clarity and stability of broad policy orientations and openness to local experimentation' (Denis and van Gestel, 2016).

Another connecting tie between governance and professions is the concept of professionalism. Professionalism may be defined broadly, including professional ethics and identities as well as professional knowledge, guidelines and standards beyond law and legally binding requirements. Professionalism is a powerful tool of governance, that allows governing people 'at a distance' and that moves beyond the institutional surveillance mechanisms and steering tools of performance management. For instance, Kroezen et al. (2014) have shown how knowledge claims and jurisdiction control have been used to negotiate nurse prescribing. Other studies have illustrated how the shared goal of health professions – namely to provide good care for patients – may serve as a policy lever to facilitate more integrated and people-centred models of care as well as multiprofessional teams and skills-mix (Burau et al., 2017; Kuhlmann, 2006). Thus, the need for transformations in medical professionalism, as highlighted by Plochg et al. a decade ago (2009), has provoked change in the professions, at least to some extent and within some professional groups more than in others. Here, too, the institutional conditions (at state and organisation levels) matter and shape the emerging new forms of professionalism.

In summary, the sociology of professions has specified the role of professional groups in the health policy process and highlighted the embeddedness in public sectors and the capacity to 'mediate' between different stakeholder interests (Kuhlmann, 2006). It has also analysed in more detail the 'tribalism' of professions as a barrier to innovation (Frenk et al., 2010) as well as the new emergent interprofessional relationships based on more inclusive professionalism and patient/population needs (Burau et al., 2017). Other examples include organisation studies that help to explore accountability mechanisms for health workforce governance (Kirkpatrick et al., 2016). Typically, a governance approach makes it possible to explore capacity building for health workforce innovation on the levels of both organisations and professions, and how these two levels of governing may be connected most effectively. However, these meso-level approaches need further investigation to be linked to systems-based (macro-level) health workforce governance dimensions. Importantly, governance increasingly includes transnational aspects (Frenk and Moon, 2013) and the governance through European Union (EU) law and policies.

2.3. Assessing the governance of human resources for health

Governance approaches are only since recently applied to HRH, although sociological studies of professions have stressed the connections since long (Johnson, 1995; Kuhlmann, 2006). The following overview is based on a convenient selection of studies to illuminate an emerging research field of health workforce governance; it is not meant to be systematic or comprehensive. To begin with review-based and conceptual work, the previously mentioned study by Dieleman and colleagues (2011) has been the first effort to systematically review the available evidence on the governance of HRH. These authors draw on data from low- and middle-income countries and highlight critical deficits. The 'evidence base needs to be improved in this field in order to better understand how governance influences HRH policy development and implementation' (Dieleman et al., 2011: 1).

A further review directed our attention to high-income OECD countries (Hastings et al., 2014). Based on data from Anglo-Saxon countries, USA and the Netherlands, these authors explored 'how governance mechanisms facilitate change in the workforce to ensure the effective use of all health providers' (Hastings et al., 2014: 1). They found six types of governance: shared governance, magnet accreditation, and types related to professional development, quality, organisational restructuring, and funding schemes. The results revealed weaknesses in governance mechanisms: 'while there are governance mechanisms that consider workforce impacts, it is not to the extent one might expect given the importance of the workforce for improving patient outcomes' (Hastings et al., 2014: 1).

Barbazza et al. introduced a conceptual framework with a focus on competencies for integrated care. This approach differentiated two levels/areas of workforce governance: processes and tools of governance that are related to the 'health system' and to 'health service delivery' (2015: 1648-9). While this process-based approach highlights relevant tools for implementation, it does not specify the connections between the different areas of 'system' and 'service delivery'-based health workforce governance.

Empirical studies and primary research are still rare but gaining momentum. A particular strength of governance studies is the capacity to assess linkages between health workforce and health systems issues

(Kuhlmann et al., 2018b) and reveal gaps between different levels and areas of governance. A German study comprising data from different policy areas (migration/mobility of nurses, educational reform of nursing, and gender-sensitive work management of hospital doctors) has illustrated health systems-based governance weaknesses. This research reveals 'a lack of connections between transnational/EU and organizational governance, between national and local levels, occupational and sector governance, and organizations/hospital management and professional development' (Kuhlmann and Larsen, 2015: 1636).

The findings echo wider calls for multi-level and transsectoral governance approach (Greer et al., 2015, 2017) and attention to the meso-levels of governance (Burau, 2016) in order to enhance transformative potential of innovations in the health workforce and 'help closing the existing gaps in governance' (Kuhlmann and Larsen, 2015: 1635). For instance, a Dutch study explored network governance in relation to inter-organisational collaboration and professional satisfaction in primary care and found that '[s]uccessful network governance was associated positively with the professionals' satisfaction with the collaboration; but not with improvements in the quality of care as experienced by patients' (Schepman et al., 2018).

Cross-country comparative governance research further illuminates the connectedness of health systems and professional development (Blank et al., 2018). Maier, for example, referred to governance in order to explore task-shifting in eleven countries. This study assessed governance through the following indicators: 'regulation of titles, scope of practice, prescriptive authority, and registration policies' (Maier, 2015: 1627). The comparative results illustrated health system differences and how different governance models may influence task-shifting practice. This research provides the evidence for policymakers to strengthen new roles and professional groups as well as task-shifting in the health workforce.

In summary, the brief discussion of selected case studies illustrates two things: the benefits of a governance approach and its capacity to reveal health systems-based weaknesses in health workforce development, and the need for more comprehensive primary research and methodological concepts to investigate health workforce governance empirically and comparatively across-countries (Kuhlmann et al., 2018a).

3. Researching and operationalising health workforce governance

A recent call for action to improve health workforce research, launched by of the European Public Health Association section on Health Workforce Research and collaborating organisations, has stressed the relevance of 'frameworks that align health systems/governance and health workforce policy/planning' as 'a priority goal to better understand the multi-level, multi-professional and multi-sectoral conditions of successful policy development and implementation' (Kuhlmann et al., 2018a). Table 10 below suggests ways to operationalise multi-level governance, building on a statement for the EU consultation (Kuhlmann et al., 2018b). One important innovation of this framework is the systematic connection between hierarchical and content-based dimensions of health workforce governance.

The matrix focuses on integration and places organisational innovation at the meso level of healthcare organisations and (with a view on the individual actors) professional development at the micro level, while both dimensions are seen in the wider context of health systems and transnational policy and governance. With regard to content four major dimensions of integration are relevant: system, sector, occupation, and socio-cultural integration, including gender equality (Kuhlmann et al., 2018b) (Table 10).

Table 10. Hierarchical and content-based levels of health workforce governance

Hierarchical levels	**Content-based dimensions**			
	System integration	**Sector integration**	**Occupational integration**	**Socio-cultural integration and equality**
Transnational (global, EU level)			Harmonisation of professional requirements; EU Qualifcation Directive	International migration; international ethical Code to avoid brain drain; EU gender equilty law
Macro-level (state/ regional)	Educational system; healthcare labour market; general labour market	Primary care; secondary care; mental healthcare; public health; social sector; informal sector/ carers and self-help networks	Relationships between different professions; professional jurisdictions, including medical dominance; gender equality	Regional imbalances; deprived, rural and remote areas; gender mainstremaing and diversity laws and policies

Hierarchical levels	Content-based dimensions			
	System integration	**Sector integration**	**Occupational integration**	**Socio-cultural integration and equality**
Meso-level (organizations/ professions)	Alignment of education, workforce and population needs	Person-centred organisation of care; performance management to reduce hierarchies	Task delegation and substitution; gender equality; diversity; teamwork settings	Integration of diverse professionals in organisations (gender, age, ethnicity)
Micro-level (actors)	Competencies for people-centred care	Cooperation; skills-mix in teams	Interprofessional education and practice; ethics; more integrated professionalism and identity	Motivation; intercultural relations

Source: adapted from Kuhlmann et al., 2018b

4. Exploring the governance of innovation in human resources for health: a European comparative case study

This case study illustrates the empirical use and the benefits of a governance approach. It seeks to explore whether and how characteristics of the healthcare system and health workforce policies shape the governance of health workforce innovation. The case brings cross-country comparison to health workforce governance research in order to connect and illuminate health system-based and operational (professional and organisational) dimensions of health workforce governance (Blank et al., 2018; Kuhlmann et al., 2018). Micro-level governance factors are usually not considered in cross-country comparative research, however. Four high-income European Union (EU) countries are selected for comparison, England, Germany, the Netherlands and Sweden, which represent different types of healthcare systems (Table 11).

England and Germany represent the two archetypical models of organising healthcare: a Beveridge-type National Health Service (NHS) and a Bismarckian-type Statutory Health Insurance (SHI) system. The NHS in England is mainly funded through central taxation with a tradition (at least in theory) of universal healthcare coverage and equal access to care, while the SHI system in Germany mainly draws on joint contributions from employers and employees. The German system is based on federalism, decentralisation and corporatism with joint self-administration based on self-governing SHI funds and SHI physicians (Blank et al., 2018).

The other two countries are positioned between these two archetypes. Sweden operates a Nordic-type healthcare system which is a strongly decentralised and regionally administered NHS-type system. Compared to the England, or other Anglo-Saxon NHS-types, there is a stronger tradition of universal healthcare coverage and more participatory governance based on a model of public corporatism. The Netherlands have established healthcare along the lines of a SHI system but with some modifications, especially stronger state intervention and more plural governance. Both hierarchy and plural governance are stronger than in Germany but weaker than in England (Blank et al., 2018; Kuhlmann et al., 2018c).

When looking at health workforce policy we can observe similar trends, albeit some variety, of increasing academisation, new roles for nurses, task-shifting and multiprofessional team approaches in England, Sweden and the Netherlands. There is also some expansion of prescribing rights as well as improved sectoral coordination and more integrated workforce planning. In contrast, Germany is still behind in relation to academisation of the health professions and does not establish new roles for high-qualified nurses, such as Nurse Practitioners (Maier et al., 2017). Workforce planning is also focused on doctors and highly fragmented, except few more integrated regional monitoring models. Yet changes in the legal framework have opened new opportunities for pilot projects and more integrated health workforce development. Some transformations are underway: for instance, Nursing Chambers are established since recently in some federal states. Also, there are some efforts to increase task-shifting, but in contrast to the other countries in our sample, the target group are healthcare assistants in primary care settings, while only few regional pilots target nurses (e.g. in the federal state of Rhineland Palatinate). The recruitment of foreign trained health workers shows a different pattern of the four countries included in our comparative case study. Here we find more similarities between England and Sweden with high levels of foreign-trained staff, and Germany and the Netherlands with lower levels, although Germany seems to move closer to the pattern typically observed in the NHS systems.

Table 11. Health systems, health workforce policy and the governance of innovation in selected EU countries

Country	Health systems	Health workforce policy	Governance of health workforce innovation
England	NHS system, tax funded, centralised, hierarchical governance with some market and public involvement; low-to-middle density of healthcare staff	Some integration across professional groups with a focus on nurses; strengthening of academic education and new roles of a wide range of health professionals, especially high-qualified nurses (Nurse Practitioners) and new roles of pharmacists; some expansion of prescribing rights; extensive recruitment of foreign-trained health professionals	Physicians and nurses as external policy players; innovation though professional development with some connection to organisational change; some integrated planning, skills-mix governance and interprofessional competence development; some integrated planning
Germany	SHI system; employer-employee funded; decentralised and federalist; corporatist governance with some hierarchy and market; sectorial fragmentation of governance, funding and planning; very high workforce density	Some integration of health professionals under medical leadership; limited academisation of nurses and therapists, lack of new roles; regional pilots to shift tasks from physicians to healthcare assistants; some efforts to establish self-governance of nurses; prescribing rights limited to physicians; foreign recruitment in a middle range but increasing; some variation with stronger workforce shortage in the Eastern parts	Physicians as insiders in health policy but very poor integration and self-governance of nurses; innovation primarily through organisational reform with some task-shifting; professional silos with little interprofessional education; fragmented governance of organisation reform and workforce innovation; comprehensive centralised planning for doctors with some regional efforts for nurses and weak integration
Netherlands	SHI-based system with some elements of a NHS system; mixed funding, centralised; network governance with hierarchy and market; high workforce density; some sectorial coordination	Integration within a medical model; integration across professions with new roles of nurses; direct access to therapists; team approaches; some prescribing rights of nurse-specialists; some sectoral integration; very low foreign recruitment	Physicians as insiders in health policy; strengthening of nurses' self-governance; some integrated competence development; advanced workforce planning and governing bodies with a focus on physicians; elements of organisational reform and competence development are relevant, but systematic coordination is weak

Country	Health systems	Health workforce policy	Governance of health workforce innovation
Sweden	Nordic-type NHS system; tax funded, decentralised governance with high variation within the country; network governance with some hierarchy, market and strong public involvement and integration/ 'public' corporatism; some sectoral coordination; health workforce density middle-to-high	Integration within a medical model with a multidisciplinary orientation and team approaches; some integrated competence development; new roles of nurses and therapists; high levels of foreign recruitment; regional variation and workforce shortages in remote and Arctic region	Physicians and nurses as insiders in health policy with strong public control; self-governance of nurses and therapists; integrated workforce planning; innovation through comprehensive organisational change with some connection to professional development coordinated through local authorities

Sources: own table, information based on Blank et al., 2018, OECD, 2016, Maier et al., 2017; Kroezen et al., 2014; indicators 'health workforce' and 'innovation' adapted from Kuhlmann et al., 2018c

In relation to the governance of health workforce innovation no clear health system-based pattern is emerging from the comparison, as described elsewhere for the primary care workforce (for details see Kuhlmann et al., 2018). England shows a governance model with physicians and nurses as external policy players and weak coordination between professional and organisational development, although change is strong in both areas. Innovation is primarily based on professional development with specialisation of nurses and new roles and tasks, similarly for pharmacists and some allied health professions. 'Some integrated governing bodies have been established, although silo approaches remain dominant in relation to physicians, alongside improved health workforce planning, skills-mix governance and competence development' (Kuhlmann et al., 2018).

The corporatist model in Germany has positioned physicians as 'insiders' in the health policy process, who enjoy strong self-administration and self-governance. Physicians represent the provider side, while other health professions are largely excluded and lack self-governing powers. Some change is underway; most recently, some of the *Länder* (federal states) are establishing Nursing Chambers. Organisational reform – based on new legal frameworks for integrated care provision – is the major policy lever for workforce innovation. However, organisational reform and workforce innovation are not systematically connected and competence development is weak. The health workforce is still primarily governed along the lines of 'silo' approaches, while integrated planning and governing bodies are mainly lacking. A few exceptions apply, as more integrated monitoring models have been established regionally (Kuhlmann et al., 2018c).

Similar to Germany, physicians are insiders in the policy process in the Netherlands. However, one important difference is a stronger position of nurses who are granted self-governing capacities. Interestingly, the governance of health workforce innovation draws on elements of organisational, professional and competence development, while planning and governing bodies continue to prioritise doctors. Finally, an inclusive governance pattern is strongest in Sweden, where we find doctors and nurses alongside with a number of other healthcare professions as policy insiders. Health workforce development shows an organisation-based approach which is increasingly combined with elements of integrated competence development, community orientation and new roles of nurses and therapists. Local authorities are responsible for establishing integrated health workforce planning and monitoring and improved coordination of the health and social care sectors. Accordingly, there is high variation between the different regions of Sweden, as strong local governing power may either facilitate or block health workforce innovation (Kuhlmann et al., 2018c).

In summary, the case study demonstrates that a governance approach is able to specify policy levers for workforce innovation and place these findings in institutional contexts. The comparative results suggest that NHS systems and plural governance (England and Sweden) seem to strengthen skills-mix and new roles, and these developments are more coherent and integrated in Sweden than in England. At the same time, these countries lack sustainability in education and planning and, therefore, heavily rely on foreign-trained human resources, especially doctors and nurses. In contrast, SHI-based systems (Germany and the Netherlands) show lower quotas of foreign-trained staff, while the effects are less clear in relation to skills-mix and integration. However, skills-mix and new roles are more advanced in the Netherlands than in Germany and more similar to the previously described patterns in the NHS systems. Germany shows a more conservative pattern of strong medical dominance with resistance against new roles but organisation-driven change in primary care and lower-qualified groups of healthcare assistants.

The results suggest that both macro-level and meso-level governance conditions matter in workforce innovation but may interact in different ways and therefore do not create coherent country or health system-based patterns. Different modes of governing health workforce innovation, as observed in the Netherlands and Sweden for instance, may create similar trends of integrated health workforce approaches although the policy levers are different.

5. Conclusions

This chapter has set out to apply a governance approach to the HRH debate and to provide an overview of the new emerging field. The findings now reveal that governance promotes the rethinking of HRH but in various ways. Two major issues shall be highlighted: firstly, efforts to strengthen more integrated professionalism and collaboration between and within health professions are relevant in different healthcare systems. Secondly, institutional settings matter and create different forms of governing health workforce innovation, and this in turn, creates different modes of collaboration, management and leadership in the health workforce. It is therefore important to strengthen sensitivity to local contexts instead of searching for a uniform big bang solution.

The results furthermore suggest that health workforce development must become a high-level policy issue and needs health system changes. It is time to take the previously mentioned suggestions of Bodenheimer and Sinsky more seriously: to add a fourth aim – taking care of the needs of healthcare providers – to the widely accepted 'triple aim' of health systems reform (enhancing patient experience, improving population health, reducing costs (2014: 573). Gauld, with a focus on primary healthcare, has stressed the failure of the 'underlying institutions behind health systems' and suggested 'disruptions' in order to reorganise the health workforce, reorient training and 'place primary care at the apex of professional development' (Gauld, 2018:6). More radical change is certainly needed, yet it is at the same time important to keep in mind that the implementation of such 'disruptions' might be possible (to some degree) in NHS systems, while more plural and corporatist-driven governance settings call for other forms of innovation and 'rethinking' of HRH.

As a guest editorial of Health Policy has argued, 'there is no one-size-fits-all model or easy solution of how to improve governance to respond more effectively to health workforce challenges. Europe needs context-sensitive health workforce policies to creatively respond to "local" needs and efficiently use existing tools and expertise, and at the same time promote cross-country learning and more standardized planning and governing models' (Kuhlmann et al., 2015:1516). The rethinking of HRH, therefore, needs to be more sensitive to the contexts of governance in order to promote implementation of health workforce innovation. If this does not happen, we will not see the 'action on the ground' to happen.

Acknowledgements

This chapter greatly benefits from collaborative work with various colleagues (Blank, Burau, Kuhlmann, 2018; Kuhlmann, Agartan, von Knorring., 2016; Kuhlmann, Batenburg, Dussault, 2015; Kuhlmann, Groenewegen, Batenburg, 2018b). I especially want to thank Ronald Batenburg, Viola Burau, Gilles Dussault and Peter Groenewegen. I also thank the European Public Health Association (EUPHA) section on Health Workforce Research for establishing a new emergent field of health workforce research, which promotes the rethinking of human resources for health in Europe.

References

1. Barbazza E, Langins M, Kluge HH, Tello JE. Health workforce governance: processes, tools and actors towards a competent health workforce for integrated health services delivery. *Health Policy*, 2015; 119(2):1645–53.
2. Bertilsson M. The welfare state, the professions and citizens. In: Torstendahl R, Burrage M (eds.). *The Formation of Professions. Knowledge, State and Strategy*. London: Sage, 144–33.
3. Blank RH, Burau V, Kuhlmann E. *Comparative Health Policy*, fifth edition, Basingstoke: Palgrave, 2018.
4. Bodenheimer T, Sinsky C. From triple to quadruple aim: care of the patient requires care of the provider. *Annals of Family Medicine*, 2014;12(6):573–6.
5. Buchan J (2006) Evidence of nursing shortages or a shortage of evidence? *Journal of Advanced Nursing*, 56, 454–457.
6. Buchan J, Wismar M, Glinos IA, Bremner J (eds.). *Health professional mobility in a changing Europe*. Copenhagen: WHO, 2014.
7. Burau V. Comparing medicine and management: methodological issues. *BMC Health Services Research*, 2016;16(Suppl 2):157.

8. Burau V, Carstensen K, Fleron SL, Kuhlmann E. Professional groups driving innovation in healthcare: interprofessional working in stroke rehabilitation in Denmark. *BMC Health Services Research*, 2017:17:662; http://rdcu.be/vUxF.
9. Campbell J, Dussault G, Buchan J, Pozo-Martin F, Guerra Arias M, Leone C, Siyam A, Cometto G. A *Universal Truth: No Health without a Workforce*, Forum Report. Geneva: Global Health Workforce Alliance and WHO, 2013.
10. Cometto G, Campbell J. Investing in human resources for health beyond outcome. *Human Resources for Health*, 2016;14:51.
11. Dent M, Bourgeault IL, Denis JL, Kuhlmann E. Introduction: The changing world of professions and professionalism. In: Dent M, Bourgeault IL, Denis JL, Kuhlmann E (eds.). *The Routledge Companion to the Professions and Professionalism*. London: Routledge, 1-10.
12. Denis J-L, van Gestel N. Medical doctors in healthcare leadership: theoretical and practical challenges. *BMC Health Services Research*, 2016;16(Suppl 2): 158.
13. Denis J-L, van Gestel N, Legape A (2016) Professional agency, leadership and organizational change. In: Dent M, Bourgeault IL, Denis JL, Kuhlmann E (eds.). ***The Routledge Companion to the Professions and Professionalism.*** London: Routledge, 215–27.
14. Dieleman M, Shaw DMP, Zwanikken P. Improving the implementation of health workforce policies through governance: a review of case studies. *Human Resources for Health*, 2011;9:10.
15. Dussault G. Bringing the health workforce challenges on the policy agenda. In: Kuhlmann E, Blank RB, Bourgeault IL, Wendt C (eds.) *The Palgrave International Handbook of Healthcare Policy and Governance*. Basingstoke: Palgrave, 2015, 273–88.
16. Dussault G, Buchan J, Sermeus W, Padaiga Z. Assessing future health workforce needs. *Policy Summary 2*. Copenhagen, WHO, on behalf of European Observatory on Health Systems and Policies, 2010.
17. Frenk J, Chen L, Bhutta ZA, et al. Health professionals for a new century: Transforming education to strengthen health systems in an interdependent world. *The Lancet*, 2010;376:1923–58.
18. Frenk J, Moon S. Governance challenges in global health. *New England Journal of Medicine*, 2013;368:936–42.
19. Gauld R. Disrupting the present to build a stronger health workforce for the future: a three-point agenda. *Journal of Primary Health Care*, 2018;10(1):6–10.
20. Greer SL, Wismar M, Kosinska M. Towards intersectoral governance: lessons learned from health system governance. *Public Health Panorama*, 2015;1(2):128–32.

21. Greer SL, Wismar M, Figueras J (eds.). *Strengthening Health System Governance: Better Policies, Stronger Performance.* Maidenhead: Open University Press, 2016a.
22. Greer SL, Wismar M, Figueras J, McKee C. Governance: a framework. In: Greer SL, Wismar M, Figueras J (eds.). *Strengthening health system governance: better policies, stronger performance.* Maidenhead: Open University Press, 2016b, 27–56.
23. Greer SL, Vasev N, Wismar M. Fences and ambulances: Governance for intersectoral action on health. *Health Policy,* 2017;121:1101–4.
24. Hastings SE, Armitage GD, Mallinson S, Jackson K, Suter E. Exploring the relationship between governance mechanisms in healthcare and health workforce outcomes: A systematic review, *BMC Health Services Research,* 2014;14:479.
25. Johnson T. Governmentality and the institutionalization of expertise. In: Johnson T, Larkin G, Saks M (eds.). *Health Professions and the State in Europe.* London: Routledge, 1995, 2–14.
26. Kirkpatrick I, Kuhlmann E, Hartley K, Dent M, Lega F. Medicine and management in European hospitals: a comparative overview. *BMC Health Services Research,* 2016;16(Suppl 2):171.
27. Kroezen M, van Dijk L, Groenewegen PP, Francke AL. *Knowledge claims, jurisdictional control and professional status: the case of nurse prescribing.* PLoS One, 2014;8(10):77–79.
28. Kuhlmann E. *Modernising Health Care: Reinventing Professions, the State and the Public.* Bristol: Policy Press, 2006.
29. Kuhlmann E, Burau V, Correia T, Lewandowski R, Lionis C, Noordegraaf M, Repullo J. 'A manager in the minds of doctors': a comparison of new modes of control in European hospitals. *BMC Health Services Research,* 2013;13:246.
30. Kuhlmann E, Batenburg R, Dussault G. Guest Editorial. Health workforce governance in Europe: where are we going? *Health Policy.* 2015;119(12):1515–16.
31. Kuhlmann E, Larsen C. Why we need multi-level health workforce governance: case studies from nursing and medicine in Germany. *Health Policy,* 2015;119(12):1636–44.
32. Kuhlmann E, Agartan T, von Knorring M. Professions and governance. In Dent M, Bourgeault I, Denis J-L, Kuhlmann E (eds.) *The Routledge Companion to the Professions and Professionalism.* London: Routledge, 2016, 31–44.
33. Kuhlmann E, Batenburg R, Wismar M, Dussault G, et al. (for the EUPHA section Health Workforce Research). A call for action to establish a research agenda for building a future health workforce in Europe. *Health Research Policy and Systems,* 2018a;16:52; https://rdcu.be/1hZv.

34. Kuhlmann E, Groenewegen PP, Batenburg R, on behalf of the EUPHA HWR section. Why Europe needs stronger health workforce research. Consultation for the next EU Research and Innovation Programme, Statement on behalf of the European Public Health Association (EUPHA) section 'Health Workforce Research'. Utrecht: EUPHA; 2018b; https://eupha.org/repository/advocacy/EU_Consultation_2018-HWR_statement_for_circulation.pdf. Assessed 22 May 2018.
35. Kuhlmann E, Groenewegen PP, Bond C, Burau, Hunter DJ. Primary care workforce development in Europe: an overview of health system responses and stakeholder views. *Health Policy*, 2018c; doi: 10.1016/j.healthpol.2018.07.021; https://www.healthpolicyjrnl.com/article/S0168-8510(18)30323-3/pdf.
36. Maier CB. The role of governance in implementing task-shifting from physicians to nurses in advanced roles in Europe, U.S., Canada, New Zealand and Australia, *Health Policy*, 2015;119(12):1627–35.
37. Maier CB, Aiken LH, Busse R. Nurses in advanced roles in primary care: policy levers for implementation? *OECD Health Working Papers No. 98*; Paris: OECD, 2017; http://dx.doi.org/10.1787/a8756593-en.
38. Moran M. Governing doctors in the British regulatory state. In: Grey A,. (eds.). *Medical Governance: Theory and Practice*. Berkshire: Open University Press, 2004, 27–36.
39. Muzio D, Kirkpatrick I. Introduction: profession and organizations – a conceptual framework. *Current Sociology*, 2011;59(4):389–405.
40. OECD (ed.). Health workforce policies in OECD countries: right jobs, right kills, right places. *OECD Health Policy Studies*. Paris: OECD Publishing, 2016.
41. Pavolini E, Kuhlmann E, Burau V, Mannion R, Speed E. Healthcare governance, professions and populism: is there a relationship? An explorative comparison of five European countries. *Health Policy*, 2018; online first.
42. Plochg T, Klazinga N, Strafield B. Transforming medical professionalism to fit changing health needs. *BMC Medicine*, 2009;7:64.
43. WHO – World Health Organization. *WHO Global Strategy on Human Resources for Health: Workforce 2030*. Geneva: WHO, 2016; http://who.int/hrh/resources/globstrathrh-2030/en/.
44. WHO – World Health Organisation Regional Office for Europe. High-level regional meeting: health systems respond to NCDs: Experience of the European Region, Sitges, Spain, 16–18 April 2018. Briefing note for presenters and panellists. Copenhagen: WHO; 2018; http://www.euro.who.int/__data/assets/pdf_file/0007/366766/HSS_NCD_briefing_note_eng.pdf?ua=1.
45. Schepman S, Valentijn P, Bruijnzeels M, Maaijen M, de Bakker D, Batenburg R, de Bont A. Do project management and network governance contribute

to interorganisational collaboration in primary care? A mixed methods study. *BMC Health Services Research*, 2018:18:427.

46. UN High-Level Commission on Health Employment and Economic Growth. Working for Health and Growth: Investing in the Health Workforce. New York: United Nations; 2016.

Flexibility in employment: work, working conditions, and dual practice

Susan Nancarrow, James Buchan

1. Introduction

Despite enormous changes in public health, population demographics and technology, the modern health workforce is still largely a derivative of the 20th century medical model which was designed to provide episodic treatment for diagnostically defined conditions. This hierarchical model is relatively expensive and strongly reinforced by historic training models, regulatory and funding frameworks (World Health Organisation 2013).

Changing population demographics, shifts in disease profiles, new models of health care and technology, increasing democratization of knowledge, alongside new management principles, place pressure on the workforce to adapt and meet the health and support needs of communities in a cost-effective way (World Health Organisation 2013; Dussault and Buchan, 2018; Crisp and Chen 2014). Therefore, innovative solutions are required to use existing workforce resources more efficiently.

Health workforce flexibilities have been introduced as a management response to increase organisational efficiency, address workforce shortages, and better meet patient needs (Buchan and O'May 2002). A flexible workforce is described as one with the ability to "employ and pay at normal rates just sufficient labour to meet the workload at any point in time"

(Collins, 2003). From a patient perspective, truly accessible care relies on the receipt of appropriate health care in the right place at the right time (Rogers et al., 1999). However, the health professional workforce supply is relatively inelastic, as demand or supply of a good or service are not much influenced by changes in the price of the good or service, because of long training times and the way that tasks and skills are bound to traditional professional role boundaries (Nancarrow and Borthwick 2005). This chapter explores the drivers, enablers and models of flexibility within the health workforce, recognising the tensions between historic drivers of workforce professionalization and the new managerial drivers.

For consistency, the health workforce referred to in this chapter includes any qualified or unqualified person involved in the paid delivery of health or social care, and they are referred to as a 'practitioner'. This includes the clinical and may include the administrative workforce in allied health, medical and nursing and social care workforce.

1.1. The health professions and social closure

A key, and relatively unique organising feature of the health workforce, is the different types of professions that comprise the labour force. Historically, the health workforce has been organised under the medical division labour, into professional groups that adopt a unifying philosophy in which pre-defined skills are codified through formal education and measured by the achievement of specific competencies (Friedson 1970). Social closure is the way that professions create a unique identity and monopoly over a specific body of knowledge (Allsop and Saks 2002). Professions use explicit and implicit strategies to prevent other groups from encroaching into their task and knowledge domains, while in some cases also attempting to adopt skills and roles from competing professions (Hugman 1991; Larkin 1983; Parkin 1979). An example of this is the uptake of foot surgery by podiatrists in Australia and the United Kingdom, in direct competition with orthopaedic surgeons, while at the same time podiatrists resisted encroachment into the management of foot problems by auxiliaries (Borthwick 2000b). Social closure is upheld by state acceptance and endorsement of professions through legislation and regulation (Friedson, 1994), and funding models that selectively recognise and reward specific professions for performing certain tasks.

This pattern is evident irrespective of if the funding model for the health system is public, private or mixed.

Consequently, professional scopes of practice have evolved, historically, through market opportunism and strategic negotiation rather than on the basis of logic, evidence or patient needs (Nancarrow and Borthwick 2005; Saks 1995; Berlant 1975). The structures that support social closure for the health professions have typically been strongly endorsed by the state (such as professional regulation and university training) and reinforced by social norms and expectations, making changes to professional boundaries often difficult and time consuming to enact. Education is an important mechanism to reinforce social closure, because entry to the professions is dependent on achieving recognised higher education credentials (Saks 2012).This feature is relevant irrespective of the location of education function in public or private sector.

1.2. The health professions and new managerial requirements

Managerial approaches to enhancing workforce flexibilities are challenging the professionally driven models of social closure. The managerial agenda has the joint goals of increasing health service safety and efficiency while responding to workforce imbalances (Duckett 2005; Hyde et al. 2005; World Health Organisation 2013; World Health Organisation 2016). Consequently the evolving, flexible workforce is increasingly a product of role-re-engineering and task allocation based on the managerial principles of risks, needs and efficiency (Smith and Duffy 2010b;) McNulty and Ferlie 2004; Borthwick 2000b), rather than historic professional values of professional ethics, expert knowledge and public credibility. This represents a fundamental shift in the nature of professionalism in the health workforce which is at odds with the more unified, Weberian approach of the professional project, in which groups establish common goals, tasks and a unifying philosophy to achieve the monopolization of professional knowledge (Saks 2013; Saks 2010; Nancarrow and Borthwick 2005; Currie et al. 2009; Timmons and Tanner 2004).

We explore the key drivers and enablers of workforce flexibilities, acknowledging the tension between the managerial and professional approaches to workforce change.

Table 12 summarises the key drivers and enablers, the domains within each, and gives examples.

Table 12. Sector Specific Drivers and Enablers of Health Workforce Flexibility

	Domains	Examples
Drivers of flexibility	↑↓ Demand for health workers	Population / demographic changes Changing epidemiological patterns Population preferences Technology
	↑↓ Supply of health workers	Policy (e.g. European Working Time Directive, training modalities) Population. Political, economic shocks: migrations, conflict, recession Outbreaks of disease
	Distribution of health workers	
Enablers of flexibility	External numerical flexibility	Training / higher education policy Migration Funding models
	Internal numerical flexibility	New models of care Organisational / HR responses
	Functional flexibility	Role flexibility, substitution / delegation
	Locational flexibility	Funding models Technology Migration policy
	Wage flexibility	

2. Drivers of health workforce flexibility

The three key drivers of health workforce flexibility are underpinned by workforce demand, supply, and distribution:

- *Changes to demand:* shifting population demographics such as ageing, obesity or outbreaks of disease; changes in population preferences;
- *Changes to supply:* ensuring sufficient workforce to meet population needs or address oversupply; *and*
- *Distribution:* ensuring the workforce is appropriately allocated to meet patient needs.

While several of the enablers of workforce flexibility, such as changes in higher education training policies and availability, will affect supply and demand, these are addressed under enablers, rather than drivers. In addition, the funding models in place to support the education of the health workforce, and its subsequent deployment can play a role, both in shaping the focus of education and deployment activity, and more specifically may be a factor in stimulating new flexibilities because of cost containment priorities.

2.1. Changes to health workforce demand and need

The concept of health workforce "demand" needs to be interpreted with caution. One interpretation of demand is the relationship between the number of workers available and the number of funded positions. However the availability of funded positions tends to be driven by social, political and economic imperatives, and does not necessarily equate to the levels of morbidity within the population.

The actual level of employability of a health workforce will depend on the availability of funded positions, or alternatively, the appropriateness of funding models that enable services to create a successful business case to address population needs.

Health workforce planning models tend to focus on epidemiological or demographic data and make assumptions about the types of workers required to meet projected population need. Workforce capacity is described in terms of nurse and doctor to population ratios. Measuring demand for other types of professionals is far more complicated because of definitional and contextual variations (Schoo et al. 2008).

Demand models tend to be driven through a profession dominant lens, which assumes that specific types of workers are required to meet population needs across multiple jurisdictions. However, health workforce demand is far more nuanced than simple workforce to population ratios, and is influenced by cultural, sociodemographic and economic factors. Demand models are further complicated because of the potential for workforce substitution and delegation.

Significant trends driving changes to health workforce demands include the growth in non-communicable diseases (NCDs) (Dussault and Buchan 2018). Shifting away from a disease focus, the complexities and comorbidities associated with NCDs call for a whole-of-life, integrated approach to prevention, management and treatment of illness. The workforce needs to be appropriately skilled, with specific competencies and credentials to meet the population needs associated with

NCDs within a framework of supportive policies and funding systems designed to support integration.

Technological advances and eHealth are continually creating new opportunities for patients to take ownership of their health care management, while creating new ways for services to interface with the community. Where medicine obtained its monopoly, in part through the exclusive access to medical knowledge, technology now means that medical knowledge is now widely available to the general population. While the effects of technology on demand for health services are only beginning to be realised, eHealth has the potential to reduce demand by increasing patient self-management; reducing demand for face-to-face visits and increasing asynchronous care; increasing remote care supported by delegated models of care; and increasing organisational efficiency (Weiner et al. 2013);Chapman et al. 2019).

Population shocks caused by outbreaks of disease or war tend to increase workforce demand while negatively impacting on workforce supply. Population shocks require rapid workforce responses which have had the effect of driving flexibility by creating new opportunities for the existing workforce; increasing workforce participation; and increasing innovation (e.g. technological responses to rehabilitation). Both world wars are widely recognised as important drivers of new workforce flexibilities (Halpern 1992). The emergence of the therapy disciplines during the First World War is a good example of workforce flexibilities driven by population shocks coinciding with the technological advancement of anaesthetics and antibiotics which meant that surgery could be performed more safely and with fewer complications, increasing the demand for rehabilitation services to survivors (Colman 1990; Murtagh 2014). Similarly, during the Second World War podiatrists accessed anaesthetics allowing them to perform minor surgery, providing a foray into podiatric surgery (Borthwick 2000b) which is now a recognised profession in Australia, the UK and the United States.

The growth of funding models that put health care purchasing in the hands of consumer or third party commissioners also appears to be changing demand for health services, with the potential to drive health care costs down and drive preferences for health care delivery closer to home (Warr et al. 2017). Similarly, workforce demands will increase when countries aim to move towards universal health coverage- expanding population access to healthcare both through the requirements for additional workers, and the expansion of the roles of the existing workforce, as highlighted in the WHO Global Strategy on Human Resources for Health (Jin et al. 2019);World Health Organization 2016). The WHO Strategy sets out a health labour market framework which highlights the need for planners and policy makers to take account of a range of labour supply and demand issues when assessing current and future requirements for health workforce numbers, location and productivity.

2.2. Changes to supply

Supply refers to the availability of appropriately trained practitioners to meet the population needs for health care practitioners. Adequate supply is dependent on training sufficient numbers of workers in the relevant professions, ensuring their participation in the workforce is sufficient to meet the needs of the population, that those workers have the appropriate skills to meet the population needs, and they are distributed appropriately.

As with demand, workforce supply tends to be measured in terms of nursing and physician to population ratios. Indeed the training and global movement of the nursing and medical professions have formed the basis of numerous domestic and global policies (Nardi and Gyurko 2013; World Health Organization 2010). However while workforce ratios are important, and relatively simple, indicators of health workforce supply, they ignore the potential for workforce substitution between doctors, nurses and other practitioners; and they focus on the medical model at a time that the global burden of NCDs calls for increased emphasis on prevention and rehabilitation – functions which require inter-agency, intersectoral and interdisciplinary input (Thompson et al., 2018).

There are several examples of workforce flexibility which have been necessitated by workforce supply shortages in certain professions that have arisen from large scale pressures on the workforce including population shocks and major policy changes, such as the European Working Time Directive (Dolton et al. 2014; Moonesinghe et al. 2011). The implications of these shortages have included the redistribution of roles to other types of workers, introduction of new workers, and ultimately an expanded repertoire of skills for some (Nancarrow and Borthwick 2005; Cameron and Masterton 2003).

The European Working Time Directive which placed a cap on the maximum number of working hours for doctors, coincided with several large workforce re-engineering projects as the gap left by medical workforce shortages was absorbed by a range of other workers, including the introduction of advanced practice roles for nurses, growth of health care support workers, extended scope allied health practitioners and general practitioners with special interests (GPwSI) (Pawson et al., 2016, NHS Modernisation Agency 2003).

Other supply considerations include workforce participation. Several factors influence health workers' participation in and departure from the workforce (Hayes et al. 2012) including organisational context, management structures and personal circumstances.

Lack of coordinated workforce planning and a lack of integration of health care training policy with health workforce planning has also led to workforce maldistribution (both oversupply and undersupply) in many jurisdictions (Zurn et al., 2004). Some countries have addressed gaps by using active international recruitment, and also looking to . introduce new cadres of worker, for example rural generalists (Schubert et al. 2018) and accredited social health activists who help connect marginalised communities with health services (Agarwal et al. 2019).

Changes to higher education funding models also have a significant impact on workforce supply. In Australia, the introduction of a demand-driven higher education system in 2011 drove the rapid and large-scale introduction of several new medical, nursing and allied health workforce programs resulting in an oversupply of new graduates in many professions and insufficient funded positions to employ these graduates. Conversely, in England, the removal of state funding for bursaries for nurses has been cited as one factor in continuing nursing shortages (Buchan et al. 2019).

Decisions on how much to pay different types of health worker, what additional incentives are made available, and how workers are paid (e.g. is there a performance related element) will also be factors that impact on health worker participation in labour markets, and the scope for flexibility- for example, s about where to work, how many hours to work, and perhaps which hours they work (Vujicic 2009)

2.3. Health workforce distribution

Workforce distribution is often seen from the perspective of geographic distribution of, primarily, doctors and nurses. However, there is more as shown by the following taxonomy of 'workforce imbalances', which recognises that workforce distribution includes:

- the relative distribution of professions, which may include shortages and/or imbalances of specific types of professions
- geographic distribution, for instance, global distribution of workers; disparities between rural and urban and poor and wealthy regions;
- institutional distribution, which is differences in workforce supply between different types of services and facilities; and
- gender imbalances (Zurn et al., 2004)

As with supply and demand metrics, many distribution characteristics can be measured, however determining the ideal ratios is often far less clear and will depend on local contextual factors. For instance, the distribution of professions may be addressed through inter and intra-disciplinary workforce substitution (Buchan and Calman 2005); institutional distribution will vary widely according to social and cultural contexts, as will preferences for gender balances. Policy and funding drivers can effectively address most of these issues.

3. Enablers of health workforce flexibility

Atkinson's model of workforce flexibility (Atkinson 1984) examines the enablers of flexibility from the perspectives of increasing supply (external numerical flexibility); organisational interventions (internal numerical flexibility); role flexibility (functional flexibility); locational flexibility; and wage flexibility.

3.1. External numerical flexibility

Until relatively recently, the most influential levers to increasing workforce supply have been increasing training and international recruitment. Atkinson called this ***external numerical flexibility*** (Atkinson 1984).

Training is the traditional route to enhancing external numerical flexibility. Despite widespread workforce shortages, there has been little debate around the relationship between the length or models of health care training and health workforce flexibility. Long training times increase costs and reduce the responsiveness of the workforce to meet changing needs (Emanuel and Fuchs 2012).

Using training to increase workforce supply is time consuming, expensive and requires forward planning. The majority of training models for accredited health professionals involve several years of university education. Paradoxically, training times have been increasing in the face of widespread workforce shortages. For instance, many allied health and nursing training programs in Australia and the United States have expanded from three to four year undergraduate (Bachelor degree) training programs, graduate entry Masters degrees or in some case, Doctoral level training (Farnworth et al. 2010; Bollag 2007; McKenna and Vanderheide 2012). In Australia and the United Kingdom post-graduate training for medical practitioners is an increasingly dominant model (Joyce et al. 2007) and graduate training for medical professionals is the norm in the United States.

With appropriate training and supervision, a great deal of health care can be delivered by more than one type of practitioner (Sharma et al. 2012). There have been several recent changes that have influenced the way that health professions are trained to increase responsiveness and cost-effectiveness.

Increasingly, training is moving away from the time based achievement of qualifications to the *incremental* achievement of specific competencies (Gruppen et al. 2012; Fong et al. 2016). Flexible training models, such as *step-on, step-off* programs allow the incremental credentialing of practitioners by providing several exit points throughout the course of professional training. This means that workers have a marketable skill, more quickly, that can be responsive to the context in which they work (Pugh et al. 2009).

Incremental training also facilitates opportunities for *micro-credentialing*. Micro-credentialing involves a short training time to learn a particular task to meet a specific, focussed (and often, high volume) need. Examples of micro-credentialing in health care include new-born hearing screening specialists, phlebotomists, cast technicians and foot care assistants.

Incremental training approaches can increase workforce flexibility by enabling practitioners to develop a repertoire of skills that are appropriate for the context in which they work, rather than dictated by historic professional boundaries. The example of the rural health generalist models is a clear illustration of a portfolio of competencies that cross traditional professional jurisdictions to meet the specific needs of the rural context (Nielson 2014; Schubert et al. 2018) .

Another source of supply is to encourage those who have left to come back into the health workforce, either from other types of employment in the country, or from no current employment; these are known as "returners". The labour market framework cited by WHO in its Global Strategy (World Health Organisation 2016) sets out the various types of workforce "flows" to and from health sector employment.

Finally, a country may look beyond its own borders to use active international recruitment to provide a more immediate solution to addressing workforce supply problems, however a strong trend for migration of workers from low-income to high-income countries has created international responses to restrict the international flow of health workers (World Health Organization 2010)

3.2. Internal numerical flexibility

Other responses include structural adjustments to the workplace that allow workforce capacity to adjust to service needs so that staff can be deployed to areas of greatest need or demand and to reduce the amount of lost activity due to down time, or ***internal numerical flexibility.***

Specialisation involves the adoption of specific expertise, generally in a smaller proportion of the workforce, as there is less demand for these skills (Nancarrow and Borthwick 2005; Stitzenberg and Sheldon 2005). To address this, there are several examples of 'hub and spoke' models of care, in which the more generalist practitioner delivers care closer to the patient with support from a more specialised practitioner who is located nearer more specialised facilities. For instance, the use of hub and spoke models of rural surgical support (New South Wales Ministry of Health 2012); the use of telehealth to deliver speech language therapy (Burns et al. 2012), and the use of interdisciplinary support workers in community based rehabilitation services whose roles incorporate tasks from range of different practitioners which they deliver directly to the patient with team based supervision.

Health care accessibility is compromised when clinicians lack access to the full range of skills or technology necessary to fully achieve their therapeutic goals and instead, have to refer to a suite of other practitioners to achieve their therapeutic or treatment goal (Nancarrow et al., 2013a). In health, therapeutic partitions arise where practitioners lack access to appropriate diagnostic investigations (such as diagnostic radiography or pathology); are prevented from performing minor procedures (such as suturing); are restricted from accessing medication that is needed to fully treat a patient; or are unable to make direct referrals to other practitioners or institutions (Young et al. 2015). The consequence of therapeutic partitions is that patients have to make multiple clinical transactions to achieve a single therapeutic goal, which can be more expensive(DAMASK Trial Team 2008), and time consuming than having treatment provided by a single appropriately skilled practitioner or co-located team.

There have been some attempts to overcome these inefficiencies by better coordinating care, and creating integrated service models(Vrijhoef et al. 2017). Interdisciplinary team work can facilitate the blurring of role boundaries, and better understanding of other workers' roles, so that team members can more flexibly meet patient needs (Courtenay et al. 2013; Nancarrow et al., 2013b).

The implementation of patient centred care relies on an unambiguous, macro (policy) level focus on meaningful, patient centred principles of health care delivery, such as accessibility (including waiting times and care close to home) and quality. For example, various international policy targets to reduce waiting times for elective surgery and in emergency care and have resulted in system changes that have successfully reduced waiting times for patients (Siciliani and Hurst, 2005, Guttmann et al. 2011; Freeman et al. 2010), several using workforce flexibilities. Performance targets based on quality and accessibility in primary health care in the United Kingdom (UK) National Health Service (NHS) resulted improvements in some aspects of care, in part, through increased workforce flexibility, although the benefits of these were not sustained under a pay-for-performance scheme (Campbell et al., 2009). Regulatory systems uphold this principle by privileging patient safety above professional protection.

3.3. Functional flexibility

Functional flexibility involves the transfer or renegotiation of worker roles within a team or organisation to ensure the appropriate deployment of skills. An efficient workforce has staff working to their full scope of practice the majority of the time and not performing tasks that can be delegated to other practitioners (Queensland Health 2013a). This principle relies on practitioners being able to delegate tasks that do not require their highest levels of expertise (Fulton et al. 2011).

There is limited published evidence that health practitioners do not work to their full scope of practice (Elwood 2013; Young et al. 2014; OECD 2018), although in many cases, unless tasks are regulated, the boundaries defining the scope of practice of a profession are unclear (Young et al., 2014). For most professions, the scope of practice is defined by competencies that are agreed by and endorsed by the professional body that oversees or regulates the workforce, adjusted to different contextual circumstances.

Several inefficiencies arise in health care when practitioners are unable to work to their full scope of practice, resulting in additional clinical transactions for the patient, additional service costs, and delays in health care delivery (Queensland Health 2013a; Queensland Health 2013b). Factors that limit functional flexibility include creating additional referral pathways for patients to access practitioners, such as referral gatekeepers; requiring practitioners to go through an intermediary to make direct referrals to other practitioners; and limiting the ability of diagnostic practitioners (such as radiographers) to comment on investigations. Task sharing is increasingly used to increase the flexibility of the health workforce (Nancarrow and Borthwick 2005; Joshi and Peiris 2019). This potential for workforce flexibility is reflected in the growth of the delegatory workforce, such as support workers, including therapy assistants, health care assistants and therapy aides (Department of Education Employment and Workplace Relations, 2012); the expansion of nursing roles and delegatory pathways (Buchan and Calman 2005). It is reinforced through competency based frameworks such as the Calderdale framework, which moves away from the traditional professional models and re-engineers roles based on patient needs and risks (Smith and Duffy 2010a). Micro-credentialing is one method used to support these approaches that move away from the profession-centric model, towards a more personalised, context specific workforce.

Functional flexibility depends on access to supportive regulatory frameworks. The National Health Service in the UK introduced a competency based framework, the Knowledge and Skills Framework (KSF) which standardised competency levels across all non-medical professionals, however the ability of this model to enhance workforce flexibility is limited by the overlaying of traditional professional boundaries and career hierarchies (McClimens et al. 2010). The separation of "medical" competencies from this framework also restricts the direct transfer of activity between a wide range of professionals, instead reinforcing the separation of medicine from non-medical professionals.

The introduction of contestability in health care funding has been a strong enabler of workforce flexibility (Borthwick 2000b; Martin et al. 2009). For example, the introduction of new-managerialism in the National Health Service (NHS), in the form of general practitioner fund-holding drove workforce changes by funding podiatric surgeons to compete with orthopaedic surgeons in the delivery of foot surgery. Podiatric surgeons provided evidence of cost effectiveness and quality of their services, demonstrating that they were able to help address a range of quality standards including waiting times and patient satisfaction. This was in the face of opposition from the British Medical Association surgeons, who proposed that surgical services should only be provided under the control of medical practitioners.

Selective reimbursement to specific professions for the delivery of certain tasks has the direct effect of limiting the scope of practice of the practitioners who are not funded to deliver those tasks. Selective reimbursement of specific professions is an important component of social closure which enables the funded professions to maintain their monopoly over the delivery of specific tasks.

However, in many cases there are no regulatory barriers to introducing functional flexibilities. For example, medication prescribing was historically the exclusive domain of the medical profession, but is now widely available to nurses and allied health professionals (Bhanbhro et al. 2011; Borthwick 2004); many allied health professionals can directly order diagnostic radiographs; and in Australia, the United Kingdom and the United

States, podiatrists have successfully competed with orthopaedic surgeons to be recognised to perform foot surgery (Borthwick 2000b). Where inefficiencies occur, they are caused by traditional ways of working, interdisciplinary role disputes, by more dominant health professions exerting control over the roles of other workers (Horrocks et al. 2000; Nancarrow 2004) the provision of state funding for some services and not others, the failure to fully delegate work to a lower cost worker when appropriate (Nielson 2014), and inefficient therapeutic boundaries.

3.4. Locational flexibility

Globalisation has meant that ***locational flexibility*** is a key factor in the accessible delivery of health services. As the health workforce shifts towards globally recognised competencies, the health workforce is becoming increasingly mobile and interdependent. At the same time, travel and technology are creating a global movement of patients through medical tourism and cross border care (Lunt et al. 2016). Within countries, geographic inequalities to health care access also exist, with a tendency towards aggregation of workers around metropolitan and urban centres and difficulties attracting workers to regional, rural, remote and underprivileged areas. Global workforce migration typically disadvantages low-income countries, as workers migrate to higher income economies. These challenges are exacerbated by the disproportionate burden of illness in lower income countries and greater in-country inequalities and accessibility challenges.

Changes in locational flexibility can be driven by global, national and profession based policies guiding workforce migration (Buchan 2007; World Health Organization 2010); incentives to work in disadvantaged areas (Johnson et al. 2018)

Increasingly, technology is providing solutions for locational flexibility with eHealth providing opportunities for health services to be delivered with more flexibility, to support delegated models of care closer to the patient home, and for new ways of accessing care (Johnson et al. 2018).

3.5. Wage flexibility

Wage flexibility is the determination of pay levels based on demand and the individual costs of employment, rather than on a collective basis. Various authors discuss the elasticity of demand for the health workforce (particularly nurses) with previous studies showing a weak, but positive relationship between wage elasticity and nursing supply (Chiha and Link 2003); however this also needs to be examined in the context of workforce motivators and quality (Fedele 2018).

Wages can drive individual decisions to remain in a profession, to return to a profession, and also influence the participation rate (Zurn et al., 2004). Wages also drive career choices and competition between professions. For example, Australian research suggested that nurses were poorly paid compared to other professionals, reducing the attractiveness of nursing as a career choice (Nowak and Preston 2001).

Wages are an important motivator of workforce mobility (Goodman and Smith 2018) between cities, from the country to cities, between sectors, and globally. This is addressed in some jurisdictions by providing 'loadings' that recognises the higher costs of living in metropolitan areas or incentives for practitioners to provide services in rural or remote areas such as housing and additional financial support or preferential work permit, visa or immigration status.

An area that has had less attention in the literature is the inter-professional competition for specific tasks. Reimbursement in the health sector is largely profession based. However the shift towards a "competency based" workforce rather than "profession based" will need to examine the idea of reimbursing tasks based on levels of *skill and risk* as opposed to a traditional scope of practice. In other words, lower risk, less skilled tasks should attract a lower fee and therefore be performed by lower cost workers (Jewell 2001). Such a model would rapidly fragment health work so that skills and risks were matched by the appropriate level of worker and reimbursement. Similarly, risks and indemnity levels would need to match specific tasks which would subsequently be reflected in pricing. Commissioning models, third party funders and patient centred fund-holding models are likely to be important drivers for this change.

Such a competency based model would begin to challenge existing occupational monopolies (Borthwick 2000a). This point is well illustrated in the earlier example of the podiatric surgeons who successfully contested the delivery of foot surgery on the basis of quality and price. The role negotiations were facilitated by a managerial policies model during a time of orthopaedic workforce shortages. The result was the development of the micro-specialism of foot surgery performed by podiatrists, rather than orthopaedic surgeons, which is now integrated with mainstream surgical services in many jurisdictions in the United Kingdom. Other analyses of workforce redistribution have illustrated how managerial pressures in primary care lead to role devolution and evolution (Charles-Jones et al. 2003).

The use of Diagnosis Related Groups is one method of reimbursement that draws on a bundle of attributes surrounding a diagnosis or procedure that is not directly linked to professions, which have the ability to reward and influence health care quality (Goldfield 2010) and could lead to efficiencies through role redesign.

4. Conclusion

Workforce flexibility aims to ensure the health workforce is designed to best meet the needs of the population it serves. In addition to the notion of skill (functional) flexibility also incorporates principles of workforce diversity and accessibility. While the notion of workforce flexibility supports the managerial principles of increased efficiency, patient focussed care and addressing workforce shortages, it is at odds with the profession-centric bundling of skills repertoires.

Workforce flexibility is an increasingly important way to respond to rapidly changing workforce needs. It is endorsed and driven at local, national and international policy level (Buchan 1998; Department of Health 2000b; Department of Health 2000a; Dussault and Buchan 2018). However, most examples of workforce change still involve localised, small scale projects that take place within the normative frameworks of the existing professional paradigms, using role negotiation between a small number of professions (Nancarrow and Borthwick 2005), rather than wholesale redesign of the workforce. There is limited, but growing research into systemic approaches to implementing large scale workforce flexibilities (Nancarrow et al. 2013c).

The introduction of workforce flexibilities impacts on service users, policy makers, planners, managers, service providers, third party payers, regulators and educators. Responsive and appropriate systems are required to facilitate changes in practice, while ensuring that the workforce is safe and effective. Health educators need to prepare the workforce to adapt to the changing requirements of modern health care systems, and be responsive to changes themselves with sufficient faculty to deliver the required training (Nardi and Gyurko 2013; World Health Organisation 2013; Frenk et al. 2010) The growth in interdisciplinary education and introduction of micro-credentialing illustrate some of this flexibility. Health care funders also need to find appropriate mechanisms to drive change while being responsive to new innovations in workforce flexibility.

Will the professions survive in an environment that demands increased workforce flexibility focussed around the needs of the patient? The sociology literature suggests that professions are robust, self-preserving entities, particularly when they are supported by the state (Abbott 1988). Professions offer some assurances around quality and the consistency and familiarity of branding that are difficult to replicate in an unregulated environment. While it is unclear how the health workforce will evolve, it is likely that in an increasingly flexible, de-regulated, competitive, consumer led marketplace, the health workforce of the twenty-second century will be very different to the workforce of today.

References

1. Abbott, A. 1988. *The System Of Professions: An Essay On The Division Of Expert Labour,* Chicago, Chicago University Press.
2. Agarwal, S., Curtis, S. L., Angeles, G., Speizer, I. S., Singh, K. & Thomas, J. C. 2019. The Impact Of India's Accredited Social Health Activist (ASHA) Program On The Utilization Of Maternity Services: A Nationally Representative Longitudinal Modelling Study. *Human Resources For Health,* **17,** 68.
3. Allsop, J. & Saks, M. 2002. Introduction: The Regulation Of The Health Professions. *In:* ALLSOP, J. & SAKS, M. (Eds.) *The Regulation Of The Health Professions.* London: Sage.
4. Atkinson, J. 1984. Flexibility, Uncertainty And Manpower Management. Brighton: Institute Of Manpower Studies.
5. Berlant, J. L. 1975. Profession And Monopoly: A Study Of Medicine In The United States And Great Britain.
6. Bhanbhro, S., Drennan, V. M., Grant, R. & Harris, R. 2011. Assessing The Contribution Of Prescribing In Primary Care By Nurses And Professionals Allied To Medicine: A Systematic Review Of Literature. *BMC Health Services Research,* **11,** 330.
7. Bollag, B. 2007. Credential Creep. *The Chronicle Of Higher Education,* 53.
8. Borthwick, A. M. 2000a. Challenging Medicine: The Case Of Podiatric Surgery. *Work, Employment And Society,* **14,** 369-383.

9. Borthwick, A. M. 2000b. Challenging Medicine: The Case Of Podiatric Surgery. *Work, Employment And Society,* 14, 369-383.
10. Borthwick, A. M. 2004. The Politics Of Allied Health Prescribing: Reflections On A New Discourse. *British Journal Of Podiatry,* 7, 31.
11. Buchan, J. 1998. Further Flexing? Issues Of Employment Contract Flexibility In The UK Nursing Workforce. *Health Services Management Research,* 11, 148-162.
12. Buchan, J. 2007. International Recruitment Of Nurses: Policy And Practice In The United Kingdom. *Health Services Research,* 42, 1321-1335.
13. Buchan, J. & Calman, L. 2005. Skill-Mix And Policy Change In The Health Workforce: Nurses In Advanced Roles. OECD Health Working Papers, No. 17. *OECD Publishing (NJ1).*
14. Buchan, J., Charlesworth, A., Gershlick, B. & Seccombe, I. 2019. A Critical Moment: NHS Staffing Trends, Retention And Attrition. *Health Foundation, London.*
15. Buchan, J. & O'May, F. 2002. The Changing Hospital Workforce In Europe. *Hospitals In A Changing Europe*, 226-239.
16. Burns, C. L., Ward, E. C., Hill, A. J., Malcolm, K., Bassett, L., Kenny, L. M. & Greenup, P. 2012. A Pilot Trial Of A Speech Pathology Telehealth Service For Head And Neck Cancer Patients. *Journal Of Telemedicine And Telecare,* 18, 443-446.
17. Cameron, A. & Masterton, A. 2003. Reconfiguring The Clinical Workforce. *In:* DAVIES, C. & OWEN, J. W. (Eds.) *The Future Health Workforce.* Basingstoke: Palgrave Macmillan.
18. Campbell, S. M., Reeves, D., Kontopantelis, E., Sibbald, B. & Roland, M. 2009. Effects Of Pay For Performance On The Quality Of Primary Care In England. *New England Journal Of Medicine,* 361, 368-378.
19. Chapman, S., Miller, J. & Spetz, J. 2019. The Impact Of Emerging Technologies On Long-Term Care & The Health Workforce.
20. Charles-Jones, H., Latimer, J. & May, C. 2003. Transforming General Practice: The Redistribution Of Medical Work In Primary Care. *Sociology Of Health & Illness,* 25, 71-92.
21. Chiha, Y. A. & Link, C. R. 2003. The Shortage Of Registered Nurses And Some New Estimates Of The Effects Of Wages On Registered Nurses Labour Supply: A Look At The Past And A Preview Of The 21st Century. *Health Policy,* 64, 349-375.
22. Collins, M. Problems Of Flexible Working Research And Theory In The New Economy. "Ebusiness And Ework" The Key Action II Annual Conference., 2003 Madrid.

23. Colman, W. 1990. Evolving Educational Practices In Occupational Therapy: The War Emergency Courses, 1936–1954. *The American Journal Of Occupational Therapy,* 44, 1028-1036.
24. Courtenay, M., Nancarrow, S. & Dawson, D. 2013. Interprofessional Teamwork In The Trauma Setting: A Scoping Review. *Human Resources For Health,* 11, 1-10.
25. Crisp, N. & Chen, L. 2014. Global Supply Of Health Professionals. *New England Journal Of Medicine,* 370, 950-957.
26. Currie, G., Finn, R. & Martin, G. 2009. Professional Competition And Modernizing The Clinical Workforce In The NHS. *Work, Employment & Society,* 23, 267-284.
27. Damask Trial Team 2008. Cost-Effectiveness Of Magnetic Resonance Imaging Of The Knee For Patients Presenting In Primary Care. *Br J Gen Pract,* 58, E10-E16.
28. Department Of Education Employment And Workplace Relations 2012. Australian Jobs.
29. Department Of Health 2000a. A Health Service Of All The Talents: Developing The NHS Workforce. Consultation Document On The Review Of Workforce Planning. London: Department Of Health.
30. Department Of Health 2000b. The NHS Plan. A Plan For Investment. A Plan For Reform. London: Department Of Health.
31. Dolton, P. J., Kidd, M. P. & Fooken, J. 2014. Get A Life? The Impact Of The European Working Time Directive: The Case Of UK Senior Doctors. *Health Economics.*
32. Duckett, S. 2005. Health Workforce Design For The 21st Century. *Australian Health Review,* 29, 201-210.
33. Dussault, G. & Buchan, J. 2018. Noncommunicable Diseases And Human Resources For Health: A Workforce Fit For Purpose. *In:* Jakab, M., Farrington, J., Borgermans, L. & Mantingh, F. (Eds.) *Health Systems Respond To Noncommunicable Disease: Time For Ambition.* Copenhagen: World Health Organisation.
34. Elwood, T. W. 2013. Patchwork Of Scope-Of-Practice Regulations Prevent Allied Health Professionals From Fully Participating In Patient Care. *Health Affairs,* 32, 1985-1989.
35. Emanuel, E. J. & Fuchs, V. R. 2012. Shortening Medical Training By 30%. *JAMA: The Journal Of The American Medical Association,* 307, 1143-1144.
36. Farnworth, L., Rodger, S., Curtin, M., Brown, T. & Hunt, S. G. 2010. Occupational Therapy Entry-Level Education In Australia: Which Path (S) To Take? *Australian Occupational Therapy Journal,* 57, 233-238.
37. Fedele, A. 2018. Well-Paid Nurses Are Good Nurses. *Health Economics,* 27, 663-674.

38. Fong, J., Janzow, P. & Peck, K. 2016. Demographic Shifts In Educational Demand And The Rise Of Alternative Credentials. *Retrieved August*, 20, 2016.
39. Freeman, J. V., Croft, S., Cross, S., Yap, C. & Mason, S. 2010. The Impact Of The 4 H Target On Patient Care And Outcomes In The Emergency Department: An Analysis Of Hospital Incidence Data. *Emergency Medicine Journal*, 27, 921-927.
40. Frenk, J., Chen, L., Bhutta, Z. A., Cohen, J., Crisp, N., Evans, T., Fineberg, H., Garcia, P., Ke, Y. & Kelley, P. 2010. Health Professionals For A New Century: Transforming Education To Strengthen Health Systems In An Interdependent World. *The Lancet*, 376, 1923-1958.
41. Friedson, E. 1970. *Professional Dominance: The Social Structure Of Medical Care*, New York, Atherton Press.
42. Friedson, E. 1994. *Professionalism Reborn: Theory, Prophecy And Policy*, Oxford, Polity Press.
43. Fulton, B. D., Scheffler, R. M., Sparkes, S. P., Auh, E. Y., Vujicic, M. & Soucat, A. 2011. Health Workforce Skill Mix And Task Shifting In Low Income Countries: A Review Of Recent Evidence. *Hum Resour Health*, 9, 1.
44. Goldfield, N. 2010. The Evolution Of Diagnosis-Related Groups (Drgs): From Its Beginnings In Case-Mix And Resource Use Theory, To Its Implementation For Payment And Now For Its Current Utilization For Quality Within And Outside The Hospital. *Quality Management In Healthcare*, 19, 3-16.
45. Goodman, A. C. & Smith, B. C. 2018. Location Of Health Professionals: The Supply Side. *Regional Science And Urban Economics*, 68, 148-159.
46. Gruppen, L., Mangrulkar, R. & Kolars, J. 2012. The Promise Of Competency-Based Education In The Health Professions For Improving Global Health. *Human Resources For Health*, 10, 43.
47. Guttmann, A., Schull, M. J., Vermeulen, M. J. & Stukel, T. A. 2011. Association Between Waiting Times And Short Term Mortality And Hospital Admission After Departure From Emergency Department: Population Based Cohort Study From Ontario, Canada. *Bmj*, 342.
48. Halpern, S. A. 1992. Dynamics Of Professional Control: Internal Coalitions And Crossprofessional Boundaries. *American Journal Of Sociology*, 97, 994-1021.
49. Hayes, L. J., O'brien-Pallas, L., Duffield, C., Shamian, J., Buchan, J., Hughes, F., Laschinger, H. K. S. & North, N. 2012. Nurse Turnover: A Literature Review–An Update. *International Journal Of Nursing Studies*, 49, 887-905.
50. Horrocks, S., Anderson, E., Parry, K., Clement, J., Archard, L., Turton, P., Stainthorpe, A., Fraser, A., Butler, C. & Rogers, C. 2000. A Randomised Controlled Trial Of The Nurse Practitioner Versus General Practitioner Vare For Patients Requestiong "Same Day" Consultations In Primary Care. *British Medical Journal*, 320.

51. Hugman, R. 1991. *Power In The Caring Professions,* Basingstoke, Macmillan.
52. Hyde, P., Mcbride, A., Young, R. & Walshe, K. 2005. Role Redesign: New Ways Of Working In The NHS. *Personnel Review,* 34, 697-712.
53. Jewell, D. 2001. Getting The Best Out Of General Practice-An Open Letter To The Minister Of Health. *British Journal Of General Practice,* 51, 523-524.
54. Jin, Y., Wang, H., Wang, D. & Yuan, B. 2019. Job Satisfaction Of The Primary Healthcare Providers With Expanded Roles In The Context Of Health Service Integration In Rural China: A Cross-Sectional Mixed Methods Study. *Human Resources For Health,* 17, 70.
55. Johnson, G. E., Wright, F. C. & Foster, K. 2018. The Impact Of Rural Outreach Programs On Medical Students' Future Rural Intentions And Working Locations: A Systematic Review. *BMC Medical Education,* 18, 196.
56. Joshi, R. & Peiris, D. 2019. Task-Sharing For The Prevention And Control Of Non-Communicable Diseases. *The Lancet Global Health,* 7, E686-E687.
57. Joyce, C. M., Stoelwinder, J. U., Mcneil, J. J. & Piterman, L. 2007. Riding The Wave: Current And Emerging Trends In Graduates From Australian University Medical Schools. *Medical Journal Of Australia,* 186, 309-312.
58. Larkin, G. V. 1983. *Occupational Monopoly And Modern Medicine,* London, Tavistock.
59. Lunt, N., Horsfall, D. & Hanefeld, J. 2016. Medical Tourism: A Snapshot Of Evidence On Treatment Abroad. *Maturitas,* 88, 37-44.
60. Martin, G. P., Currie, G. & Finn, R. 2009. Reconfiguring Or Reproducing Intra-Professional Boundaries? Specialist Expertise, Generalist Knowledge And The 'Modernization'of The Medical Workforce. *Social Science & Medicine,* 68, 1191-1198.
61. Mcclimens, A., Nancarrow, S., Moran, A., Enderby, P. & Mitchell, C. 2010. 'Riding The Bumpy Seas': Or The Impact Of The Knowledge Skills Framework Component Of The Agenda For Change Initiative On Staff In Intermediate Care Settings. *Journal Of Interprofessional Care,* 24, 70-79.
62. Mckenna, L. & Vanderheide, R. 2012. Graduate Entry To Practice In Nursing: Exploring Demographic Characteristics Of Commencing Students.
63. Mcnulty, T. & Ferlie, E. 2004. Process Transformation: Limitations To Radical Organizational Change Within Public Service Organizations. *Organization Studies,* 25, 1389-1412.
64. Moonesinghe, S., Lowery, J., Shahi, N., Millen, A. & Beard, J. 2011. Impact Of Reduction In Working Hours For Doctors In Training On Postgraduate Medical Education And Patients' Outcomes: Systematic Review. *Bmj,* 342, D1580.
65. Murtagh, D. L. 2014. Occupational Therapy: First World War Centenary-Growth From Conflict. *British Journal Of Occupational Therapy,* 77, 329--330.

66. Nancarrow, S. 2004. Dynamic Role Boundaries In Intermediate Care Services. *Journal Of Interprofessional Care,* 18, 141-151.
67. Nancarrow, S., Roots, A., Moran, A., Grace, S., Lyons, K., Hulcombe, J. & Hurwood, A. 2013a. Queensland Health Practitioners' Models Of Care Project": Evaluation, Learning, And Upscaling Of Results For A National Audience. *Health Workforce Australia.*
68. Nancarrow, S. A., Booth, A., Ariss, S., Smith, T., Enderby, P. & Roots, A. 2013b. Ten Principles Of Good Interdisciplinary Team Work. *Human Resources For Health,* 11, 19.
69. Nancarrow, S. A. & Borthwick, A. M. 2005. Dynamic Professional Boundaries In The Healthcare Workforce. *Sociology Of Health & Illness,* 27, 897-919.
70. Nancarrow, S. A., Roots, A., Grace, S., Moran, A. M. & Vanniekerk-Lyons, K. 2013c. Implementing Large-Scale Workforce Change: Learning From 55 Pilot Sites Of Allied Health Workforce Redesign In Queensland, Australia. *Human Resources For Health,* 11, 66.
71. Nardi, D. A. & Gyurko, C. C. 2013. The Global Nursing Faculty Shortage: Status And Solutions For Change. *Journal Of Nursing Scholarship,* 45, 317--326.
72. New South Wales Ministry Of Health 2012. Rural Surgery Futures. North Sydney.
73. NHS Modernisation Agency 2003. Changing Workforce Programme: Developing Support Worker Roles In Rehabilitation And Intermediate Care Services. London: NHS Modernisation Agency.
74. Nielson, I. 2014. Rural And Remote Generalist: Allied Health Project. Greater Northern Australia Regional Training Network.
75. Nowak, M. J. & Preston, A. C. 2001. Can Human Capital Theory Explain Why Nurses Are So Poorly Paid? *Australian Economic Papers,* 40, 232-245.
76. OECD 2018. Feasibility Study Of Health Workforce Skills Assessment: Supporting Health Workers Achieve Personalised Care. . Paris: OECD.
77. Parkin, F. 1979. *Marxism And Class Theory: A Bourgeois Critique,* London, Tavistock.
78. Pawson, R., Greenhalgh, J. & Brennan, C. 2016. Role Change: General Practitioners With A Special Interest–Can They Control And Shape Demand? *Demand Management For Planned Care: A Realist Synthesis.* NIHR Journals Library.
79. Pugh, C. M., Watson, A., Bell Jr, R. H., Brasel, K. J., Jackson, G. P., Weber, S. M. & Kao, L. S. 2009. Surgical Education In The Internet Era. *Journal Of Surgical Research,* 156, 177-182.
80. Queensland Health 2013a. Blueprint For Better Healthcare In Queensland,. *In:* QUEENSLAND HEALTH (Ed.). Brisbane.

81. Queensland Health 2013b. Ministerial Taskforce On Health Practitioner Expanded Scope Of Practice - Consultation Paper. *In:* ALLIED HEALTH PROFESSIONS OFFICE QUEENSLAND (Ed.). Brisbane.
82. Rogers, A., Flowers, J. & Pencheon, D. 1999. Improving Access Needs A Whole Systems Approach. *BMJ,* 319, 866-867.
83. Saks, M. 1995. *Professions And The Public Interest: Medical Power, Altruism And Alternative Medicine*, Psychology Press.
84. Saks, M. 2010. Analyzing The Professions: The Case For The Neo-Weberian Approach. *Comparative Sociology,* 9, 887-915.
85. Saks, M. 2012. Defining A Profession: The Role Of Knowledge And Expertise. *Professions And Professionalism,* 2.
86. Saks, M. 2013. Regulating The English Healthcare Professions: Zoos, Circuses Or Safari Parks? *Journal Of Professions And Organization.*
87. Schoo, A. M., Boyce, R. A., Ridoutt, L. & Santos, T. 2008. Workload Capacity Measures For Estimating Allied Health Staffing Requirements. *Australian Health Review,* 32, 548-558.
88. Schubert, N., Evans, R., Battye, K., Gupta, T. S., Larkins, S. & Mciver, L. 2018. International Approaches To Rural Generalist Medicine: A Scoping Review. *Human Resources For Health,* 16, 62.
89. Sharma, S., Ward, E., Burns, C., Theodoros, D. & Russell, T. 2012. Training The Allied Health Assistant For The Telerehabilitation Assessment Of Dysphagia. *Journal Of Telemedicine And Telecare,* 18, 287-91.
90. Siciliani, L. & Hurst, J. 2005. Tackling Excessive Waiting Times For Elective Surgery: A Comparative Analysis Of Policies In 12 OECD Countries. *Health Policy,* 72, 201-215.
91. Smith, R. & Duffy, J. 2010a. Developing A Competent And Flexible Workforce Using The Calderdale Framework. *International Journal Of Therapy And Rehabilitation.,* 17, 254-262.
92. Smith, R. & Duffy, J. 2010b. Developing A Competent And Flexible Workforce Using The Calderdale Framework. *International Journal Of Therapy And Rehabilitation,* 17, 254-262.
93. Stitzenberg, K. B. & Sheldon, G. F. 2005. Progressive Specialization Within General Surgery: Adding To The Complexity Of Workforce Planning. *Journal Of The American College Of Surgeons,* 201, 925-932.
94. Thompson, S., Watson, M. & Tilford, S. 2018. The Ottawa Charter 30 Years On: Still An Important Standard For Health Promotion. *International Journal Of Health Promotion And Education,* 56, 73-84.
95. Timmons, S. & Tanner, J. 2004. A Disputed Occupational Boundary: Operating Theatre Nurses And Operating Department Practitioners. *Sociology Of Health & Illness,* 26, 645-666.

96. Vrijhoef, H. J., De Belvis, A. G., La Calle, M. D., De Sabata, M. S., Hauck, B., Montante, S., Moritz, A., Pelizzola, D., Saraheimo, M. & Guldemond, N. A. 2017. IT-Supported Integrated Care Pathways For Diabetes: A Compilation And Review Of Good Practices. *International Journal Of Care Coordination,* 20, 26-40.
97. Vujicic, M. 2009. How You Pay Health Workers Matters: A Primer On Health Worker Remuneration Methods. *World Bank, Washington DC.*
98. Warr, D., Dickinson, H., Olney, S., Hargrave, J., Karanikolas, A., Kasidis, V., Katsikis, G., Ozge, J., Peters, D. & Wheeler, J. 2017. Choice, Control And The NDIS. Service Users' Perspectives On Having Choice And Control In The New National Disability Insurance Scheme. *Melbourne: Social Equity Institute, University Of Melbourne.*
99. Weiner, J. P., Yeh, S. & Blumenthal, D. 2013. The Impact Of Health Information Technology And E-Health On The Future Demand For Physician Services. *Health Affairs,* 32, 1998-2004.
100. World Health Organisation 2013. Transforming And Scaling Up Health Professional's Education And Training: World Health Organisation Guidelines 2013. Geneva: World Health Organisation
101. World Health Organisation 2016. Global Strategy On Human Resources For Health: Workforce 2030 Geneva: World Health Organisation.
102. World Health Organization 2010. User's Guide To The WHO Global Code Of Practice On The International Recruitment Of Health Personnel. Geneva: World Health Organization.
103. World Health Organization 2016. Global Strategy On Human Resources For Health: Workforce 2030.
104. Young, G., Hulcombe, J., Hurwood, A. & Nancarrow, S. 2015. The Queensland Health Ministerial Taskforce On Health Practitioners' Expanded Scope Of Practice: Consultation Findings. *Australian Health Review,* 39, 249-254.
105. Young, G., Hulcombe, J., Hurwood, A. & Nancarrow, S. A. 2014. The Queensland Health Ministerial Taskforce On Health Practitioner Expanded Scope Of Practice: Consultation Findings. *Australian Health Review.*
106. Zurn, P., Dal Poz, M. R., Stilwell, B. & Adams, O. 2004. Imbalance in the health workforce. *Human resources for health,* 2, 13.

PART IV

STRENGTHENING INFORMATION SYSTEMS ON HRH

National health workforce accounts

Mathieu Boniol, Khassoum Diallo, Aurora Saares

1. Introduction

A health workforce (HWF) of adequate size and skills-mix in place to deliver quality and equitable services is critical to the attainment of any population health goals, including the Sustainable Development Goals (SDGs), the Universal Health Coverage (UHC) and primary health care (PHC) (World Health Organization, 2016a; Dussault et al., 2018). Managing the HWF requires a good understanding of issues such as gender, ageing, mobility and equity (World Health Organization, 2019; WHA63.16). The importance of health workers is recognized across the WHO's thirteenth general programme of work (GPW13) and its triple billion goals: one billion more benefitting from universal health coverage; one billion more better protected from health emergencies; and one billion more enjoying better health and well-being (WHA71.1). Given that health workers are central to any health systems, countries need strong HWF data and evidence to guide policy making and planning towards UHC and to support the attainment of universal accessibility, acceptability, coverage and quality of HWF within strengthened health systems.

Availability, quality and use of HWF data has been positioned at the centre of the global health agenda by numerous resolutions and frameworks calling for strengthened HWF information. The Global Strategy on Human Resources for Health: Workforce 2030 (GSHRH) adopted in

May 2016, urges all Member States: (i) "to strengthen the data, evidence and knowledge" on health workforce; (ii) "progressively implement the National Health Workforce Accounts (NHWA)" and; (iii) "report annually to the Global Health Observatory" (WHA69.19).

- Data on Human Resources for Health (HRH) will be critical for the monitoring and reporting on:
- SDG 3 (indicator 3.c.1 on HWF density and distribution)
- The GSHRH milestones (WHA69.19);
- The recommendations of the High-Level Commission on Health Employment and Economic Growth and its five-year action plan (World Health Organization, 2016b; World Health Organization, 2018a);
- The 2 million CHWs initiative (No author, sd);
- World Health Assembly resolutions on strengthening nursing and midwifery (WHA64.7); and
- The Global Code of Practice on the International Recruitment of Health Personnel (WHA63.16).

These global frameworks and initiatives, assessing the progress of countries on various health topics, call for improved availability, quality and timeliness of HRH data.

In spite of global acknowledgement of the importance of health workforce data and evidence, the availability and quality of HWF data and evidence still remains a global challenge. WHO launched the NHWA as a system strengthening approach for countries to address the challenges they face in producing and using quality HWF information and evidence. The NHWA introduces 78 HWF indicators for improved collection, reporting, analysis, monitoring and use of harmonized and comparable statistics on HWF with multi-sectoral and multi-stakeholder approach, adapting the health labour market (HLM) framework for UHC (Sousa et al., 2013).

2. National Health Workforce Accounts – why?

Availability and use of HWF data of good quality is essential for strengthening health systems and HWF in countries through evidence informed planning and policy making. Despite health workforce and information systems being crucial health systems building blocks, HWF data availability and quality have been generally poor in many countries until recently. Existing human resources for health information systems (HRHIS) might capture only public-sector workforce or information limited to few occupations or indicators, thus failing systematically to produce comprehensive quality data needed for planning.

The HWF data challenges include fragmentation of systems, lack of standardization, unclear data flows, multiplicity of sources, lack of systematic dissemination products and channels, and poor governance with unclear roles and responsibilities without clear accountability mechanisms. The HWF data might be produced by multiple stakeholders through several mechanisms, hence the key policy makers might not be aware of all the available information nor have access to it. Instead of routine data production on key indicators, HWF information is often characterized by ad hoc collection initiatives. In addition, a lack of feedback loop between different actors involved with data collection, analysis and use can result in mismatch between information produced and needed. Lack of comprehensive understanding of the scope of HRH, including its various stakeholders and data sources involved, is often the reason behind above mentioned challenges in data availability and quality.

Achieving UHC in any country will require sound evidence on HWF and its use for decision making. NHWA was established to support and guide countries towards this aim. It is a system by which countries progressively improve the availability, quality, and use of health workforce data through monitoring of a set of indicators to support achievement of health objectives. To address the HWF data challenges, NHWA proposes a system strengthening approach that enables countries to develop or improve systematic collection and use of relevant HRH information from multiple sources in a multi-sectoral, standardized and sustainable manner. This requires involvement of all relevant stakeholders within and beyond the health sector. NHWA advocates for the analysis, use and dissemination of HWF data and evidence to inform policy making and planning processes in countries. The implementation of NHWA is grounded on countries' realities, i.e. what kind of information is needed in the countries based on their key HRH issues. The NHWA approach reflects the change of culture: from an international mandatory reporting exercise seen as an administrative burden by countries, to a fit-for-purpose data collection and use based on countries' needs and originated from their major HRH issues and policy questions.

3. National Health Workforce Accounts & health labour market framework

The Health labour market (HLM) framework for UHC (Figure 18) is instrumental for appropriate understanding of the HWF data needs in countries since it captures the comprehensive picture of dynamics and changing processes of HWF including the different flows from education to employment of health workers. The HLM framework encompasses several domains such as education, labour market dynamics, financing, governance, policies and regulations necessary for HWF planning processes to attain UHC with safe, effective, person-centred health services. NHWA indicators are aligned with the various domains of the HLM framework covering topics such as HWF education, distribution, migration, and gender.

Figure 18. Health labour market

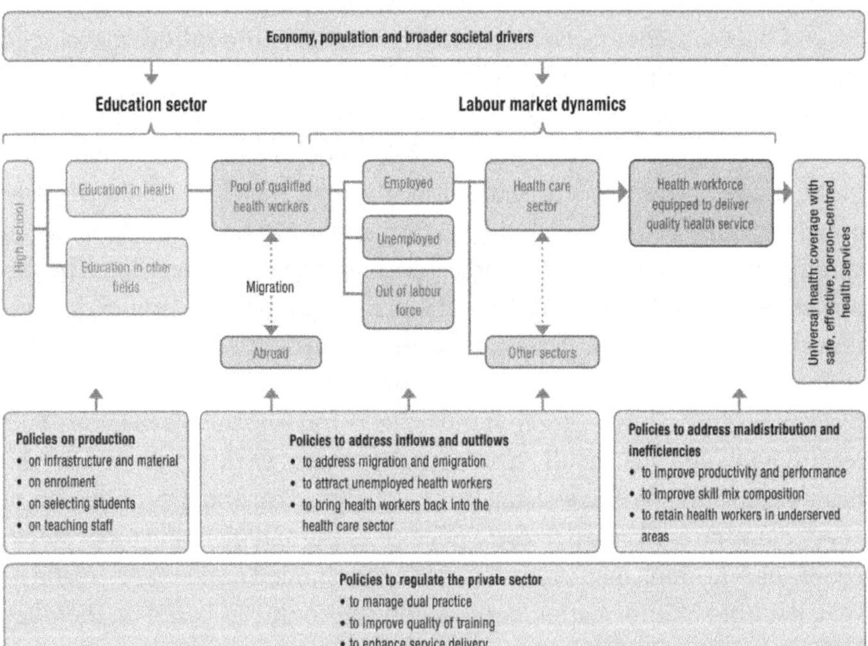

Sousa et al., 2013

Once the NHWA system is developed and progressively implemented at national level, it shall result in improved measuring and monitoring of trends of HWF indicators and guide evidence-based policy making and planning. The application of the HLM framework in collection and use of HWF data calls for a multisectoral approach and for information beyond traditional data sources to produce an inclusive assessment of the HRH in countries. To enlarge and attain a fit-for-purpose health workforce, collaboration with all the sectors involved with the health labour market is essential.

Figure 19. HRH issues in countries

Box 1: NHWA guiding principles

- Countries in the driving seat: countries can pick and prioritize NHWA elements that are relevant to their needs.
- Not reinventing the wheel: NHWA implementation does not replace existing systems, nor lead to the creation of additional organizational structures if these structures and mechanisms are already in place.
- Flexible terminology: No need to replace existing terminology that describes the HRH information systems, such as HRH registries, HWF observatories or other equivalent systems.
- "Do-no-harm": activities should not have any detrimental effect on current health status and other initiatives improving global health.
- Multisectoral collaboration: to be effective, activities to strengthen HRH data within the NHWA framework should be collaborative bringing together all relevant stakeholders across sectors.

Timely and quality HWF data can assist decision makers in addressing policy questions around key HRH issues, such as HWF production, financing, governance, regulation, distribution and migration (Figure 19). The key issues depend on country-context and should be identified and discussed within the multisectoral HRH governance mechanism. NHWA implementation suggests a mapping of existing resources and key stakeholders which will guide the data collection, sharing, triangulation and analysis to inform the identified challenges. NHWA will therefore be instrumental for answering key policy questions, such as:

- How to improve planning through better alignment of HWF production and needs?
- How to address geographical imbalances and improve access in underserved areas?
- How can the HRH challenges be addressed by better resources allocation?
- How to monitor and address HWF migration?
- Can the national production of health workers replace the losses caused by exits, such as retirement, mortality and migration?

4. National Health Workforce Accounts indicators

NHWA encompasses 78 indicators organized into 10 modules covering three health labour market dimensions: education, labour force and serving population health needs (Figure 20); these correspond with major types of policies required to provide 'UHC with safe, effective person-centred health services. NHWA includes both 'capability' indicators, which provide information on regulations and other mechanisms related to the health workforce, and numeric, i.e. computable indicators. Module 1 is the key starting point to strengthened HWF information and evidence as it collects the most important information on the HWF stock and distribution. Modules 2, 3 and 4 provide information on education and training, including related regulations and financing. Modules 5, 6 and 7 give more in-depth information on the labour market, including in- and outflows, employment characteristics, working conditions and spending on the health workforce. Modules 8, 9 and 10 are to inform policies to address the outcome dimensions of the HLM framework, i.e. serving population health needs, including skill-mix, governance and information systems. All the NHWA indicators and their metadata are presented in the NHWA Handbook, as well as examples on how the indicators can be utilized to answer HWF policy questions (World Health Organization, 2017).

The NHWA indicators have been defined with policy relevance in mind. They can be progressively collected and used in a flexible, modular way based on country prioritization and needs (i.e. key HWF issues) and as per the maturity of their information systems to generate HWF evidence. The more indicators available at national and subnational level, the better the scope for an overview of the HWF landscape will be, along with the potential for more sophisticated analyses, more effective HWF policies, and progress towards UHC.

Much of the data relevant to NHWA indicators are already collected in many countries through different mechanisms, but not systematically compiled and analysed. One of the purposes of NHWA is to facilitate the standardization and interoperability of HWF information, i.e. the ability to exchange HWF data within broader subnational or national health information systems, as well as within international information systems. To facilitate this, the NHWA indicator definitions are based on agreed international classifications when available, e.g. International Standard Classification of Occupations (ISCO-08) (International Labour Organization, 2012), System of health accounts, and System of education accounts.

The NHWA approach and indicators were developed through a stepwise process that included several phases of consultation on preselected indicators from diverse sources of international and sub-regional literature. The global consultation comprised over 70 experts from around the world, including deans of faculty, academics, teaching instructors, information systems experts, policy planners, and health professionals. Experts of a Technical Advisory Group, representing various institutions engaged in human resources for health (HRH) data monitoring, collection and management, discussed and interpreted the results of the global consultation in a series of workshops which finally resulted the final list of indicators and definition of NHWA approach. The NHWA indicators are aligned with and built on existing tools and mechanisms such as WHO minimum data set for health workforce registry (World Health Organization, 2015) and the joint data collection by OECD, Eurostat and the WHO

Figure 20. NHWA modules

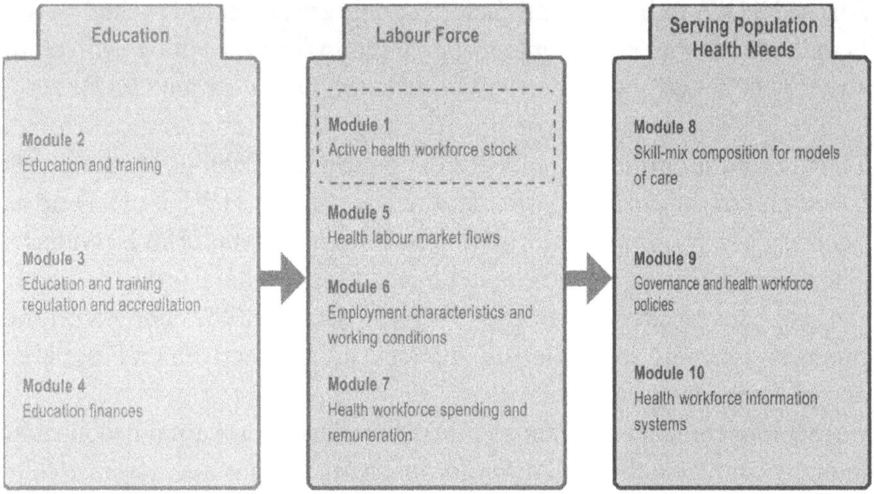

Regional Office for Europe to the greatest possible extent to minimize the potential for duplication in data collection and to enable integrated data collection and subsequent analysis.

5. Data sources and triangulation

The sources of HRH information and evidence vary from country to country and are often characterised by fragmentation and lack of standardization. Information relevant for one HRH issue or indicator might be captured through several different information systems which do not necessarily talk to each other at national level. To attain a comprehensive assessment of HRH, a wider variety of information sources could be considered especially since data from secondary sources might include specific information not available elsewhere (Table 13) (World Health Organization, 2010). Aligned with the HLM framework, NHWA recommend the inclusion of stakeholders beyond the health sector and expanding the data gathering beyond traditional HRH data sources.

The traditional HWF data sources include Ministry of Health databases and data collected by regulatory bodies, councils and professional associations. However, this information might be partial (e.g. only includes public-sector employees) or unfit for the purpose (e.g. includes all licenced health workers without specifying who are actively practicing). In order to generate evidence on all active health workforce in the country health workers employed by private and non-profit sectors should be captured with data collection. In addition, some health workers might be employed by training institutes and academia, military services, or ministries and other government entities in non-clinical assignments.

Additional potential sources for HWF data include administrative records such as payrolls, tax data bases and pension funds. Some countries have established central registries pooling together information from different sectors and mechanisms to have a comprehensive picture of the available health workforce. Although professional councils are in many countries the "gate-keepers" for the health labour market entries through their licencing mechanism, they rarely capture permanent and temporary voluntary and involuntary exits including emigration, death, retirement, and practicing other profession in their registries. There are several other examples on relevant HRH information which can be obtained from "non-traditional" sources, such as data on HWF production in education sector, financing and remuneration data in other ministries (e.g. Finance, Labour, Defence) and health facilities, and information on international mobility of health workers captured by professional councils or ministries other than health. Other data sources like census and labour force surveys (LFS) may complement the information on the characteristics of the HWF, including age and sex distribution and provide labour market related details on issues such as dual practise and working hours. Information from different data sources once pooled together and cross validated i.e. triangulated, can generate a comprehensive country profile with of the key HWF indicators. An example from Brazil regarding use of LFS data in HWF evidence generation is illustrated in Box 2.

Planning and coordination at the sub-national and national level is required to identify, collect, analyse, use and report harmonized HRH information and evidence in sustainable way. Given that data quality depends on the source, quality and eligibility criteria are required to define which data is fit for purpose. In cases of multiple sources of information for the same indicator, data triangulation should guide the establishment of a hierarchy of data sources which will guide the prioritization of data selection. It is essential that relevant meta-data (e.g. information on the source; data collection methodology; detailed description of individual elements and indicators; and computation methods for rates, percentages and ratios) are available to guide the analysis and interpretation of the results. These meta-data are also critical for triangulation and selection of the "best" data source for monitoring and indicator.

Table 13. Commonly Used Health Workforce Information Sources: Strength and Limits

Source	Strengths	Limits
HWF registry or database	If advanced, can pool together information from different sources for a comprehensive database	Often limited to one (MoH) or few sources and indicators
Civil service payroll	Information on public sector employees Usually routinely updated	Only limited to public sector employees Might double count some employees while similarly maintaining some "ghost-workers" in the system
Other ministries (e.g. education, finance, labour, defence)	Can provide information on HWF production, financing, labour market and migration	Often the systems do not speak to each other and there might be difficulties in gaining access to the data
Registries of professional regulatory bodies (council/ chamber/association)	Mandatory registration for most of health professions Commonly available across countries Might host information on HWF migration (mainly entrants)	Disconnected with active workforce due to one-off life-long registration in some countries Limited level of disaggregation possible Can be limited to highly skilled health professionals
Labour force surveys	Nationally representative data on occupations Includes details labour force activity (e.g. unemployment, wages, dual employment) Standardized methods globally (including ISCO) Requires less resources than census	Often small sample limits analysis Sometimes occupations only reported on 3-digit level The frequency of survey period varies between countries Not tracking labour force entries and exits
Population census	Whole population Subnational data Additional demographic data (e.g. urban vs rural)	Long period Requires extensive resources Occupations rarely reported with sufficient precision or only using national classifications Not tracking labour force entries and exits

Source	Strengths	Limits
Health facility data (routine administrative records, Health Management Information System, District Health Information System census and/or survey, health facility assessment)	Data on health facility staff Can provide detailed information, including geographical area, wages, absenteeism, unfilled posts etc. Often routinely updated	Might not include community-based workers Might double count some employees while similarly maintaining some "ghost-workers" in the system Variable quality of data across countries and over time
Other administrative records including Tax registries, insurance or pension fund registries	Information on expenditure (wages, pension) Information on labour market flows	Often the systems do not speak to each other and there might be difficulties in gaining access to the data

Box 2: Human Resources for Health Statistics from Labour Force Survey: the example of Brazil

Survey characteristics

Country: **Brazil**

Year: **2017**

Occupation definition: ISCO-08 4th digits

National continuous household survey

Whole population 14+ (excl. institutionalised)

Sample size: **2,279,742** out of which 927,501 active workers representing approximatively 88 million* active workers

Stock

Overall **43,155** health workers were included, representing 4,560,000* health workers†.

They represent **4.65%** of the active workforce (95%CI 4.61%-4.70%).

Occupation	Percentage (number in survey)	Estimated national stock* [95% CI]	Estimated density* per 10,000 inhabitant [95%CI]	Density per 10,000 †
Physicians (generalists and specialists)	7.1% (3062)	397000 [383000, 411000]	19 [18.3, 19.6]	21.8
Nursing and midwifery personnel (P&A)	27.4% (11823)	1252000 [1230000, 1275000]	59.8 [58.8, 60.9]	
Dentistry personnel (P&A)	6.9% (2972)	338000 [326000, 350000]	16.1 [15.6, 16.7]	
Pharmaceutical personnel (P&A)	3.7% (1587)	172000 [163000, 180000]	8.2 [7.8, 8.6]	
Community health workers (3253)	13.3% (5737)	437000 [425000, 448000]	20.9 [20.3, 21.4]	
Home based personal care (5322)	12.0% (5176)	575000 [559000, 590000]	27.5 [26.7, 28.2]	
Other health workers	29.7% (12798)	1394000 [1370000, 1418000]	66.6 [65.4, 67.8]	

P&A= Professionals and associate. NR: Cells with less than 5 respondent not reported

† Triangulation: from Demografia medica no Brasil 2018 (p148).

Distribution

Age & Gender

76% of health workers were women, significantly higher than in other sectors (40% p<0.01).

This percentage varies between occupations, for example being 42% of women for physicians, and 87% for nursing and midwifery personnel.

HWF age and gender distribution

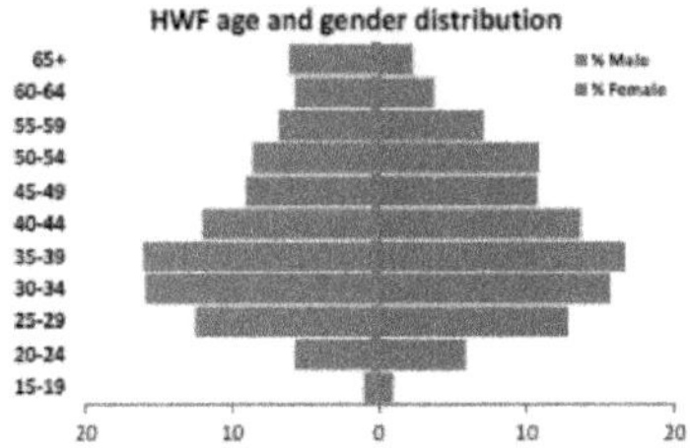

Youth employment (15-24) represented 7% among health workers, and 13% of health workers were aged 55 and above.

The median age of men and women was similar (37 years), although the distribution significantly differed (p<0.01) with 17% of men in the older categories 55 years and more, and 12% for women.

The median age differed between occupations and was for example 42 for physicians and 37 for nursing and midwifery personnel.

Urban/rural

No data on rural vs urban areas available.

Education

The education level classified with ISCED-97 showed variability.

Health workers employed in the private sector had a lower education level as compared to health workers in public sector (p<0.01).

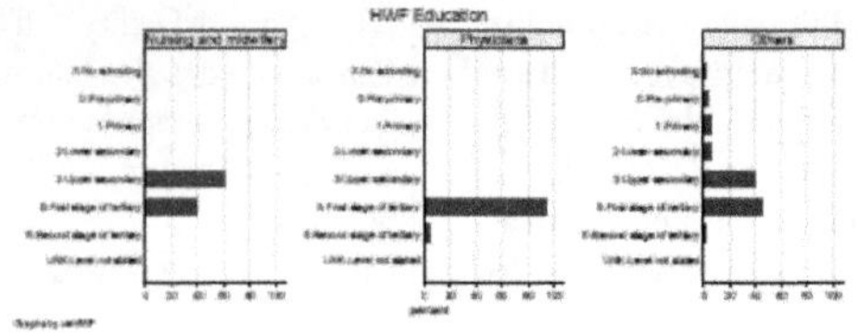

Labour Market

Unemployment

No data on previous occupation available.

Sector

62% of health workers were employed in the private sector.
Health workers represented 17% of the employed workers in the public sector.

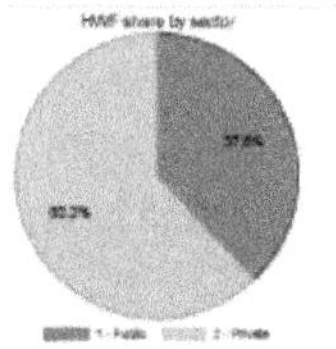

The employment in the private sector varied by occupation and it was 53% of physicians, 46% of nursing and midwifery personnel, 75% of dentists, 77% of pharmacists, 2% of community health workers and 99% of home based social care personnel.

Women were more frequently employed in the private sector (56% of women) than men (52%) p<0.01. Workers in the private sector were also younger (median age of 37 in private vs 42 in public, p<0.01).

Working conditions

67% of health workers worked full time, which was less than for non-health workers (71% working full time p<0.01).
Most health workers were employees (88%) as compared to 62% in other sectors (p<0.01). Health workers declared an average weekly working time of 39 hours** which was higher than non-health workers (38 hours, p<0.01).
Data on earning were available only in local currency
The median monthly earning was 1600 BRL and the median hourly earning was 9.51 BRL.

Occupation	Part time workers (%)	Employees ICSE 93 (%)	Average working hours per week	Median monthly earning (BRL)	Median hourly earning (BRL)
Physicians (generalists and specialists)	42%	73%	43	10,000	52.9
Nursing and midwifery personnel (P&A)	34%	99%	40	1,600	9.5
Dentistry personnel (P&A)	33%	59%	38	4,000	26.4
Pharmaceutical personnel (P&A)	21%	90%	41	3,000	17.4
Community health workers	16%	100%	37	1,200	7.2
Home based personal care	33%	96%	40	937	5.4
Other health workers	38%	80%	36	2,400	13.2

P&A= Professionals and associate. NR: Cells with less than 5 respondent not reported

Gender Pay Gap: The unadjusted gender pay gap between men and women was 29.6%, it was 11% for equivalent occupations. The pay gap varied by occupation and was 20% for physicians, 12% for nursing and midwifery personnel, 10% for dentists, and 5.7% for pharmacists.

** Weekly working hour was missing for 931 health workers. Monthly earning was available for 42910 (99%) health workers and hourly earnings for 41982 (97%).

6. National Health Workforce Accounts implementation

The WHO Health Workforce Department has developed a number of tools and guidance including the NHWA Handbook, the NHWA implementation guide, the NHWA online data platform and a public NHWA web portal, to enable countries to properly understand, implement, use and report on NHWA (https://www.who.int/hrh/statistics/nhwa/en/). The implementation of the NHWA should be a country-led activity, based on national needs and priorities. It builds on national systems and existing mechanisms to progressively strengthen country capacity to collect, analyse, use and report HWF indicators to inform policy making. Countries with strong statistical capacity might only have need to strengthen coordination, networking and communication. In other countries further actions may be required. Several countries are already effectively implementing NHWA. Key implementation success factors include establishment of an inter-sectoral multi-stakeholder collaboration and utilization of already existing coordination systems and mechanisms, as demonstrated in the example of Mozambique (Box 3) (Waters et al., 2016).

Implementation of NHWA requires multi-stakeholder collaboration within and beyond the health sector. The stakeholders may include, but are not limited to, representatives from the Ministries of Health, Employment and Labour, Economy and Finance, Education, and Defence; National Civil Service Commission; National Institutes of Health; legal bodies; national statistical organizations; academia and training institutes; health worker organizations and other interested parties; public and private health facilities; and health professional councils and associations. The involvement of different stakeholders is vital to identify key HRH issues and policy questions, and to map all potential HWF data sources. It also enables a better accountability by sharing responsibilities on HWF information compilation throughout the HLM framework. A successful stakeholder involvement will support all the other areas of NHWA implementation as well, including data sharing and collection from multiple sources, data analysis and the dissemination of results and key messages.

The NHWA implementation guide proposes three phases and eight steps (Figure 21) to strengthen availability and use of quality HRH data and evidence in countries. The proposed steps should be considered as non-sequential and complementary to those mechanisms already in place, if any. More detailed information on implementation steps is available in the NHWA implementation guide (World Health Organization, 2018b).

The three phases of NHWA implementation are:

I. Conceptualization: enabling political buy-in, establishing a multi-sectoral governance and assessing the availability and quality of HRH information.
II. Operationalization: covering all aspects of data gathering, flow, validation and dissemination under an enabling legal framework.
III. Process revision: revising the NHWA roll-out on a regular basis to account for changes such as in data availability or stakeholders involved.

Figure 21. NHWA implementation

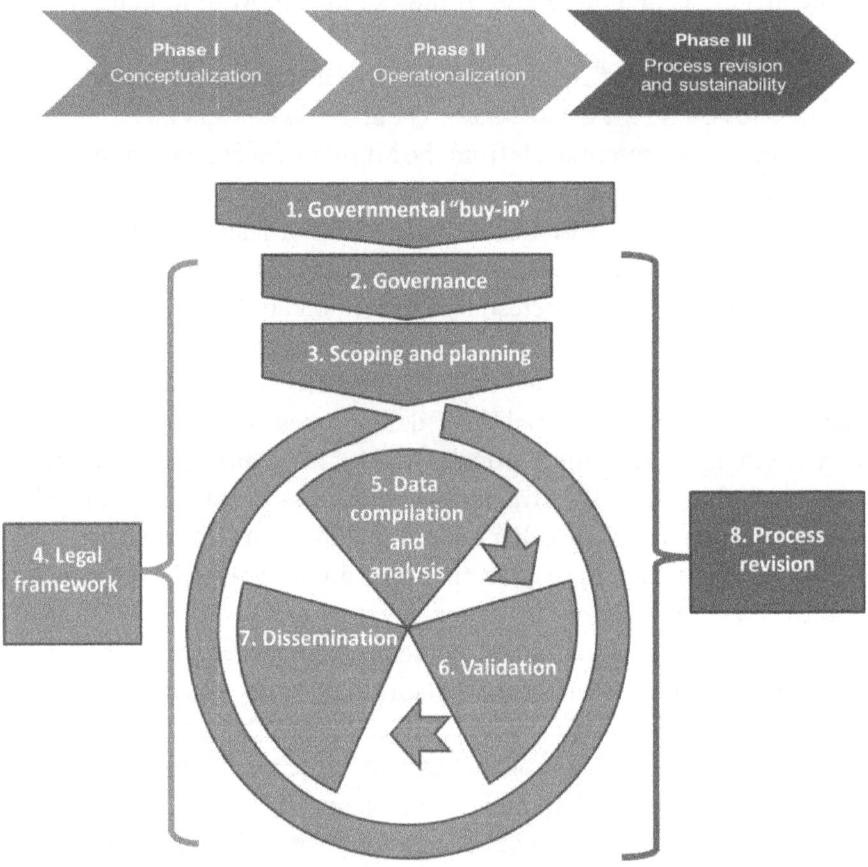

Box 3. Strengthened HRHIS through NHWA implementation: Mozambique example

Building upon the government's commitment for the use of HRH information in policy-making, Mozambique is strengthening the existing system of integrated HRIS (human resources information system) and HRH Observatory in line with NHWA and global recommendations for improved HRH data and evidence.

The HRIS, called eSIP-Saúde, includes HRH data mainly on public-sector employees and information on pre-service and in-service training. Inter-sectoral collaboration between different line ministries and among partners has been one of the success factors in strengthening the HRIS, as well as building upon and linking the integrated HRIS with existing government systems. Another success factor has been the production and dissemination of strategic information by the HRH Observatory, bringing together stakeholders across the sectors and triangulating HRIS data with service delivery data to improve health service delivery and guide strategic HRH planning and policy making.

An exercise of assessing available data against the 78 NHWA indicators was conducted in 2018 by the HRH Observatory to guide the progressive implementation of NHWA, building upon already existing systems of integrated HRIS and HRH observatory. Results suggest that almost two thirds of the NHWA indicators are available. The main deficits in data availability against NHWA indicators were on education regulation and financing, health labour market flows, employment characteristics and working conditions.

Availability of NHWA indicators in Mozambique across the 10 modules in 2018.

Indicator	Available		Not Available	Total
	N	%	N	N
1- Active health workforce stock	8	89%	1	9
2- Health workforce in education	6	86%	1	7
3- Education regulation	2	22%	7	9
4- Education finances	1	13%	7	8
5- Health labour market flows	4	57%	3	7
6- Employment characteristics and working conditions	4	40%	6	10
7- Health workforce spending and remuneration	7	100%	0	7
8- Skill mix composition for models of care	6	75%	2	8
9- Governance and Health workforce policies	4	80%	1	5
10- Health workforce information system	8	100%	0	8
Total	50	64%	28	78

The NHWA indicators, for which the data is currently available, are being integrated with the regular HRH data gathering and reported in the NHWA Online Platform utilizing the automatized mapping between Mozambique health occupations classification and the ISCO-08.

Recognizing the key role of systematic collection of quality data, and production and dissemination of strategic information, Mozambique has substantially improved the availability and use of HRH data and evidence for policy making. Further implementation of NHWA will assist the country in identifying data needs and use to address current HRH challenges, and will guide strengthening of the existing HRIS.

7. Data dissemination and use

The global monitoring of NHWA indicators as per the WHA resolution and GSHRH milestones is expected to occur on an annual basis, although more regular monitoring schemes are possible at national and regional level. However, data collection, analysis and use in country level should be a continuous process. To assist with this, WHO has developed an online data platform for countries to serve as a data management, analysis, visualization and reporting tool. It can be used by countries both for keeping track of the HWF trends and characteristics and for informing national evidence-based HWF policy making, especially if there is no other national HWF data management system in place. NHWA online data platform can be used by several stakeholders in the same country to enter and manage data, but only the nominated NHWA focal point can approve the data uploaded on the platform. After data collection, analysis and validation, the findings should be disseminated and communicated to inform planning and decision-making processes and to raise awareness on HRH issues among stakeholders and the general public. A clear and realistic communication plan is essential to guide the dissemination of findings nationally and internationally to relevant audiences such as government bodies, academia, and media. The dissemination products such as policy briefs should be tailored to the audience (e.g. ensure that the findings and their implication are understood and adequately interpreted by appropriate policy makers). Dissemination can also include periodically published report on the state of the HRH in the country with key messages to be disseminated to a wider audience.

As proposed in the NHWA implementation guide, the data collection and analysis should be guided by the evidence needed to support decision making on key HRH issues identified by the multi-stakeholder collaboration, thus there should be no mismatch between the data collected and analysed and that needed. The multi-stakeholder collaboration increases the information sharing between different actors involved and provides a feedback-loop for further revision of data analysis and collection. Furthermore, it can foster and support policy dialogue and multisectoral action towards UHC.

One of the main benefits of NHWA, when adequately implemented, is a more comprehensive understanding of the HWF, including its size, characteristics and distribution, which allows countries to recognize gaps, needs and possibilities for HRHIS and HWF strengthening. The findings can inform actions towards strengthened HWF in all aspects of the health labour market while also addressing cross-cutting issues such as gender, equity and ageing. Actions may target HRH governance and policies, education and training, social protection, working conditions, etc.

There are several other possible benefits associated with NHWA implementation and improved availability and use of HWF data and evidence. NHWA implementation can support national health labour market analysis to better forecast and plan for health worker needs of the future and address the root causes of key workforce shortages and other challenges (World Health Organization, s. d.), as illustrated by the example from Iran (Box 4). Through NHWA implementation countries can generate evidence and information for the transformation and scale-up of HWF education and training. The evidence generated can inform investment cases advocating for resource mobilization. Sex disaggregated data on HWF can be utilized to guide policies and investments to foster gender equity and increase female labour participation, which can further contribute to economic growth. As per the recommendation of the UN High Level Commission on Health Employment and Economic Growth, HWF information and evidence could be utilised in country level for mobilization of domestic and international resources to implement evidence-informed HWF strategies. Investments coupled with the transformation and expansion of education, skills and decent job creation can contribute towards economic growth with sustainable HWF, and in doing so, to targets across SDGs 3, 4, 5 and 8 (World Health Organization, 2018c).

NHWA can inspire countries to address or reconsider major policy questions related to current HWF challenges and to optimize planning systems. The availability of HWF information enables systematic research on health system developments and resilience at national, regional and global level. NHWA may facilitate cross-country capacity-building, information and knowledge exchange, as well as more sophisticated research about future trends of HWFs within and across regions through analysis and use of high-quality and standardized data in regional and global level.

Beyond the national dissemination and use, country-validated and aggregated key HWF data and figures will be published in NHWA web

Box 4. Human Resources Requirement Projection through Health Labour Market Analysis in Iran

In Iran, the Ministry of Health & Medical Education conducted a health labour market (HLM) analysis in order to estimate human resources requirements for 2025 and produce a HRH supply & demand policy document for 14 occupational groups based on optimum scenarios. This projection is to guide the balancing of the number of HWF needed and students to be trained.

The baseline analysis identified nearly 600,000 health workers, out of whom 160,000 in the private sector. In addition, the analysis captured non-health related staff employed by the health sector, total health sector labour market thus representing more than 735,000 full-time equivalents.

The HLM analysis followed a 7-stage approach in three parts: part one covering the estimation of demand, part two supply, and part three balancing the first two. The first stage was to identify affecting assumptions, which included assumptions related to growth of health sector resources, working hours distribution, and HWF stock. The second stage was to calculate the required workforce based on existing national policy requirements, service delivery structure, financial resources, wages and working hours, demographics, and burden of disease. The third stage was to conduct a feasibility evaluation to select the most feasible scenario based on projected costing and fiscal space available. Stage four was to identify the optimum scenario and provide policy recommendations for funding and optimizing utilization of existing workforce. The workforce supply estimation in stage five was calculated based on current stock, graduates and estimated loss rate (retired, dismissed, resigned, deceased and migrated workers). The last part of the analysis was to estimate required supply for projected demand for 2025.

The outcome of the exercise was that based on the optimum scenario there is a need for more than 400,000 additional health workers within the 14 main groups by 2025. These calculations were further utilized to inform the planning of HWF education and training, HRH financing and resources allocation, health facility staffing and policies on other areas such as migration and unemployment.

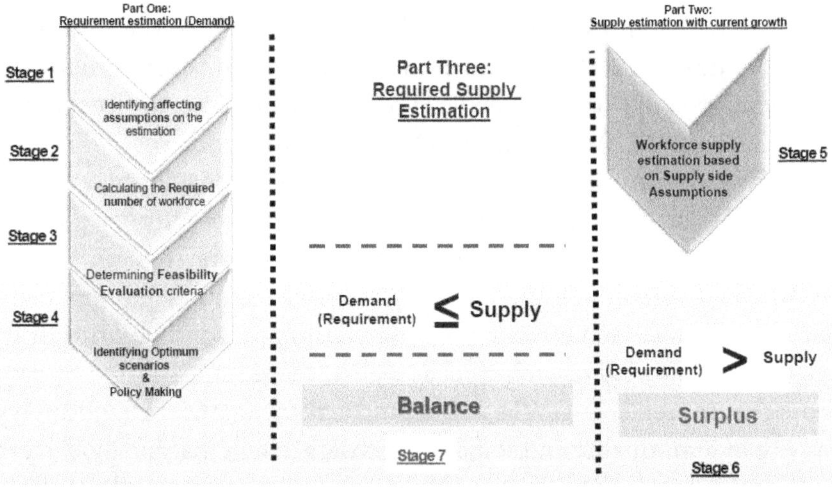

portal. This publicly available portal serves as a global public good for the dissemination of globally harmonized HWF data while also providing data to the WHO Global Health Observatory and other global reports such as World Health Statistics, UHC, World Bank and SDGs reports.

8. The way forward

The implementation of NHWA can provide countries with high-quality information on the HWF. The data and evidence generated and disseminated can inform policy decisions and planning according to the country's needs and key HRH challenges. Effective implementation of NHWA will contribute to building a stronger health system in any country through identifying challenges, bottlenecks, requirements and opportunities for significant improvements in health service coverage and health outcomes through investment in HWF.

For the sustainable implementation of NHWA, the capacity of data producers, analysts and users should be strengthened, as NHWA implementation calls for a system strengthening approach for HWF data and evidence generation instead of ad-hoc data collections. The governance mechanism for NHWA including multisectoral collaboration for dialogue and data sharing should be fostered to ensure involvement of all key actors and data sources. Guidance and capacity building for strengthened HWF data and for NHWA implementation is provided by WHO and partner agencies. WHO provides tools and guidance to countries and stakeholders as well as capacity building and trainings such as webinars and workshops. There are several networks and collaborations focused in improved HWF data and evidence, in particular Global Health Workforce Network (GHWN) and its Data and Evidence Hub[2], which brings together HWF experts around the world for knowledge sharing and guidance on how to further improve HWF data collection and use in national, regional and global level.

References

1. [No author] SD 2 million African community health workers — Harnessing the demographic dividend, ending AIDS and ensuring sustainable health for all in Africa http://www.unaids.org/sites/default/files/media_asset/African-2mCHW_en.pdf

[2] https://www.who.int/hrh/network/en/

2. Dussault G, Kawar R, Castro Lopes S, Campbell J. Building the primary health care workforce of the 21st century - Background paper to the Global Conference on Primary Health Care: From Alma-Ata Towards Universal Health Coverage and the Sustainable Development Goals. Geneva : World Health Organization; 2018. https://www.who.int/docs/default-source/primary-health-care-conference/workforce.pdf?sfvrsn=487cec19_2
3. World Health Organization sd.: A Labour Market Approach to Investing in the Health and Social Workforce to achieve the SDGs https://www.who.int/hrh/labour-market/HLMAleaflet2018.pdf?ua=1
4. World Health Organization 2010: Monitoring the building blocks of health systems: a handbook of indicators and their measurement strategies. https://www.who.int/healthinfo/systems/WHO_MBHSS_2010_full_web.pdf
5. World Health Organization 2015: Global reference list of 100 core health indicators, World Health Organization http://apps.who.int/iris/bitstream/10665/173589/1/WHO_HIS_HSI_2015.3_eng.pdf
6. World Health Organization 2016a: Health workforce requirements for universal health coverage and the Sustainable Development Goals. (Human Resources for Health Observer, 17) https://apps.who.int/iris/bitstream/handle/10665/250330/9789241511407-eng.pdf?sequence=1
7. World Health Organization 2016b: Working for health and growth: investing in the health workforce. Report of the High-Level Commission on Health Employment and Economic Growth. I https://apps.who.int/iris/bitstream/handle/10665/250047/9789241511308-eng.pdf?sequence=1
8. World Health Organization 2017: National accounts: a handbook. https://apps.who.int/iris/bitstream/handle/10665/259360/9789241513111-eng.pdf?sequence=1
9. World Health Organization 2018a: Five-year action plan for health employment and inclusive economic growth (2017–2021) https://apps.who.int/iris/bitstream/handle/10665/272941/9789241514149-eng.pdf?ua=1
10. World Health Organization 2018b: National health workforce accounts: implementation guide. https://apps.who.int/iris/bitstream/handle/10665/275473/9789241514446-eng.pdf?ua=1
11. World Health Organization 2018c: Five-year action plan for health employment and inclusive economic growth (2017–2021) https://apps.who.int/iris/bitstream/handle/10665/272941/9789241514149-eng.pdf?ua=1
12. World Health Organization 2019: Delivered by women, led by men: A gender and equity analysis of the global health and social workforce. (Human Resources for Health Observer Series No. 24) https://apps.who.int/iris/bitstream/handle/10665/311322/9789241515467-eng.pdf?ua=1

13. WHA63.16 Sixty-third World Health Assembly: WHO Global Code of Practice on the International Recruitment of Health Personnel https://www.who.int/hrh/migration/code/code_en.pdf?ua=1
14. WHA64.7 The Sixty-fourth World Health Assembly: Strengthening nursing and midwifery http://apps.who.int/gb/ebwha/pdf_files/wha64/a64_r7-en.pdf?ua=1
15. WHA69.19 The Sixty-ninth World Health Assembly: Global strategy on human resources for health: workforce 2030 http://apps.who.int/gb/ebwha/pdf_files/WHA69/A69_R19-en.pdf
16. WHA71.1 The Seventy-first World Health Assembly Thirteenth General Programme of Work, 2019–2023 https://apps.who.int/gb/ebwha/pdf_files/WHA71/A71_R1-en.pdf
17. Sousa, A.; Scheffler, R.; Nyoni, J. & Boerma, T. 2013: A comprehensive health labour market framework for universal health coverage. Bull World Health Organ 2013;91:892–894. https://www.who.int/bulletin/volumes/91/11/13-118927.pdf
18. International Labour Organization 2012: International Standard Classification of occupations ISCO-08. https://www.ilo.org/public/english/bureau/stat/isco/docs/publication08.pdf

KEY MESSAGES AND WAY FORWARD

Gilles Dussault, James Buchan, Inês Fronteira

The previous chapters presented a discussion of the main structural issues and challenges that policy-makers face to ensure that their health workforce is fit to meet the needs of the population. This is critically important in the context of global economic, social, demographic and epidemiological changes that require a continuing adaptation of health services and therefore of the competencies and behaviours of workers who deliver them. This last chapter brings together the main messages conveyed by the various authors. In doing so, we want to reinforce the objectives of the book, e.g. (1) to foster a common understanding of what needs to be done and of what can be done, and help frame the policy debate in a more rational and less ideological manner, (2) to raise awareness of the need for more proactive policies to address the causes of these problems and of examples of good practices, and (3) to stimulate engagement in policy development and implementation of actors who have a stake in improving health workers' education, conditions of employment and work environment to optimize their performance.

Message 1: Human resources matter

Human resources matter to provide "socially just, timely, integrated, people-centred and ethically delivered services" which will contribute to the well-being of the population in an effective and efficient manner. While other inputs are essential, such as financial resources, infrastructures, equipment, medicines and other consumables, and knowledge and information, a health workforce available in sufficient numbers, accessible and acceptable to all and performing at the highest quality standards possible is indispensable. Health workers' decisions and behaviour determine how well the other inputs will be used. Competencies, e.g. knowledge, skills and attitudes, and motivation influence these decisions. Other factors are also at play, such as how the work is divided and organized, the quality of the working environment and of management, and the regulatory framework which can make these effective or be a constraint to good performance. Here the message is that not paying sufficient attention to health workforce development has a cost; without well performing health workers, a health services system will not perform and collective health will suffer (Campbell et al. 2013).

Message 2: More of the same will not meet changing needs

Changing demographics and epidemiological profiles, technological advances, higher expectations of users, all imply necessary changes in service delivery modalities. As populations grow older, the prevalence of non-communicable diseases and of multi-morbidity augments and demand for services changes. This requires new services, delivered in new locations, sometimes at a distance, by a different mix of personnel. Just training more of the same types of health workers as is currently done will not be an adequate or effective response to these new needs. The education system must be adapted accordingly to ensure that it equips future health workers with the right competencies, and to work as an integrated team member. Those currently in practice also need to adapt through life-long professional development activities (Dussault, Buchan 2018). As demand for services such as mental health, public health, rehabilitation, nutrition or home care and palliative care becomes more prominent, education institutions need to make sure that they produce sufficient numbers of qualified professionals to respond to this demand. Also, provider organizations may need to retrain some of their current staff and even reallocate them to new areas of service.

Message 3: How work is divided among the various occupational groups is critical to the performance of the health workforce.

The building of an optimal mix of occupations with complementary competencies is not an option; it is a policy responsibility. This means that the composition of the workforce is as efficient as possible, that it is capable of the highest productivity levels, at the lowest cost, and meeting the required service quality and security standards. Efficiency can be improved in two ways. First, by fully using the competencies of each professional at all levels of the care system. In practice, physicians, the most qualified professionals, should not deliver services that can be safely delivered by nurses or pharmacists for example. Similarly, nurses or pharmacists should not deliver services that can safely be delivered by personnel with shorter training but with the required competencies, and so on. In many countries, nurses perform, under defined conditions, services traditionally reserved to physicians, such as prescribing medicines, analyses and exams, or manage cases like normal pregnancies or stable chronic diseases, in an autonomous manner. There is abundant literature showing that these nurse practitioners or advance practice nurses deliver services of the same quality of physicians' and that these save time that can be devoted to more demanding tasks. (Maier et al. 2017; Maier, Buchan 2018).

The second strategy is to identify the most productive numerical balance between health workers of different cadres corresponding to the needs of services. For example, the ratio of nurses to physicians ranges from more than 4 to 1 nurses in Japan, Ireland, Finland, Switzerland and the United States, to less than 1.5 to 1 in Greece, Italy, Portugal and Spain (OECD 2019). There is no prescribed ratio, but it is self-evident that there are efficiency gains associated to higher ratios of nurses, and even health gains (Aiken 2018).

Both strategies are not easy to implement as they imply challenging the interests of powerful professional organizations. They indicate the right direction towards improved efficiency; they may take time to implement, but they clearly needed.

Message 4: Recruitment, deployment, retention and mobility of health workers are fundamental aspects to take into account for the development of a sustainable health workforce.

Numbers are important when we assess the performance of a country's health workforce, but other dimensions are just as critical. Recruitment refers both to attracting qualified students to the health professional education programs and to employing graduates. Generally some programs are more sought after, like medicine, and others find it more difficult to attract candidates. Also, within the health professions, some areas are less popular, such as mental health, geriatrics, palliative care, and special efforts are needed to convince students to choose them when they reach the stage of specializing. As to the recruitment of graduates, if it is not timely or if working conditions are not attractive, there is a risk that some will not enter the domestic labour market.

Deployment refers to the distribution of health workers by level of services and type of provider organization, and to geographical coverage. The overconcentration of personnel in hospitals and in urban areas lead to poor efficiency (hospitals used for services that should be delivered at primary care level) and lower equity of access (people in rural or remote areas with no access to health workers). In most countries, the deployment of health workers is not balanced, hence the need for policies such as strengthening primary care services –as recommended by the World Health Organization (WHO 2018)- and designing and implementing interventions to attract health workers to areas with unmet needs and to retain them. Retention in such areas is a constant challenge that is best addressed by packages of professional, financial and personal support incentives rather than by mandatory posting or by single measures such an increased remuneration.

There is also the challenge of retaining health workers in the country itself, at a time when the health labour market has become global. Many higher-income countries experience shortages of physicians, nurses, and other professionals and use international recruitment to fill the gaps. In the European Union, moving to another country that offers better working conditions is relatively easy and many countries, mainly those from Central and Southern Europe, but also Ireland have lost hundreds of physicians and nurses to the benefit of higher-income countries. Other countries, such as the United States or the Gulf countries are also actively recruiting.

This leads to the message that policy-makers who are responsible to make the best use possible of the available health workforce need to pay attention to how health workers are recruited, deployed, how they make decisions in relation to where they plan to practise.

Message 5: Training and employing health workers is a cost, but if done strategically it can be a wise investment.

Expenditures on health services and on the workforce that delivers them are an important element of national budgets in European countries. The perception that it is only a cost, rather than also an investment is widespread, but it is not correct. If spending on the health workforce is effectively targeted, that is training and employing the right numbers and types of workers and providing them with motivating and supportive working environment, can produce benefits well beyond the protection and improvement of the health of the population. It can contribute to increasing direct and indirect employment, to productivity gains and to economic growth. In addition, equitable access to competent and motivated health workers strengthens social protection and cohesion. Countries known to have good quality health services accessible to all offer protection from poverty risks generated by health problems and are better prepared to respond to shocks like epidemics. They are also more attractive to foreign investors and to qualified immigrants.

Message 6: A good understanding of the dynamics of the health labour market helps design and implement workforce policies in a more effective manner.

It is critical that policy-makers and planners, and other stakeholders such as leaders of professional associations and users' representatives, understand what influences the demand and supply for health workers. This refers to how health workers decide to opt for a type (primary care, specialty) and location (provider organization, geographical zone) of practice, to what motivates them, and to what are determines their performance in terms of productivity and quality of service. A good knowledge of what influences the decisions of employers is just as important. Decisions of workers and of employers are motivated by various factors other than population health needs. Actors (individual, collective, organizational) in the market have different objectives, interests, and preferences. The power to influence the market is not distributed evenly, and the balance of power can change over time. This is why a valid reading of the political landscape in the health sector is critical to policy-making.

The understanding of the functioning of the health labour market helps deal with questions such as: how many health workers does the country need now, and will need in 5-10-15 years, of what type and how many of each occupation, with what competencies; how to ensure that they will maintain and improve their competencies all along their career; how to keep them motivated and avoid that they leave the health sector or emigrate; How much developing an adequate workforce will cost; where the resources will come from?

There are analytical tools available to help answer these questions and an investment in research prior to making strategic workforce policy decisions may avoid costly misguided interventions.

Message 7: Strategic planning is needed to bridge the gap between need, demand and supply of HRH, and to mitigate its consequences.

Shortages lead to inadequate services and unmet healthcare needs, overworked practitioners, unfilled public positions and higher costs. Oversupply or surplus of certain categories of health workers generates a waste of human resources and leads to declining average incomes. Health workforce planning is critical to try to avoid these problems, particularly in a context of limited resources. Changes that may affect the demand for health services, the structure and organization of service delivery, and eventually the demand and supply of health workers are hard to predict. We know the main trends in demographics and in the burden of disease as the pace of their change is relatively slow, compared to advances in technology which are increasingly rapid. Political and economic changes are not easy to forecast, but scenarios can be identified. It is important to stress that planning and projections are not predictions of the future. Sudden shocks, such as the economic crisis of 2008 and beyond, or the coronavirus pandemic of 2020, represent unpredicted and total challenges to health systems and their workforces.

Planning is not limited to forecasting as when the number of future retirees is used to estimate the replacement needs. This is important information, but it is far from sufficient. A strategic approach starts by assessing demand, and projecting which services will be needed in 5-10-15 years, how they will likely be organized and delivered. Scenarios can be envisaged as how the scopes of practice can be adapted and tasks be distributed among the various groups of health workers. This type of planning is more demanding in terms of data collection and analysis time and expertise, but it is well worth the expense. In the end, it provides decision-makers with more comprehensive information and limits risks of negative consequences of inappropriate interventions. This is critical because decisions in relation to the health workforce, such as augmenting or diminishing the number of entries in a specific profession, have long-term effects.

Message 8: Data and knowledge matter

Planning and policy development and implementation are as good as the data and information on which they are based. In the last 10-15 years, data on the health workforce and knowledge on the dynamics of health labour markets have increased exponentially. However, major gaps still remain in most countries, for example on the private sector (education institutions, provider organizations), on mobility flows between countries or on working conditions. The production of NHWA offers a response to the need of quality data to inform decisions that impact the size, composition, distribution and performance of the health workforce. The effective implementation of NHWA can contribute to building a stronger health system through identifying HRH challenges, bottlenecks, requirements and opportunities for significant improvements in health service coverage and health outcomes. As the development of NHWA requires time, expertise and financial investment, countries can progress in that direction by incrementally developing simpler information systems, which overtime can become full NHWA. The production of valid, reliable, updated and easily accessible data requires the collaboration of several key stakeholders, such as registration bodies, professional organizations, employers and others who have access to data on health workers. Supporting data holders to use standard definitions, periods of reporting and validation procedures can be a major step forward in harmonizing the production of data. A number of countries – notably in South-America – have created HRH Observatories with a function of collecting data from different sources and conducting analyses and research to feed the policy process. Lessons can be learned from their experience.

Message 9: Governance matters

The growing importance placed on providing holistic and personalized forms of care will require a new approach to delivery of services and a re-organization of the workplace, not simply introducing new technologies but reengineering work processes, infrastructure supports and human resource development tools. This in turn requires significant new thinking about the structure and functioning of governance mechanisms that determine who decides how work will be regulated, organized and performed in the health sectors. The responsibility for governance is usually shared between government ministries and agencies, professional councils and associations, and other actors, for example accreditation bodies. Depending on the context, it can be more or less centralized.

Challenges include breaking the "silo approach" whereby planning, policy-making and management are conducted occupation by occupation rather than in taking into account the whole set of interdependent links between the various categories of workers, and of the need to emphasise teamwork. This is needed to increase organisational efficiency to better meet population needs. For example, making the right decisions at the right level can facilitate the introduction of health workforce flexibilities as a management response to the current rigid division of labour that does not make optimal use of the capacities of some categories of health workers. A more flexible work environment can address low motivation that generates poor productivity and dissatisfaction, leading to high attrition through early retirement, exit of the health sector or emigration. Good governance means to design and put in place functionning regulatory mechanisms, such as accreditation of education programs and surveillance of the quality of practice, to create flexible management structures and processes and employ competent managers to make them work, and to have a planning strategy based on solid data and information and on active involvement of the various stakeholders.

Message 10: Policy matters

One of the most frequent, if not the most frequent, recommendation to improve the performance of the health workforce, it to formulate a comprehensive and sustained approach to health workforce performance. Such a policy should cover all occupations contributing to the delivery of health services, because of the systemic nature of their interactions. An intervention targeting a specific occupation will likely affect the other occupations which interact directly or indirectly with it. Comprehensiveness also means to consider of the whole cycle of professional life, from entrance in an education program, to employment, to retirement. Recruitment, deployment, management, retention are also aspects to take into account. The issue of which type of governance should be developed comes on top of the reflection of policy-makers. A comprehensive policy sets priorities and realistic objectives that the country commits to achieve. Then strategies to implement it are designed taking into account their affordability, acceptability and the organizational capacity available. Research tends to conclude that single interventions have only limited effects and that policies should be defined in accordance with the specific context of the country. Clearly, designing and implementing an effective health workforce policy remains a daunting challenge, but it can be overcome. A common understanding of what needs to be done and of what can be done, based on valid data and information helps frame the policy debate in a more rational and less ideological manner.

The development of an effective and efficient health workforce is only possible if it is high on the political agenda. This requires public engagement and stakeholder support. A common foundation of such is "health workforce literacy", e.g. familiarity with the issues and problems, understanding of their causes, access to information on policy options, and a strong and shared commitment to making health services more responsive to people's needs and expectations.

References

1. Aiken L H (2018), Evidence-based Nurse Staffing: ICN's New Position Statement, International Nursing Review, 65 (4):469-471; https://onlinelibrary.wiley.com/doi/full/10.1111/inr.12499
2. Barriball KLB, Buchan J, Craveiro J, Dieleman I, Dix M, Dussault G, et al. (2015) Recruitment and retention of the health workforce in Europe: Final Report. Luxembourg: Publications Office of the European Union; https://ec.europa.eu/health/sites/health/files/workforce/docs/2015_healthworkforce_recruitment_retention_frep_en.pdf
3. Campbell J, Dussault G, Buchan J, Pozo-Martin F, Guerra Arias M, Leone C, Siyam A, Cometto G. (2013), A universal truth: no health without a workforce. Forum Report, Third Global Forum on Human Resources for Health, Recife, Brazil. Geneva, Global Health Workforce Alliance and World Health

Organization. http://www.who.int/workforcealliance/knowledge/resources/hrhreport2013/en/

4. Dussault G, Kawar R, Castro Lopes S, Campbell J. (2018), Building the primary health care workforce of the 21st century - Background paper to the Global Conference on Primary Health Care: From Alma-Ata Towards Universal Health Coverage and the Sustainable Development Goals. Geneva : World Health Organization; https://www.who.int/docs/default-source/primary-health-care-conference/workforce.pdf?sfvrsn=487cec19_2
5. Dussault G., Buchan J. (2018), "Noncommunicable diseases and human resources for health: A Workforce Fit for Purpose", in Jakab M, Farrington J, , Mantingh F, Borgermans L (eds) Health Systems Respond to Noncommunicable Diseases: Time for Ambition. WHO Regional Office for Europe, Copenhagen: 182-198; http://www.euro.who.int/en/publications/abstracts/health-systems-respond-to-noncommunicable-diseases-time-for-ambition-2018
6. Maier CB, Aiken LH, Busse R. (2017) Nurses in advanced roles: policy levers for implementation. OECD Health Working Papers, No. 98. Paris: OECD Publishing, 2017. http://dx.doi.org/10.1787/ a8756593-en
7. Maier C, Buchan J (2018) Integrating Nurses in Advanced Roles in Health Systems to Address the Growing Burden of Chronic Conditions. Eurohealth 24 (1) 24-27 http://www.euro.who.int/__data/assets/pdf_file/0005/365972/EH_v24n1.pdf
8. OECD (2019), Health at a Glance 2019- OECD Indicators, Paris, OECD Publishing; http://www.oecd.org/health/health-at-a-glance.htm
9. WHO (2018) Declaration of Astana, Geneva, World Health Organization; https://www.who.int/docs/default-source/primary-health/declaration/gcphc-declaration.pdf